History Anew:

Innovations in the
Teaching of History Today

Edited

by

Robert Blackey

The University Press
California State University, Long Beach
1250 Bellflower Blvd. • Long Beach • California • 90840-1901

Copyright © 1993 by
The University Press
California State University, Long Beach
1250 Bellflower Boulevard
Long Beach, CA 90840

Distributed by arrangement with
University Publishing Associates,^{SM} Inc.

4720 Boston Way
Lanham, MD 20706

3 Henrietta Street
London WC2E 8LU England

Library of Congress Cataloging-in-Publication Data

History anew : innovations in the teaching of history today / edited
by Robert Blackey.
p.   cm.
1. History—Study and teaching (Higher)—United States.
I. Blackey, Robert.
D16.3.H57   1993   907'.1'173—dc20   92–34909 CIP

ISBN 1–878981–03–X (cloth : alk. paper)
ISBN 1–878981–04–8 (pbk. : alk. paper)

 The paper used in this publication meets the minimum requirements of
American National Standard for Information Sciences—Permanence
of Paper for Printed Library Materials, ANSI Z39.48–1984.

For
T. David Blackey
and
I. James Blackey,
my brothers, my friends.

Contents

Introduction

IN HISTORY there is, inevitably, a history to virtually everything, and this collection, along with the "Teaching Innovations" column in *Perspectives* (the newsletter of the American Historical Association), is no exception. These brief introductory remarks serve the dual function of highlighting that history and recognizing the vital roles played by its leading participants.

In the early 1970s the annual meetings of the AHA began to include sessions on the teaching of history, while the popularity of these sessions reflected a growing awareness and an appreciation of the importance of classroom teaching. In 1974 William H. McNeill directed the transition of the old AHA Committee on Teaching, which he chaired, into the current Teaching Division, complete with an AHA vice president at its head. McNeill also arranged to have space set aside in the *AHA Newsletter* (now *Perspectives*) that would be devoted to teaching. The resulting column, initially called "Innovations in Undergraduate History," was edited by Myron Marty and Henry S. Bausum, and they helped to give life and form to this collective wish of a number of concerned historians.

That first year, September through May 1974-75, the column consisted of remarks, each month, by anywhere from two to five teachers of history, all but one of whom were from colleges and universities. In September 1975, in a marriage of ideas, new and old, the column took on the name it would hold for more than a decade, "Teaching History Today," and with it came individually or jointly written articles much as they appear today. Beginning in 1980 the baton of editorship — surely in the form of a red pen — was passed to Jeanette Lauer, who a year later started sharing the job with Mildred Alpern.

Alpern was a high school teacher, and her appointment was indicative of the AHA's wish to bring secondary school teachers of history more actively into the membership fold. Also with that in mind, a new column was introduced in the fall of 1982, called "Advanced Placement Teaching." As past Chief Reader of European History Advanced Placement, I wrote the inaugural article and subsequently became that column's editor. Soon thereafter the two teaching columns appeared in alternate issues. Then, in 1986, they were recast into a single column, called "Teaching Innovations," with the team of Alpern and Lauer leapfrogging months for publication with me and sharing editing responsibilities. They retired in 1988, and I handled editing chores alone until 1991 when Howard Shorr, another secondary school teacher, joined me.

During these nearly two decades of active attention to teaching history key members of the AHA's full-time staff have played vital overseeing and editorial roles, and they deserve recognition, especially Executive Directors Paul Ward, Mack Thompson and Samuel R. Gammon, Deputy Executive Directors Eleanor Straub, Edmund Worthy, Jr., Charlotte Quinn, Jamil S. Zainaldin and James B. Gardner, and *Perspectives* editors Janet H. Hearne , Janet E. Hartman, Eleanor Straub, Kathleen Swiger, Judith Minz, Ira E. Carrel, Meredith H. Fields, Marilyn C. Finley, and Kathy Koziara-Herbert.

As we enter the 1990s and head toward the turn of a new century, the need to recognize and encourage effective teaching is increasingly pronounced. Several sessions at the annual meetings of the AHA and the Organization of American Historians are routinely devoted to teaching, summer NEH fellowships and programs of the History Teaching Alliance abound, there is activity focusing on teaching by such groups as the Society for History Education (which publishes *The History Teacher*), the Committee on History in the Classroom, the Organization of History Teachers, and the National Center for History in the Schools, and there is increasing university dialogue, and even action, toward weighing teaching more heavily vis-a-vis research in considerations of retention, promotion and tenure. Another signpost may be reflected in the "Teaching Innovations" column itself, which this volume honors. A recent survey by the AHA, for example, pointed to the wide readership the column has been enjoying. And then there is the subject of manuscripts.

In her retirement statement (*Perspectives*, December 1988), Alpern lamented the slimness of the pickings we editors had been facing; they "barely trickled in," she wrote, and manuscripts had to be solicited, almost like donations to a charity. My experience mirrored Alpern's and Lauer's, at least until about 1988. I hustled, I pleaded and I called on friends and strangers, and still there were months when no column appeared because I had none to forward to the AHA. Thankfully, that has changed. I still solicit columns, as ideas for subjects come to mind or as I try to help convert convention papers and panels into articles. But I am also sent significant numbers of papers, by secondary school teachers in the hinterlands, by prominent scholars at major research institutions, and by people in between. (Undergraduates have not yet tried their hand, but a couple of graduate students have been co-authors with professors.) Perhaps the most telling indication of the heightened interest in teaching that the column reflects is the delay time between finished/edited papers and publication. What used to be a matter of from two to four months is now a year to 18 months, and each of the last several academic years has begun with articles for the entire year in place.

The 43 articles in this collection cover a panoply of teaching-related topics, from the broad to the specific; with four exceptions as noted, all come from

"Advanced Placement Teaching" and "Teaching Innovations" columns, from 1983 to 1991, that I have had the pleasure and good fortune to edit. (An earlier collection of 14 articles, published between 1975 and 1984, was issued in 1985 by the AHA's institutional services program and edited by Henry S. Bausum.) If I have been at all successful at editing, then the articles should have at least one characteristic in common: they are of value to teachers. This has been the guiding principle motivating my work. I strive to make the column a conduit whereby ideas, philosophies, techniques and methods can be transmitted among us. Each time I take pencil in hand to edit a new manuscript my overriding concern is: if I wanted to replicate or in some way make use of what I am reading, what would I need to know in order to be successful? Each reader will be his or her own judge in determining whether I have asked the correct questions and helped to extract the best answers. I can only hope that as the articles are read no one will see a kinship between what I have done and role of editor as defined cynically by Elbert Hubbard (author, editor and printer, 1856-1915): an editor "is a person ... whose business it is to separate the wheat from the chaff, and to see that the chaff is printed."

I wish to extend my heartfelt thanks to a number of people who have played, and are still playing, influential roles in my life as a teacher of history: to Miss Ruth Kowalsky of Junior High School 60 and to Miss Sennet of Seward Park High School, both in New York City, who first awakened in me a love for history and an appreciation of effective teaching; to Professor Howard Adelson of the City College of New York and to Professors John W. Wilkes and L. Jay Oliva of New York University, after whom I modeled my own teaching; to my colleagues and students at California State University, San Bernardino; and to the hundreds of Advanced Placement teachers and Readers, from all over the United States and Canada, with whom I have been working for more than 20 years, including a very special historian of my recent past and my future, Carol Pixton.

Robert Blackey
San Bernardino, California

Chapter I:

Thinking and Rethinking History

History and Humanities: Teaching as Destructive of Certainty

Russell H. Hvolbek

"Better a mended sock than a torn one — not so with self-consciousness."
— G.F.W. Hegel

TWO ISSUES HAVE EMERGED from recent studies of American higher education: 1) students graduating from American colleges and universities "lack even the most rudimentary knowledge about history, literature, art, and [the] philosophical foundations of their nation and their civilization"; 2) many of those who teach the humanities are not teaching effectively. I will address these points with special emphasis on the teaching of history and the humanities, outlining the fundamental problems hurting our ability to teach effectively and then discussing teaching as a means to destroy certainty.

I believe that the underlying presuppositions of our profession have skewed our vision and hindered our ability not simply to teach students (for all of us have information to offer), but to impart the desire to learn. This is where our problems lie — we are no longer able to inspire in students the predilection to comprehend and see the full value of our cultural, intellectual, and social past.

There are many reasons for the decline in inspired and inspiring teaching, the most damning being the perseverance of the "wretched pedantry, the meanness of motive, the petty rancors of rivalry, the stultifying professionalism," and the fact that good teaching is generally not rewarded financially or socially. But I believe there is a deeper reason. In a profession that claims to impart human values, we often ignore these for an "objective" knowledge divorced from the existential conditions of life. Losing touch with the fundamentally human element in history, what we study does not touch our own lives; indeed, we intentionally design studies to prevent too close a personal involvement in our subjects. But if our investigations lack serious importance to our own lives, if they are simply knowledge acquisitions, how can we have an inward connection to them? And how can we expect to touch and stimulate our students?

It is important therefore to reevaluate our motives for teaching, and to become absolutely clear about what we are doing when we engage ourselves in the study of culture and the past and teach students about them. Is the aim of teaching history and the humanities the transmitting of precise information? Do we really want history to be "scientific"? Is it really better to know absolutely or is it better to be in doubt? What are we educating students for in the humanities? Do we study the past to confirm our own views; and do we seek to condition the views of our students? Does all the information we now impart have any serious connection to the lives of the people we teach or even to ourselves? Do we suppose it could affect the lives of our students? Even asking such questions has become anathema. What guides our ultimate motives for teaching?

It is my contention that the primary purpose of teaching history and the humanities is to make students more aware of how their lives connect to past human experience. Teaching is a means to entice students to question actively their own beliefs and certainties, and thus participate in their own education. The first step in doing this involves, as Hegel implies, "tearing" self-consciousness. What Hegel means by this is that the psychological, intellectual, and social growth of an individual depends on a continual questioning of the presuppositions around which lives, societies, and civilizations are formed. The cultural/historical beliefs we have adopted help determine who we are; the extent to which we become aware of our unquestioned sociocultural assumptions is the extent to which we become creative independent individuals. In order to become free we have to have our "prejudices" torn. Hence "destruction" becomes a metaphor for education.

Let me begin to develop these ideas by recalling a similar issue discussed by Plato in his dialogue *Euthyphro*. Socrates meets Euthyphro (the straight thinker) on the steps of the law court in Athens. Euthyphro, lawyer, community leader, theologian, is prosecuting his own father for manslaughter and is convinced he is correct in doing so. He knows the law and what is right and pious. Socrates, gadfly, penniless philosopher, himself about to be put to trial for "corrupting the youth of Athens," asks Euthyphro to define piety so he may learn enough to convince the judges of his improved behavior. Euthyphro replies, "Piety consists in just what I am doing." Socrates then confounds the straight thinker with a series of questions that prove Euthyphro does not know what piety is, but rather, he just assumes he knows. Euthyphro has strong opinions he has never questioned. He represents the state, the right, the maintenance of the laws; he does not reflect or question his opinions. He is sure of himself. He is "uneducated."

Socrates desires the "destruction" of Euthyphro, that is, the destruction of "straight thinking." He wants to rend a seam in the consciousness of Euthyphro in order to make him self conscious. Until Euthyphro becomes self-conscious he cannot carry on a dialogue; Euthyphro's chatter is monological. Rigid, he acquires new information only insofar as it supports his opinions. He never listens, he only narrates. He never grows more aware; he only states what is for him the obvious.

Socrates on the other hand is the wisest man in Athens because, unlike the "Euthyphros," he knows he does not know. He is unclear about answers to important questions. Plato's point is that intellectual confusion, including error, is a component part of the process toward knowledge. Socrates can carry on a dialogue because the answers are not always there. Knowing you do not know, or even that you might be wrong, leaves you open to new experiences that may change your consciousness. The purpose of the dialogue is not to teach what piety is, but to undermine the reader's faith that he actually knows what piety is. Undermining presuppositions, having one's consciousness torn, allows one to receive a new idea or to develop an old one.

Socrates' dialogue with Euthyphro clarifies the fundamental problems facing the teaching of history and the humanities, and suggests an alternative premise from which our studies and our teaching might evolve. The purpose of education as practiced by Socrates is to steal away the assurance (dullness?) of mind surrounding the vast amount of data students have been forced to assimilate and which they assume to be important. Just as the dogmatic "correctness" of Euthyphro prevented him from creative involvement with alternative ideas, so too our educational practices aim at creating "Euthyphros," individuals with vast amounts of absolutely correct information but with little awareness that that information has been historically interpreted and is therefore open to interpretation.

The reasons for this are historical. For the past fifty years or so many of those who study and teach history and the humanities have been doing their best to emulate the hard sciences by aspiring to a comparable realm of truth. Objectivity, distance, and strict methodological principles have become our ideals. This means that much of history is perceived as a "social science" concerned with exact quantitative research and the erection of scientific models through which investigations are to be undertaken. The problem, it seems, is not the acquisition of positivistic knowledge but the use, or lack of use, of that knowledge. In our attempt to establish levels of truth that are "objective" and "timeless" (similar to scientific laws), we have begun to approach a subject which is in time as if it and we were out of it. We believe we can escape our own biases by creating theories (linguistic mediums) that purport to allow what is to be known in an unbiased fashion. But the theories themselves are part of our own historical biases toward timeless objectivity. By adopting this particular form of engagement with our subject, we advance our own personal estrangement from it.

Moreover, educational theory and practice have conflated the conception of knowledge recognized in the natural sciences and the means toward acquiring it with what knowledge is and how it is acquired in history or the humanities. Modern education is now modeled on a theory of knowledge lying at the heart of and practiced most successfully by the scientific enterprise. The assumptions are that knowledge begins at a low level with basic information, theories, formulae, and advances to more complex plateaus. Achievement is recognized as a building-up, an improving, a making more "intelligent" through the imbibing of more exact and complicated information. The denouement of contemporary educational practices is the "achievement test" that supposedly determines whether the student has mastered the material in order to proceed onto the next level. Such tests represent the entire range of thinking about modern education as the quantifiable absorption of information leading to a specific end, the passing of an exam.

Unfortunately, what achievement tests purport to determine (i.e., command of information) has little to do with achievement or intelligence in the humanities. In fact, the *a priori* assumption of modern scientifically-based educational practices — that knowledge is a progressive absorption of information that can be measured and has an end — is the antithesis of the process toward and the goal of knowledge in the humanities. The end of an education in the humanities (if we can speak of such a thing) is itself not the passing of a test or the advancement of the business or science industries. That is, an education in the humanities turns students both inward as individuals and outward as members of a society and culture, to shake them free of fixed ideas. As such it is not constructive but, frankly, "destructive," although this is no ordinary destruction. Individuals pursuing the study of the humanities seek continually to have their presuppositions confronted. What an education in the humanities should consist of is the continual confrontation with the truths and ideas that students and teachers hold self evident, and not simply the memorization of social/cultural information about the past.

Our love of and need for information are not to be scoffed at or scorned, but perhaps our love has prevented us from fully realizing and making a distinction between understanding and information. Information is just that, no more. But understanding involves synthesizing information into comprehensible relationships; and when we understand something about the past we have more than information, we have a story about human life, and that story can tell us something about our lives. This, not the memorization of states on a map or important names and events, should constitute cultural literacy. To exaggerate the point — What good does it do us to know a few more facts about George Washington or the American Revolution? Would it not be more instructive if we knew that revolutions, orginating in thought, ultimately redefine the way human beings conceive of themselves, their world, and their relationship to the world? That when thought changes the world changes, and that applies to then as well as to now? That Washington's role, symbolic or otherwise, helped create a new idea about the individual and his relationship to his society and government? And then, perhaps, to discover the extent to which that idea is present and influential in American society today? The dynamic interaction of the thought and action of the past has, indeed, shaped our ideas, regardless of whether we react for or against it. The extent to which we become aware of this shaping determines how we can decide about it. Information itself is not the goal. Understanding the ideas and actions that have shaped the world, and putting information into a coherent story about how human beings have made their world, is the goal. As this is accomplished the information becomes important.

Alas, history is now a "social science," the humanities are now the "human sciences," and universities are filled with professors seeking to become more practical, useful, and scientific. Teachers of subjective personal material have become scholars, objective and aloof from the object of their study — human life. By consciously seeking to subsume the ideals of their discipline into the natural sciences, the "human scientists" have lost touch with the humanities. And they have perhaps driven students away as well. In part this is because as "social scientists" we often transmit information that appears dull to students who really cannot see the relevance of some particular fact about the past. It is all information, equally valid and without any serious connection to their lives. At least the natural sciences seem to offer us the power to control nature.

In our science-based educational practice, what is "useful" is that which can be known in such a way that it can be controlled and manipulated for human good. But what is "useful" in history and the humanities and the type of educational practices I am advocating is that which strikes at self-assurance and urges self-consciousness. The task of the humanities professor is to make the student aware of the fact that thoughts are conditioned and fixed by society and culture so that confidence in the "this is the way things are" is undermined. The teacher must seek to undermine confidence in the obvious, to destroy "common sense," that *horrendum pudendum*, as Nietzsche called it, of all forms of training "education." For when something is taken as "common sense," when something is accepted as absolutely right and an end in itself, conversation is over. Conversation is over because one's own biases are not being questioned. And without the recognition of questions, fresh creative involvement is impossible.

In the humanities, answers are less important than questioning answers. And questioning must be self-reflective. To be educated in the humanities (and the sciences) is to be made aware of what one is lacking, it is to be made aware that one must continually generate new questions and do away with the confidence that one's own ideas are absolutely correct. This leads to questions, and questions are what precipitate fresh approaches to things. We discover in the latter part of the Socratic dialogue that when the dogmatic Euthyphro tries to turn the table on Socrates by asking him questions, he cannot do so. He has nothing to ask. He is closed. The point I am making can also be illustrated by recognizing that nothing is more depressing than trying to engage in a dialogue with an individual who knows all the answers (such as Euthyphro). Such an individual will seek to win an argument, to place his view over another's. Unwilling to recognize an opposing consideration, such an individual cannot carry on a dialogue. You cannot really "talk" with such an individual until he is able to recognize that his knowledge might be incomplete. Unless he becomes aware of the questionableness of his views, his relationships with others will always be over and against, never with, the other.

I am not advocating "cultural relativity." It is really not an issue. Most students will spout the "well-everything-is-relative-man" theme because it is part of their historical heritage; they have been conditioned and are trapped in that idea. That too is a "value." But is the way to get rid of "relativism" to force feed them other, what some believe are superior, values? Would it not be better to let them realize that their "relativism" is a history-conditioned value they need not accept? In my experience all students want values and will seek them out. No one lives without some values. If the "value" of relativism is hurting them, and I believe it is, the problem is not that they do not want values. No — rather it is that they have no idea "relativism" is a value, that "relativism" is their "objectively" clear "value," and that there might be other ways to consider the world. Like Euthyphro, they are stuck; unconsciously conditioned by a "value," they are closed to the educational experience.

The legacy of Descartes that every step to knowledge has to follow a "clear and distinct" path, and that of Galileo who defined the scientific method as the study of the world as if it were without life, without consciousness, has stifled us.

In studying history and the humanities we are talking about consciousness as it evolves in time. The student should be forced to walk in the dark, in the abyss of an idea, and not in the white light of some assumed objectivity that consciously seeks to deny consciousness. This will encourage receptivity and openness to life and values. Then the sense of despair students feel living in the value of objectivism and the relativity of innumerable facts will recede. Nietzsche was correct when he stated that an educated person "lies servilely on one's stomach before every little fact, always to be prepared for the leap of putting oneself in the place of or plunging into, others and other things — in short the famous 'objectivity' is bad taste, is ignoble par excellence." When every idea is "clear and distinct," when we have totally divorced ourselves from a personal inward relationship with life, we will have lost history and the humanities entirely.

When one teaches the history of science, for example, the goal is not to chronicle accurately the series of events leading up to contemporary thought structures. This serves only to solidify fundamental contemporary conceptions and rigidify thinking (the relativity of values, for example!). The narrative line of historical events should be merely the structure through which one pulls apart the presuppositions behind a particular thought pattern and then discusses the implications and meaning behind those presuppositions.

It serves very little purpose for undergraduates to know that Isaac Newton, following the pioneering genius of Johannus Kepler and Galileo, derived the first law of motion. His discovery has been in our culture so long that high school students know "intuitively" that an object will continue in motion or remain at rest unless acted upon by an outside force. To stress this and other "facts" about history of science as statements of the gradual progress of truth only substantiates contemporary thought structures. I am not saying we should ignore data; but this should not be our primary focus. It is more important that students realize that this was a totally new way to see and live in the world that departed radically from prior orientations to reality. It makes a significant difference that they know that the first law of motion is totally counter to the immediate experience the individual initially has with nature, and that there is no such object in the world that continues in a straight line without stopping; all things in our world are acted upon by outside forces. It makes a difference that students know that Newton's science indicates growth in the West of a new theory of knowledge, a new relationship to nature, and a new conception of our place in nature that has fundamentally altered our world. It makes a significant difference that students realize that the absorption of these theories has altered their orientation to reality and hindered alternative conceptions of reality. To destroy their belief that this is the way things are, and thus to tear into their self-consciousness, is to open them to new worlds. To add more information that affirms the dull and dreary world of "objective" reality — which is a direct product of our intellectual history — is to stifle creativity.

In my experience, once students glimpse that the way they have been thinking about things is not necessarily the way they have to think about them, they become inspired to learn. This does not happen overnight, of course, and it does not happen to every student. But it is astonishing how open and desirous of new ideas college students can become as a result of one "consciousness-tearing" course. College can be the most intellectually stimulating period of most people's lives. When they become aware that there are alternative ways to think about things, lights go on. Students begin to want to understand their lives, their history, and their place in the world. They want to see connections between themselves and the past and how it has affected them. At that point, teaching becomes easy and all students become good students.

Exciting teaching and active learning are possible. Education in history and the humanities has the greatest potential for challenging and inspiring students when it abandons certainty. Giving students the possibility of having their consciousness torn is giving them the possibility of freedom. And this freedom is freedom from the "known".

▼

Editor's Note: This article appeared in the "Viewpoints" column in *Perspectives*. It was edited by Robert Blackey, and he wishes to express his gratitude to Carol Pixton of the Polytechnic School, Pasadena, and a Ph.D. candidate at Columbia University by acknowledging her constructive criticism and vital contributions to the editing of this article.

The Challenge of "Historical Literacy"

Peter N. Stearns

GROWING CONCERN WITH HISTORICAL LITERACY and demonstrations of the power of literacy-like standards in actual school curricula form one of the striking currents in history education in recent years. The historical literacy phenomenon is of course part of a general extension of "literacy" impulses in the major disciplines, a means of calling attention to deficiencies in basic preparation and providing a definable set of benchmarks by which education can be evaluated. The superficial rigor of the literacy movement constitutes its central challenge, as it affects not only pre-collegiate education but also the teaching possible in the early college years plus the training provided to new teachers. In history, literacy advocates have not only produced lists of crucial facts that any educated person must know, they have also moved to reduce flexibility in history curricula in the name of essential coverage. They have won apparent adhesion even from a wider range of historian-teachers, as witness the decision to label yet another exercise in historical literacy with what is in fact a diverse collection of essays surrounding the "Guidelines" prepared by the Bradley Commission on History in Schools. Literate historians surround us at every turn.

Yet the historical literacy approach rests on a number of highly questionable premises. It follows from a nostalgia for a century past, when improving mechanical reading ability seemed the key to personal and social progress, a notion that does not fully conform to historical reality. It rests, certainly, on an equation of reading skills with the features of a complex discipline like history that is dubious in the extreme. Literacy advocates often imply, further, that historical knowledge has deteriorated over recent decades, which allows them to trumpet remedial action without bothering to prove the facts of their proposition. The amazing ignorance demonstrated by sizable minorities of World War II draftees — about a quarter, for example, unable to name the existing President, then in his third term — suggests that some genuine problems may not be as novel as the panic-pushers would have us think. Even if some kinds of social knowledge have deteriorated, causation is surely complex.

Some historical literacy gurus suggest that new kinds of historical inquiry, diverting from the great men and great achievements whose history will convert callow youth into American citizens, constitute the villains of the piece. Yet most school history has apparently changed very little, despite admitted attempts at reform, which might suggest that new approaches, rather than more of the same, fit the pedagogical bill. On the whole, provocative assertion surpasses careful demonstration in the current halls of literacy. New views of history mislead; students have fallen from standards, with resultant if not fully specified pathologies. The remedy is reemphasis on recounting the basic achievements of past heroes, warts carefully removed.

Most of the practicing historians who have spoken out on the subject have rejected the literacy approach, or at least have seriously modified it in practice. Even the reports that fed the Bradley Commission, while something of a hodge-podge, largely urged non-literacy values, even if the literacy flag was hoisted on the report's binding. While attacks on historical literacy should not divert from more constructive teaching goals — the task of providing alternatives is far more exciting — they constitute an essential first step.

Dissent rivets on two key points, the first factual, the second analytical.

Extreme literacy advocates want a taught history that elevates the achievements of Western society, and of selected statesmen and intellectuals within Western society, as a means of socializing students to an agreed-upon version of what the past really means and how it determines what is true and beautiful. What is involved here is essentially a semi-democratized version of the Renaissance idea of history teaching by example, wherein educated men had a common fund of information about past deeds of greatness and past artistic standards that would provide identifiable levels of elite cultivation and that would guide their own actions. In the literacy vision, students more generally are to be exposed to an inspirational past, which will provide necessary common knowledge in an otherwise-diverse society and which will promote values that should underlie responsible political behavior. The problem is that this approach ignores, and downplays, most human experience, leaving even Western history unanalyzed in a comparative context. Implicitly, I fear, students are to be taught the inferiority of other traditions — a lesson that many American students, whatever their own deficiencies, may already learn too well. Within the Western tradition itself, the approach leaves out the social history dimension, which has added to our understanding of the past through attention to groups out of power and activities not immediately related to the generation of great deeds or great ideas. As a discipline, history today reaches out unprecedentedly to a variety of civilization stories and to a sense of the richness of the groups and experiences that make up even our national story, yet historical literacy would largely ignore this new range of material. Literacy advocates, riveting on hortatory themes such as the rise of democracy, clearly fear dilution from examination of other cultures or Western experiences that do not illustrate democracy's triumphant surge — or they fear the results of such inquiry directly.

The literacy movement also converts history from analytical instrument to memorization enforcer. The best historical research has always sought more than a good story. It has aimed at using facts not to provide tests for levels of sophistication or of patriotism, but as data for analytical efforts to understand social change. It works, in other words, to provide better understanding of how societies function. This analytical purpose has been enhanced, over the past generation, by the expansion of history's range and by cross-fertilization with other disciplines in the social sciences and, most recently, with the newer kinds of cultural studies as well.

These gains, in turn, raise a central question, which the historical literacy movement answers without addressing: is history primarily a set of facts, whose mastery presumably enhances the credentials of the memorizer, or is it an active interpretive tool, providing habits of thought, based to be sure on expanding data, that assist in grasping how institutions function, or how officially-approved ideas relate to popular beliefs and actions, or how and why groups may decide on significant shifts in demographic behaviors? The question can be converted readily to pedagogy. Should students concentrate, in dealing for example with the Industrial Revolution, on lists of inventions, or should they explore the issues involved in technological causation, in this and other important cases? (Most American students absorb from their culture a rooted belief in technological determinism, but almost never know the implications of their belief, or that they have the belief in the first place.) Should they note all the legislation of the New Deal as part of a litany of presidential administrations, or should they understand how one major law, such as Social Security, altered the relationship between state and society?

Most historian-researchers do not see themselves mainly as memorialists, repeating or modestly adding to the store of timeless truths. They value their discipline's engagement in an effort to use data to answer significant questions about how society works. It is no accident, in this regard, that recent concerns have prompted new attention to historical contributions to an understanding of the function of gender in society, or that political sociologists have joined interested historians in renewing questions about the impact of changing government functions. Historical analysts will, of course, disagree about what levels of their craft can be taught to nonspecialist students, and at what ages. They will grant the need to develop a mastery of certain factual data before much analytical progress can be made, and they will urge that their approach to social research requires attention to particular contexts of time and place. But they will agree on the importance of addressing questions, not memorizing hallowed facts for their own sake. And to this extent, they will clash head-on with the historical literacy movement.

Partisans of literacy measurements can, to be sure, address the first of the two great objections to their approach by expanding the facts-to-be-learned to encompass non-Western and social data. It is not entirely unproductive to think of amending some of the recent formulations about what must be known to include highlights from Asian, African, and Latin American history as well as from Western, and to note major developments in family structure or protest behavior along with great philosophers and classic treaties. This already forces important reconsideration of teaching coverage, requiring important reductions of the conventional canon — omitting, for example, one of the Jacksonian bank episodes in favor of understanding the process of commercialization of the American agricultural economy in the early nineteenth century, or moving more quickly through Greek philosophy in favor of some understanding of the Confucian legacy as well. These are adjustments that some of the more ambitious recent curricula are undertaking, and they constitute important improvements over historical literacy in its most belligerent formulations. Even these adjustments, however, risk confirming the basic approach, altering the list of questions that can be answered through multiple choice rather than challenging the idea of such a list. The question of what kind of history, social inquiry or factual survey, remains untouched.

The defects of the historical literacy approach, in distorting and reducing the value of the discipline, have not prevented substantial alterations of history teaching in the literacy direction. A teaching discipline already defined primarily in terms of factual coverage — Johnny should know what I think I had to learn about the Constitution — is becoming increasingly rigid. Teachers report decreasing leeway to depart from elaborate state requirements concerning coverage. Tests — out of apparent necessity, machine-gradable — drive home the importance of making sure that students memorize as much as they can. Whether the result is improved factual mastery cannot yet be determined, but one thing is clear: many students have less reason than ever before, at least as they enter college, to see history as a vehicle for exploring analytical questions.

Yet, tragically, the literacy movement has not been widely challenged before a wider public or educator audience. Historians ridicule the lists of a thousand essential facts to each other, but they have not mounted a vigorous counterthrust. In persuading an education-school group of the limitations of the literacy approach — an encouragingly easy task — one can be brought up short: if this is so, why has a historian not written a rebuttal? Why, as far as the interested public is concerned, has Allen Bloom been allowed to cultivate and define the historical garden? Why, beyond its amorphous ultimate message, has the Bradley Commission report generated such scant reaction?

The challenge is valid, and it should provoke some real soul-searching. The historical literacy movement has addressed some genuine problems, which may mute response. All serious historians must be concerned about the dilution of social studies classes with practical programs such as how to write checks (commercial economics); social studies, it seems, can become a catch-all to the detriment of rigorous study of any sort. The continued prevalence of coaches who teach (but who really teach to coach) among the ranks of social studies teachers is another issue of importance to historical literates and to those of analytical bent alike, as is the need in many cases to consider serious expansion of total social studies requirements in the schools. Further, even historians ultimately interested in their discipline as a means of evaluating social change can be caught short by the widely-publicized findings about student ignorance. Most of us, after all, were trained to value some knowledge of the Renaissance or the Founding Fathers, and it is disconcerting to find students bereft of these staples while also no further along in the more analytical uses of the discipline. It is tempting, in this situation, to go along with the coverage crowd.

It takes some courage, additionally, to oppose an approach so cunningly labeled as literacy. Some historians may fear that, deprived of its credentialling function, history's popularity might suffer, given the obvious fact that its analytical claims differ in precision and in forecasting potential from those of science.

Some historians, further, may be daunted by the political charge accompanying the historical literacy movement. There is no question that many literacy partisans hope to use history to enforce conservative national loyalties, against the immigrant, feminist, and other tides that threaten. Correspondingly, suggestions of a different approach to history teaching have undeniable political implications, even if its proponents argue in terms of higher truths. Analytical history involves revisionism, for the warts on culture heroes get put back on. On another front, many researchers may be content with a de facto division of their discipline, in which school history is simply different from real history, with college history courses presumably serving as a time of implicit transition for those students whose education goes that far. A division of this sort follows from the primary responsibility of education departments, rather than history departments, in training teachers. It also provides a convenient excuse for many imaginative historians to get on with their principal research tasks. The current excitement of historical research, quite apart from more prosaic goads to publish lest perish, has diverted many practitioners from paying much attention to the pedagogical implications of their work. The discipline has, quite simply, put far more creativity into research than into teaching during recent decades, and the lack of systematic opposition to the historical literacy movement both reflects and potentially furthers this disparity.

This situation may of course continue, given the ongoing interests of the research community and the undeniable strength of the literacy surge, feeding wider interests in developing simple forms of accountability for teaching in various fields and in making sure that students replicate the historical coverage many adults are familiar with. Yet the triumph of the literacy approach is not only undesirable, but also avoidable. Granting the validity of some historical literacy concerns, and the appeal of making young people toe the memorization mark, alternatives can be envisaged.

The first step, of course, is to prevent historical literacy from preempting the field. There are different ways to construe what history teaching should convey, and they must be more widely articulated. The second step is to project viable options that would provide genuine grounding in a history used as part of social analysis. Several suggestions are already possible.

1.   Historians should project several variants of contemporary history courses that simultaneously provide some coverage of later twentieth-century developments (recent-history literacy, if you will) and a real linkage with larger historical trends and analogies from past periods. If history is to contribute to an understanding of how society works, this is the kind of course that must be offered, in principle at several different levels. It is well known that survey courses typically run out of gas before the recent period, and this dilemma needs to be countered explicitly. In the process, the contributions of history to social understanding can be directly developed.

2.   Historians should project analytical segments that can be used as options within a survey context, at least by middle- and high-school levels. Even if coverage goals cannot be entirely recast, they can profitably be modified, freeing regular class periods for what are essentially history laboratories. In these labs, in turn, students would be asked to gain experience in dealing coherently with primary evidence (this is one ingredient already present in some teaching frameworks), but then to move on to engagement with key types of interpretive issues, such as analyzing official value structures and their interaction with subcultures, or determining the relationship between causes and results of key pieces of legislation or policy. In these labs, conceptual training would join with skills in managing data, not only through textual criticism but also via quantitative techniques. Just as science teaching uses problem sets to illustrate scientific method and selected theories and laws, as relief from rote learning, so the installation of the history laboratory modifies straight survey coverage in favor of utilization of case studies that provide insight into central analytical problems. Thus problems involving comparative frameworks will be introduced to interpretations of cultural variables without the necessity of laboratory work on each civilization segment of a world history course. Case studies that involve explaining the sources and impacts of change would not, therefore, require a survey of every major historical time period. The laboratory highlights issues, not undifferentiated memorization.

The proposal of regular history labs is not intended to assert scientific status for history, for the discipline's claims are different. It follows, however, from a need shared by history and the sciences to leaven textbook treatment with serious introduction to the discovery aspects of the disciplines — in this case, discovery qualities that emerge in learning to manage data and to grasp analytical issues in the case-study format.

3.   College-level historians should take the lead in rethinking (again!) the purposes of the entry-level history course. Here is another point at which historical literacy goals are particularly tempting — at last, one can rescue former high school

students from ignorance — but also particularly unfortunate. To replicate coverage goals, often complete with gigantic textbooks and multiple-choice examinations, risks deadening an interest in history at the college level plus inhibiting any real ability to use history in approaching social topics.

The entry-level course may, to be sure, require certain coverage elements, for example in insisting on some international history exposure, but its principal goals should surely be analytical. A survey semester to provide essential survey context, itself leavened by analytical training, could thus be followed by a deliberately topical semester in which the case study approach takes pride of place. Or the whole introduction could be organized around historical problems, capped perhaps by a contemporary history segment. The bulk of the introductory survey should build on defined types of historical situations whose analysis especially pays off in terms of abilities to grasp social processes more generally: types of change, organized perhaps between cases in which the state initiates and cases in which the state is acted upon; issues of causation in comparative context; implications of "silent" processes such as demographic patterns; again the question of competing value systems within single societies — the list of potential foci for exemplary analytical experience is considerable. Different groups of historians will generate different preferences, and ideally can move from this to the provision of models and some casebook material that will enable other instructors to follow suit.

Precisely because the pressures on the schools to emphasize coverage learning are mounting, it is vital for college instruction deliberately to introduce students to the additional functions of history, at the expense of some conventional survey time, and at the expense, certainly, of the comfort of some familiar teaching routines. What analytical exercises are possible, beyond some exposure to primary documents, and how they combine with what may still seem essential coverage ought to organize creative debate. In the process, imaginative college curricula can provide at least indirect guidance to those history teachers in the schools who struggle to offer something more than textbook mastery.

The essential ingredients involve a willingness to open vigorous debate about history teaching and the provision of some real effort in developing and fleshing out analytical options. Proponents of historical literacy, while calling legitimate attention to a series of issues in the presentation of the discipline, have miscast the kind of thinking that should be engaging history teaching. The "essential elements" of history — to use phrasing from the state of Texas — do not really consist of factual gems, but rather exposure to the kinds of historical situations that help students sort out some of the complexities of the human social experience. History requires data; it is no mere exercise in context-free critical thinking. Yet coverage goals are so deeply ingrained in the way most educators think of history teaching, and at the same time by themselves risk such sterility, that the strongest possible case for experimenting with realistic means of meeting the essential analytical purposes of history is not misplaced.

Ultimately, the emphasis on historical literacy risks demeaning historical study. Converting history to the memorized mastery of monuments from the past diverts from history as a means of discovery, as a basis for expanding insights and understandings of the past and what the past can tell us. Precisely because history permits discovery, it is essential to promote innovation in history teaching that matches its achievements in other domains. Here, once the literacy blinders are removed, the need for renewed commitment not just to good teaching but to imaginative educational planning becomes essential. Many universities have pulled back from much creative attention to history teaching save as accomplished by individual instructors; they have thus resanctified the survey course because of its convenience in meeting the laudable goal of an identifiable history requirement. They must now be called upon for the more ambitious task of stimulating new debate and rewarding well-reasoned innovation. The challenge of matching history's research achievements with appropriate teaching strategies has not yet been met in the contemporary educational context.

Chapter II:

Critical Thinking Skills

Demystifying Historical Authority: Critical Textual Analysis in the Classroom

Robert F. Berkhofer, Jr.

ALTHOUGH HISTORIANS urge the close, critical reading of documents in their own work and in the classroom, they rarely treat the textbooks, paperbacks, and articles they assign and review in the classroom to the same rigorous and detailed analysis. Even less do they show the impact of modern literary theory upon the very representation of the past as a form of text or narrative. Failure to show students the constructed side of history through a critical analysis of the assigned readings as textual wholes promotes two false impressions of how historians convert the past into history and how contemporary theorists in the social sciences, philosophy, and literature view the nature of historical understanding.

One false impression may be labeled *historical fundamentalism* in analogy to religious faith. Students seem to treat their assigned readings and textbooks, if not their teachers, as divinely inspired. All history is basically a matter of facts in this view, all students need do is memorize enough data by reading the assignments in the course. These students do not tolerate ambiguous interpretations of data, let alone multiple perspectives upon the past. Such an approach to representing the past as formal history presumes at base only one great story told from a single omniscient viewpoint. These students need to learn, in my opinion, how to treat textbooks and assigned readings as textual constructions subject to the same kinds of analysis as any other piece of argument or literature and, therefore, that the construction of history as an overall narrative is subject to the same biases and problems as any other intellectual production.

On the other side are the students who learn all too well the many interpretations given any major event or period of history by professional historians. To them such conflicting interpretations too often seem the picayune squabbles internecine to a profession in need of mental leaf-raking to keep its members in business. These students do not see the larger issues about human behavior and understanding at the core of the divergent interpretations historians give events and periods.

These students also need to learn that history textbooks and other assigned readings can be treated as textual constructions but, in this case, in terms of how they embody major controversies about the nature and causes of human behavior, the moral and political purposes of learning, and the role of narrative and rhetoric in the expositions humans give their understandings of themselves. Just as other persons cannot stand outside some universe of discourse, so these students must learn that they too make certain claims by their intellectual stance.

Both types of students should learn that historians construct history as if it were really an omniscient narrative that can be read as a single, great story of the past. In actual practice that great story is constituted by historians' books and articles through their representation of the past as formal history. Students learn this lesson best through becoming critical and close readers of their various assigned readings and textbooks as part of this discourse. Students should learn to move from reading assignments as textual constructions to reading all of history as a text. To modern literary theorists the word *text* designates not only the written work itself but also the framework of presuppositions that produce its form as well as content. In this sense of the word, a textbook, like a famous document or great book, invites interpretation as well as embodies interpretation, hence calls for a more active reader.

In my own classrooms, whether for first-year, upper-division, or graduate students, I try to achieve such an approach through a lengthy handout that offers guidelines to what I see as a more active approach to reading secondary sources than the usual suggestions for reading (and reviewing) a history book or article. Advanced Placement (AP) students will learn, like their college peers in history courses, that the discipline is a thinking person's field. In fact, they might study the whole AP examination as a textual production itself, using the guidelines to discover definite sets of presuppositions about the nature of history and whether the exam embraces but one version of the great story.

In the following version of my handout, I offer some additional commentary in brackets after each section of the original.

The purpose of analytical or deep reading (and reviewing) is to see through the surface text of a book or article to its inner workings. A simple recapitulation or summary of the work's contents as the author organizes it does not usually provide you as a reader or anyone with whom you discuss the piece an adequate under-standing of the contents as a set of arguments or a narrative embodying a cluster of presuppositions. You should examine authors' main points, how they went about explicating them, and the sets of assumptions that made for their works being exactly the way they are. In books, for example, authors have several hundred pages to make their points, but in preparing a review you have only a few double-spaced pages to make your points. Thus you must reorganize the author's scheme of exposition and framework of argument and assumptions for your own purposes according to your own needs for understanding and/or presentation. The following topics and questions aim to help you do this, to examine the book or article as a whole according to the larger framework of assumptions that generates its contents.

Comparing the author's goals and achievements. What are the chief goals of the work as announced by the author in the preface or introduction to the book or the first few paragraphs of the article? What are the actual major themes or ideas of the work in your own opinion? Does your analysis of the goals and themes agree with the aims as expressed by the author? Do the author's explicit goals (if any) and his/her major themes or arguments match both in their logic and in their exposition as represented in the book's or article's organization? Are the goals, themes, and arguments shown clearly in the organization of the book or article? Does, for example, the structure of the book — its parts, chapters, or other subsections — follow closely or loosely from the author's stated goals, or does the structure derive more from implicit judgments about morality, politics, or other concerns? Does the author, in short, prove her/his argument(s) and how well and by what means? Does the author's style enhance or detract from the main arguments or the overall contents of the work? What rhetorical ploys does the author use to further the argument or story? From whose viewpoint and with what literary devices does the author present the story or frame the argument? Why do you think the author chose that particular viewpoint or voice? Do conspicuous silences occur in the work about topics you think should have been covered? Why do you think the author omitted what you think so important to the work's argument or narrative?

[This section calls the students' attention to the overall message(s) of the book or article as stated by the author and whether they see the total text in the same manner. By focusing upon the comparison they examine the work as a whole in terms of its implicit as well as explicit messages and how the many layers of text embody and thus (re)present those messages.]

Morals, uses, politics. What are the author's moral and political judgments and how do they influence the text? For what political, moral, intellectual, or other purpose does the author argue and shape the material? (Philosophical, religious, and professional concerns can shape material as much as economic, political, or other interests.) Are the author's uses made explicit or are they implicit in how he/she told the story or made the argument(s)? Even an explicit denial of political or moral ends may have moral and political consequences.

[These questions direct the students' attention to their and the author's largest concerns in the political and moral realms. Such questions connect the work's contents to the world of ethics and politics, whether through philosophy, political theory, economic self-interest, partisan argument, or otherwise. Not only can the students use knowledge gained in other subjects, at home, or in still other ways to explore the presuppositions of an author, but, in the process, they connect a history text to their own larger perspectives as well. They also learn that all secondary sources have present-day political and moral implications even if the author argues for the appreciation of the past for its own sake.]

Models of society, economy, polity. What does the author presume about the nature of social, economic, or political arrangements in the society being examined? How are social groupings and their relationships determined? Does the society have classes as well as groups? What does the author argue explicitly or implicitly about the structures of power and the means of social control or domination? Does the author presume consensual agreement or conflict is natural among social groups and the overall workings of a society? Is the author a pluralist who believes in the wide distribution of power throughout the society or a power elitist who sees a small integrated group dominating the society? Does the author present supporting evidence or only theory in her/ his exposition of social arrangements?

[To ask what is presumed about the state, the economy, or the social organization in a text or interpretation exposes certain basic presuppositions that may or may not be uncovered in the preceding set of questions about uses, but the morals of the preceding part and the models of this part are often inextricably connected in an argument. These questions once again give students a chance to apply knowledge from other subjects and disciplines and to compare their versions of their own or another society with those presented by the authors they study.]

Plots, stories, metastories. From whose viewpoint does the author tell the story or make the argument? How does the author employ (or organize) the underlying narrative (conceived broadly)? To what extent does the author presume progress, decline, cyclic, or other basic modes of comprehending time through history? What story or logic does the author employ to move his/her argument or narrative forward? Of what larger story or history does the text or interpretation presume its story to be a part? Why does the author begin and end the history when she/he does? Do the beginning and end points build in certain biases in the making of the argument? At bottom, how does the author view the nature of history as a way of comprehending the past? To what extent do the author's arguments and story depend upon her/his evidence and what upon larger assumptions about human nature and society, ethics, and political uses? How does the author divide time in her/his story? What periodization does the author presume or explicate and how does the author know it or prove it?

[This section attempts to have students apply some of the current interest in literary theory and philosophy to the nature of historical narrative and the structure of the story. They should explore the author's viewpoint and voice as well as the literary motifs or rhetorical devices employed in the text. Even social science texts use plotting and rhetoric to make their arguments. How metaphors and narrative structures shape present-day social understanding as well as the history of ethnicity is argued delightfully in Werner Sollors, *Beyond Ethnicity: Consent and Descent in American Culture* (New York: Oxford University Press, 1986).]

Model(s) of human nature and causation. Does the author presume that human beings change their ways and outlooks easily or are they fundamentally hostile to change? To what extent do changes stem from willed human agency, that is, from goal-oriented human action individually or collectively? Or does change come from unanticipated consequences of aimed-for actions or from larger forces and/or structures working upon human beings? Can humans change their circumstances easily or only with difficulty? Does society in a sense create human beings and their actions or vice versa in the author's opinion? How does the author see the particular society, culture, or time as coming into being, and how does that society, culture, or time reproduce itself according to the author's arguments? To what extent are humans constrained by their culture or society or times and to what extent are they free to create what they will? Are all human beings alike over time in their interests, outlooks, and capacities, or do they vary by time and culture? Does the author, in other words, presume human nature is universal or a cultural and temporal creation? Are certain drives and interests considered common to all human beings, or do these vary by individual human beings, by cultures, by times?

[If students' attention was called to political and literary theory earlier, these questions focus on social theory and the "psychology" of human behavior in the explanation or interpretation of human activities and thoughts. Many of the questions revolve about the relationship — even the conflict — between voluntary human agency and social structure or impersonal factors like demography or physical environment in the explanation of past and present human behavior.]

Uses of evidence and proof. Does the author have all the kinds of evidence needed for all parts of her/his case as explored in the preceding topics? Are the basic facts presented by the author determined more by the evidence used or by the author's premises and presuppositions about human nature, models of society, or political and moral uses? Does the author, in other words, employ the types of evidence she/he needs to prove her/his case in the larger sense of the argument? Or is much of the evidence presented in the book or article beside the point(s) actually argued or implied? Does the author employ sophisticated methods of analysis in the manipulation of data? If the methods are quantitative, are they the proper or best methods? Does the author assert and then prove a strongly framed version of her/his case or argument but assert the stronger one is proven?

[Historians regard evidence as crucial in their own work, so too with the reading of secondary works as narratives and sets of arguments. How does the author use evidence, and is the right kind of evidence employed to prove the argument? For example, evidence of behavior may not prove the thoughts, let alone motives, of a person, just as statements of intention do not prove that such an activity occurred or was done for that reason. The conflict between human agency and structural explanation only complicates this matter. In the end, matters of evidence are matters of logic, and frequently the lack of the right kinds of evidence for the arguments or stories offered undermines the validity of the whole book. Similarly with methods of analysis these days, improper statistical manipulation of variables may nullify the most voluminous accumulation of data.]

    This guide to reading and reviewing, in my experience, improves students' critical reading abilities at the same time that they learn to think about the construction of history as ways of thinking. Most students react with happy approval when they realize that this approach to thinking about history works also for understanding human affairs in the present. Likewise they come to appreciate the present-day significance of the many arguments about the past. Students also find they read with more interest as they become more active in questioning authors. They also discover they have far more than they previously thought possible to discuss or write about an article's or book's organization and its author's presuppositional framework when they follow the guidelines. Even more importantly, they experience profound satisfaction in realizing how all the sets of questions fit together as a totality in the pages of an author's work and, as the semester progresses, in their own and other students' thinking.

    I have used this handout with equal success for students ranging from first semester freshmen in the survey course to graduate students in a readings seminar. In discussions of required reading, the guidelines broadly orient the students to the assignments. As a result, they frequently can carry the class discussions by themselves because they have thought through the reading. They also seem to retain the so-called factual material better than if they tried to learn the facts apart from the larger intellectual frameworks that give them meaning. If I give undergraduates a quiz on the reading, I ask a question that brings out major themes of the reading according to the guidelines. Students find such an intellectual exercise more satisfying than the typical quiz because it shows how deeply they understand the assignment and its relationship to the total course.

    If I require analytical book reviews as part of a course, the guidelines form the basis of the students' reviews. But, as I warn them, the questions cannot be applied mechanically. The guidelines offer students suggestions for thinking about a book and framing their essays in their own manner, not a step-by-step manual for easy application. Students soon learn their own book reviews are constructed according to the same presuppositional frameworks they find in the authors they study. They too must make decisions about how to construct their arguments, choose the moral or political uses of their reviews, and rally evidence for their own cases. As I tell students, neither they nor I can stand outside the universes of discourse we say others use. That the guidelines apply as much to themselves (and me) and to their (and my) ways of framing things comes as an important self-discovery to students. (In fact, I urge students to watch the logic and presuppositions of their professors' arguments and lectures as much as the authors they read.)

I have even organized an entire semester course around the guidelines. In "Myths and Models In (And Of) American History," I arrange a sequence of paperbacks covering the span of American history. By reading short monographs that have strong models and morals shaping their messages and organization, the students soon gain an awareness of the constructedness of history as an intellectual activity. Not only do the students therefore get a chance to understand each text for itself, but they also begin to see over the semester that the larger story of history presumed by the different authors (and the historical profession) embodies similar or conflicting presuppositional choices. Since this class was a required writing course at the University of Michigan, I assigned a short paper every other week. The students were asked to write five to ten typed pages on questions that probed the core of the author's presuppositional frameworks in terms of one or two sections of the guidelines. The discussions were always energetic and frequently intense. Most of the twenty students said it was the most exciting class they had taken in their college career. The best student was only a sophomore, but he and half of the other students produced reviews of the assigned books better than most of the reviews that appear in professional journals.

Building Critical Thinking Skills in an Introductory World Civilizations Course

Ruth F. Necheles-Jansyn

I HAVE TAUGHT the required history survey course for twenty-five years with mixed results. During this time, both its content and the background of the students to whom it was offered have changed markedly.

The greatest difficulties I encounter are too much material (hence the need to skim superficially over the surface); inadequate textbooks overloaded with trivial, pedantic information; a mechanical approach to studying often learned in high school; and the consequent boredom of most students who have no personal interest in history.

In 1986-1987, I participated in a Cognitive Skills Project at the Brooklyn campus of Long Island University. The discussions in a weekly faculty seminar and released time helped me review the problems of teaching a broad historical survey at an institution where largely minority and/or foreign-born students are vocationally oriented and ill-prepared for college.

Before restructuring the world civilizations course, I redefined my purpose as developing students' ability to read, discuss, and write about the past, stressing communications skills, and deemphasizing the accumulation of factual data for the sake of the students.

Abandoning a rigidly chronological approach, I used as an organizing principle the theory that civilizations develop in stages and that most societies evolve in a similar fashion. The class, I decided, would first look at prehistoric society. Then, even though civilizations did not begin simultaneously everywhere, students would read about the origins of two or three different civilizations and compare the historical process at work. The same treatment would be given to other major stages of pre-modern world history: urbanization; development of religions or world views; empire building; invasion and assimilation of outsiders; recovery and stabilization; and first steps toward a world civilization. Which civilization would be discussed at any stage would depend on its ability to illustrate the characteristics of the period and provide a model for comparison.

Finding a textbook amenable to such treatment was difficult. Since the Cognitive Skills Project students came out of our remedial program, I chose the short text, *The Human Venture: The Great Enterprise: A World History to 1500*, by Anthony Esler, that had a socioeconomic rather than a political-philosophical approach. I also selected two issues of *National Geographic* in order to expose students to longer discussions of specific topics.

Looking for an approach that would develop students' ability to think critically about historical material, I decided to focus on explaining changes rather than on specific events or figures. Students would be introduced to the idea that all societies are made up of social, economic, cultural, political, and religious institutions. In all class discussions and written assignments students would be expected to use institutions to describe past civilizations, trace social evolution and change through institutional change, and compare societies by their institutions. Institutions then would provide the basis for students to use for interpreting stages of development, (for example, by comparing political structures; by explaining the direction that change takes [such as through the use of technological innovations]; and by attributing significance to past events in terms of institutional impact).

Cognitive skills to be developed during the semester were: to become aware of how we *know* history; to ask what sources are available for each stage of civilization; and to see how societies develop different perspectives, depending on both their past and such external conditions as geography, climate, and resources. I hoped that by the end of the semester students would be able to criticize other observers' (historians) theories about how and why a society developed by taking a look at their methods, evidence, and assumptions.

On the first day of my classes, I usually had detailed study guides, listing questions to be discussed and techniques to be developed. This time I decided to distribute only a brief overview of the semester's work and a list of due dates for written assignments. I would develop separate study guides for each unit building on class experience. Students' grades would be based on essays, tests composed of essay questions and identifications, and group participation.

Because a few students generally dominate discussions and many do not profit from lectures, I decided occasionally to use collaborative learning techniques. For each stage in the evolution of civilizations, the entire class would study and discuss one "master" civilization, one about which the most is known or in which they had the most interest. Then, for one or two sessions, the class would divide into several groups, each of which would read about another civilization at the same stage. During the class the groups would discuss their reading among themselves, and the instructor would circulate among them to answer questions and participate in discussions. Then each group would summarize its findings for the class; all students would be expected to know this information.

In the fall of 1986 I implemented these ideas in two very different classes: one small day section that met one hour three times a week in which fourteen of the seventeen students were enrolled in our remedial program; the other a once-weekly two and a half hour night section with thirty-three students who ranged from outstanding to apathetic to unprepared. When possible, both classes were given identical assignments.

To start, I gave students an issue of *National Geographic*, 168, 1985, devoted largely to prehistoric man. Unlike most in this journal, the articles, "The Search for Our Ancestors," by Kenneth Weaner, Jay Maternes, and David L. Brill and "Homo Erectus Unearthed," by Richard Leakey, Alan Walker, and David Brill, used many technical terms that remedial students could not follow. I therefore required them to read only the boxed feature sections, illustrations, charts and captions, although I recommended reading the complete articles.

Several of the day students were Pentecostals who refused to consider the concept of human evolution. Since my purpose was to teach about nonwritten sources of history, I left the issue of biological evolution to their anthropology class and presented a slide lecture on how archaeologists uncover and interpret information about prehistoric man. In this lecture I briefly surveyed what we learn from various types of artifacts. Then I showed slides of work scenes and findings from an art historical dig in which I had participated. Students were fascinated by the idea that we learn directly from physical evidence and need not take someone else's word; they asked many questions and throughout the semester remained aware of the issues of sources and interpretation of evidence.

I did not assign primary sources in the first part of the semester; stilted language or excessive length precludes using such material as Gilgamesh, Egyptian inscriptions, or Greek tragedies. Late in the course I gave the students Henry VI of England's description of Joan of Arc's trial and asked them to compare it with the textbook account. Their self-confidence increased when they found that not only could they discover contradictions, but they could figure out why King Henry, although an eye witness, was an unreliable source.

High among my goals was the desire to train students to view societies institutionally and to use institutions to compare civilizations. Early in the semester they wrote in class a description of a civilization based on its institutions, and for their first paper compared two civilizations. All students who successfully completed the course understood the institutional approach.

I also wanted students to look behind authors' words to their intentions, and I devised two exercises in which students would identify and criticize interpretations. For the first of these exercises, I summarized four theories about the fall of the Roman Empire, trying to avoid editorial comment and insure that the different theses were clear. After discussing the theories in class, I assigned an essay in which students were to select the most plausible one and justify their choice, based on evidence from their text.

Most students successfully completed the Roman Empire assignment. The more able ones grasped the difference between a descriptive statement and an interpretive one, a skill that we had practiced in class by analyzing whether quotations cited in the text were fact or opinion. As long as the differences between interpretations were obvious, students were able to criticize weak ones on the basis of the author's assumptions, methods, or internal contradictions. Writing an essay in which they looked for assumptions and evidence and exercised their own judgment signaled to the students that these were skills they were expected to master.

I was, however, dissatisfied with the Roman Empire assignment because the theories were "predigested" and the weaknesses rather obvious. Consequently, I devised a more difficult exercise. Students were given an issue of *National Geographic* which described several scientists' efforts to trace Christopher Columbus' exact route. (Joseph Judge and James L. Stanfield, "The Island of Landfall," and Luis Marden "Tracking Columbus Across the Atlantic," *National Geographic*, 170, 1986.) In class we discussed the role played by such disciplines as geography, archeology, and marine sciences in historical investigations. Students were assigned a paper in which they discussed whether Columbus' route merited study and how scientists attempt to resolve such a controversy. Then they were given a short critique of the *National Geographic* study, "Columbus was Here. Or was He?," by Mark Cherrington, *Expedition News: Quarterly Earthwatch Report*, November 1986, and for their final exam they were asked to explain which conclusion they accepted, that of the *National Geographic* or its critics. I advised them that this problem resembles the Roman Empire exercise in that they had to select from among alternative interpretations on the basis of evidence from their readings. Most students expended considerable effort in understanding the *National Geographic* theory and thus had a vested interest in it. Some believed themselves incapable of judging the critique because it lacked supporting details, but a few looked carefully at the arguments raised by the critics and evaluated them according to clearly defined criteria.

Students in the two sections responded differently. The day students followed the skill-development scheme more readily, expressed enthusiasm, and attended regularly. All fifteen day students who completed the course performed satisfactorily; there was one "earned" failure among the night students.

I found the emphasis on writing and communication skills to be worthwhile, as was the decision to deemphasize the accumulation of historical facts. The students' ability to communicate about history improved markedly, and several developed an interest in the subject. By the end of the semester, frequent writing assignments had accustomed students to describing civilizations and institutional terms. Thinking clearly and writing coherently are connected and, because I also teach English composition, I used the same techniques and standards for criticizing these papers as for English assignments. By the end of the semester most students were able to write credible descriptive, comparative, and critical essays.

The collaborative learning technique was less successful, however. The day students could not complete their work in one hour. Some groups failed to work together; members frequently were unprepared and used the time allotted for discussion to read the assignment. Because students failed to take their colleagues seriously, they neither paid careful attention to the reports nor asked questions.

Collaborative learning worked fairly well in the night section, where groups could meet for a longer period and all could present their reports in the same session. Perhaps maturity and increased responsibility were additional reasons why the night students worked together more successfully. In small groups, they asked questions and raised issues that they hesitated to bring up before the entire class. In their papers, some compared the information given in reports to the civilizations that had served as models.

On the whole, I believe that small groups cannot effectively impart information to the rest of the class. But because small group discussions discourage dependence on articulate students and encourage broad participation, they should be used for discussing interpretations and controversial points.

The text presented a final problem. Its brevity did not compensate for its subtlety. The author's literary allusions confused and frustrated students whose native language was not English. Occasionally I assigned chapters from another text by Edward McNall Burns, Philip Lee Ralph, Robert E. Lerner, and Standish Meacham, *World Civilizations: Their History and Their Culture*, 1986, which, although considerably longer, students understood better and willingly read.

In the spring of 1987, I taught a modified version of this course to a larger day section of twenty-nine students. Of the innovations adopted in the fall, I retained the emphasis on writing and interpreting skills and the requirement that students write two or three essays at home (that semester, a comparison between two civilizations, and a Roman Empire and a Chacoa Indian exercise.) I assigned short accounts of recent scientific explorations illustrating how discoveries affect our understanding of the past. Another text that focuses on social and institutional history and falls within our students' linguistic abilities was used, John P. McKay, Bennett D. Hill and John Buckler, *A History of World Societies I, to 1715*. Finally, the exercise on the Roman Empire was rewritten to make it more sophisticated, and students were required to view a museum exhibit on Southwestern American Indians to develop their own interpretation of a civilization that was not discussed in class.

I have continued to experiment with this format, even though the spring 1987 changes solved some problems. For example, I have changed the order of the written assignments to postpone looking at historical interpretations until the end of the semester. The Roman Empire is a "natural" for such an exercise, but it is better to wait until students are equipped to handle such a difficult task. On the basis of this ongoing experiment, I believe that the overall goal of merging cognitive and historical skills is a realistic one, worthy of further development.

Teaching Analytical Thinking Through the "AHR Forum" and The Return of Martin Guerre

Phyllis A. Hall

PANSETTE HAS DONE IT AGAIN. The sly trickster who impersonated Martin Guerre in the sixteenth century and subsequently fascinated generations of storytellers, readers, and scholars, has captivated two sections of freshman history. I assigned the "AHR Forum: The Return of Martin Guerre" as supplementary reading in the "History of Europe to 1715" survey at the College of William and Mary. Students loved it, and it also proved to be a useful tool for teaching analytical thinking.

In introductory survey courses, instructors have two main missions. They must teach students about the past and, at the same time, help them to develop analytical skills. During more than twenty years of teaching, I have used a variety of methods and books to present opposing interpretations of historical evidence.

I have used books of readings, such as the Heath series, *Problems in European Civilization*, and more recently, J. Kelley Sowards' *Portraits in European History*. These college texts present differing opinions on historical problems. I have discussed such readings in the classroom and required students to write papers in which they describe a problem and the opinions surrounding it. They then must select one of the opinions to support with a rational argument based on the evidence. I have had success with this approach to teaching critical thinking and writing but I am always looking for something new.

I found a heated and scholarly debate between two contemporary and respected historians, Robert Finlay and Natalie Zemon Davis, in the "AHR Forum" of the June 1988 *American Historical Review*, pages 553-603. The debate concerns Davis' book, *The Return of Martin Guerre*. Finlay accuses Davis of "refashioning" the story of Martin Guerre by using interpretation to stray from the facts; Davis responds with justification for her interpretation. Unlike some of the other readings I have used to present differing opinions on historical problems, the Finlay-Davis exchange involves a point-by-point criticism and rebuttal, and the overall theme concerns the extent to which historians can legitimately embellish fact with interpretation.

The Martin Guerre story is an intriguing one. An impostor, Arnaud du Tilh, also called Pansette, passed as Martin Guerre for three years. Both Guerre's wife, Bertrande de Rols, and his family accepted Pansette as Martin Guerre until the pseudo-Guerre claimed his inheritance. Pansette then was accused of deception, brought to court, and had nearly exonerated himself when the real Martin Guerre returned. The court found Pansette guilty and he was executed. The traditional version of the story, based on sixteenth-century accounts, most notably that of Jean de Coras, a judge of the Toulouse parlement, portrayed Pansette as a charlatan and Bertrande as a dupe and a victim. The story itself is compelling, and just as compelling are the essays in the "*AHR* Forum" by Finlay and Davis.

In his essay, "The Refashioning of Martin Guerre," Finlay argues that Davis has gone beyond the evidence to transform Bertrande from a dupe to a willing accomplice. He claims Davis is guilty of an excess of invention and does not respect the sovereignty of the sources. After reading Finlay's criticism, I was convinced that Davis had over-stepped the bounds of acceptable historical scholarship. I agreed with Finlay until I read Davis' point-by-point rebuttal in her essay, "On the Lame." Davis defends her historical reconstruction by showing how she overcame the limitations of early sources through knowledge of sixteenth-century French peasant life and psychology.

If I could be caught up first by Finlay's arguments, and then do an about-face when I read Davis' reply, I judged that reading and discussing the "*AHR* Forum" might be a useful exercise for students. The story itself is hard to beat. And, although other historical disagreements may be as great as that between Finlay and Davis, seldom are they so current or so persuasively presented. Additionally, the "Forum" has the advantage of Davis responding point-by-point to Finlay. Such direct debate — including personal jibes — probably would heighten student involvement in the issues.

In the fall semester I assigned the reading for a class discussion to compliment textbook material on early modern Europe. The film, *The Return of Martin Guerre*, was shown at the local public library a week before the reading assignment was due. I recommended viewing, but did not require it because students were already burdened by a heavy work load for the course.

I had set up the discussion to accomplish several things. I wanted students to understand the use of evidence and the complexities of interpreting the past, and I wanted them to grasp some of the dimensions of peasant life in sixteenth-century France. The vehicle for all of this was the Finlay-Davis debate.

First, students needed to understand the story. Then, I wanted to be sure they understood the traditional interpretation of the case and both Finlay's criticism of Davis and her rebuttal. Once they understood the story and the issues raised in the "AHA Form", I could find out whether they found Finlay's or Davis' assessment more convincing. Most students favored Davis' interpretation. Students — and one vocal woman in particular — did not think Bertrande was a dupe. They agreed with Davis that Bertrande must have known "the touch of the man." She must have realized from body size, foot size, and overall appearance that Pansette was not her husband.

Student discussion touched on issues relating to sixteenth-century life when they considered why Bertrande would pretend to recognize the imposter. She had been abandoned and could not remarry. It was a male dominated society and marriage conveyed both social status and property rights. Students suggested that if Pansette had not tried to claim Martin Guerre's inheritance, Bertrande's uncle probably would not have questioned his identity. According to the students, Pansette's deception was allowable only as long as he enhanced the family fortunes.

Part of the discussion focused on the use of evidence. We discussed documentary evidence such as legal records and Davis' use of contextual arguments, psychological arguments, and sources not consulted by Finlay. Most students favored Davis' contextual approach. When the balance of student opinion clearly favored Davis' historical reconstruction, I introduced Finlay's question, "In historical writing, where does reconstruction stop and invention begin?" (p. 569). In one class, a student adamantly supported Finlay's contention that Davis had refashioned the Martin Guerre story. He argued, as Finlay does, that of the 180 witnesses in the trial, not one suggested Bertrande was an accomplice. The records further revealed that Bertrande was a plaintiff in the charges of imposture against Pansette. How, then, could she be an accomplice? Other students countered that Davis' essay and her book had been an exploration of truth and doubt. The purpose of Davis' book had been to raise questions about the traditional interpretation.

At the end of the discussion, we had reached no clear conclusions, but we had, like Davis and Finlay, raised important questions. To sum up, I explained that I had assigned Martin Guerre because it was a darn good story and because I wanted students to see the dynamics of scholarly disputation. I also stressed that I wanted them to see the complexity of interpreting the past. Their textbook made the past look clear, factual, and simplistic, when in fact, it is just the opposite. The fun and the business of history comes in trying to make sense of the complexities.

Student response to the "AHR Forum" in both sections of the class was enthusiastic. I thought reading the "Forum" had worked well for the classroom discussion, but I still wondered what the students had actually gotten out of it. To find out, on the final examination, I asked a fifteen-point essay question on the Guerre problem. Students had to discuss either 1) Finlay's criticism of Davis or Davis' response to Finlay, or 2) what they had learned about history from the "AHR Forum." Before grading, I was struck by the length of answers to the questions. The Guerre question carried the least points of the essays, and yet students wrote their responses at greater length than on some of the weightier essays. Here are some typical excerpts:

"The most important thing learned was that of writing a persuasive, argumentative essay. Both Davis and Finlay are brilliant.... They carefully hide their weaknesses while systematically exploiting the weaknesses of their opponent."

"On almost every historical event and person, opposing views such as these can be found. As Davis admits in the 'Forum,' we need both views."

"Finlay was correct in saying that Davis used conjecture. However, Davis' conjecture was not taken out of the blue. Davis shows the reader her style of the "New Research" wherein she used not only historical evidence of the time, but social and anthropological evidence in determining French customs of the time, psychological evidence in reconstructing the thought and logic process of Bertrande and Arnaud, as well as evidence from a variety of other social sciences."

"Two people may see the same event, but record it totally different from each other. The reasons for this are that some people may see something from a different angle or perspective. Finlay feels that Bertrande was a `dupe' who was tricked by Arnaud.... Davis bases her ideas on the assumption that Bertrande played along with Arnaud. Davis feels that Bertrande had to have been able to make the distinction between the real Martin Guerre and the impostor...."

"Davis clarifies the failures in Finlay's analysis, namely, that he believes there is a black and white in the situation. He claims to have discerned the truth from Coras' *Arrest Memorable*, her principle source, but she asserts that Coras did not come to absolute decisions, and there were many uncertainties in his perception of Bertrande. She also points out that Finlay did not even look at one of her sources and therefore cannot make judgments on the validity of her statements."

"Dedicated to a factual and logical evaluation of historical material, Robert Finlay exposes what he perceives as weaknesses and misrepresentations in Davis' *The Return of Martin Guerre*. His attack on Davis' use of self-fashioning, psychology, and anthropology exemplify his belief that Davis has gone beyond facts to a fictional interpretation of Martin Guerre."

"... from the obviously different points of view between the sixteenth century and the twentieth century and between two twentieth-century views, it is easy to see how an event can be changed by the historian's point of view."

"Davis was a promoter of 'self-fashioning' and she credited Arnaud with having experienced such a transformation. Finlay says this was ridiculous and that Davis was simply using it because it was a new word."

▼

I was pleased with the above responses. In rethinking the assignment, I would like to require students to see the film in addition to reading the "Forum"; then, the essay on the final exam could count for more points. The problem will be in eliminating something else from the busy schedule of a course that covers Europe from the Greeks through 1715. I even have considered expanding the exercise by requiring students to read the December 1988 "*AHR* Forum" focusing on Robert A. Rosenstone's essay: "History in Images/History in Word: Reflections on the Possibility of Really Putting History onto Film." The use of a film like *The Return of Martin Guerre* in class raises lots of important questions beyond the Finlay-Davis debate.

Whether or not I use the film, reading the "*AHR* Forum" on Martin Guerre has served my students well. I was satisfied that they had crossed the boundary of benign acceptance and entered the fertile realm of analytical inquiry. They had learned that historical facts contribute to an historical context, and the context may enhance the facts. Yet there are limitations to both the facts and the context in explaining human events. Pansette, even after his execution more than 400 years ago, with the able assistance of Davis and Finlay had taught my students to doubt, to question, and to weigh arguments. They learned that wisdom may be more in seeking than in certainty.

Writing In The Major:
A Novel Approach That Works

Robert Blackey

Edited by Jeanette Lauer and Mildred Alpern

IT IS A TRUISM among teachers of writing that the only way for their charges to improve is to write, rewrite, and then write some more. Writing, of course, is not only valuable for its own sake, but as a vital educational tool as well: the best way to understand something fully is to write and rewrite what we think we know. "He who writes badly thinks badly," wrote William Cobbett. And, according to John Updike, "Writing and rewriting are a constant search for what it is one is saying." For their part, most teachers of history acknowledge the value of student writing and routinely assign term papers, book reviews, and other writing projects; most of us also utilize essay exams.

But how much written work can history teachers assign each semester? How much dare we assign? We usually have more than enough to keep us busy each day, so there is a clear limit to what we will require of our students and be able to grade constructively. Besides, we are not English teachers! Some of us might think twice, moreover, before asking our students to work significantly more than do our colleagues. We could, as an alternative, devote additional time to extensive written suggestions and criticism of fewer papers, but this solution too is fraught with problems, since both the amount and frequency of writing is vital for learning. So, to borrow Lenin's pre-revolution words, "what is to be done?"

At California State University, San Bernardino, we are engaged in what appears to be a novel and effective solution that goes beyond the domain or responsibility of a single department The program at CSUSB has its origins in an April 1976 directive by the Board of Trustees of the twenty campuses of the California State University mandating that all graduates demonstrate writing proficiency prior to graduation. Each campus subsequently developed a method of defining and certifying that writing ability for all degree candidates.

CSUSB came to offer five courses, all numbered 495, through the Schools of Administration, Education, Humanities, Natural Sciences, and Social and Behavioral Sciences, which in 1981-82 became part of our upper-division general education requirements. Prerequisites for 495 are freshman composition and upper-division standing. Significantly, most of the courses are taught by teachers from within the schools themselves. And this is how I, a historian, came to teach Social Sciences 495 to history and other majors from the school.

Social Sciences 495 takes more time than any other course I teach, but I gladly offer a couple of sections each year, as do several of my colleagues, for one simple reason: it works! Most students leave the course improved writers, more aware of the relationship of writing to thinking, of language, nuance, style, grammar, and what generally makes for good writing. Those who begin the class with poor skills can, with effort, leave with minimum levels of competency, while those with ability have the opportunity to refine their skills.

Most students think of writing in superficial ways — consisting primarily of spelling, grammar, and punctuation. But I try to help my students become aware, both implicitly and explicitly, of the vital link between writing and thinking. They learn, I hope, that writing *is* thinking, which means that every time they write they have another opportunity to discover just how perceptive they are, or are not. That is, there really is no writing equivalent of "the gift of gab"; we may be able to fool ourselves and others with our spoken words, but with writing, if no thought is in our minds, nothing substantial reaches the page.

My particular qualifications, apart from willingness and enthusiasm, include my own writing and publications (in several fields and to diverse audiences), seven years as editor of CSUSB's annual self-study and accreditation reports, current editorship of the "Advanced Placement Teaching" column in this newsletter, and my participation in a series of faculty seminars (funded by an NEH grant and supported by CSUSB's Writing Reinforcement Program) designed to assist college teachers in improving their own assignments and the written work of their students. Other teachers with less writing and editing experience are trained by a program coordinator, and most of us exchange materials and ideas.

The course itself (four quarter units, meeting four hours per week, with class size limited to a maximum of twenty) is one in expository writing, and it emphasizes the techniques of analysis, summary, review, research, and argumentation. Students are instructed to consider the class a writing workshop where they write, edit, and rewrite their own work, criticize the writing of others, and discuss the critiques of their own writing. Grades are A, B, C, and No Credit, with the latter meaning that students must repeat the course.

Students are required to develop and complete four short papers (three to four typed pages) and one longer paper (about ten pages), as well as take midterm and final exams, which, like the other assignments, are geared to enable them to work in and think about their academic majors. Papers are initially drafted in class, criticized by fellow students, edited and rewritten at home, and then handed in for grading.

My comments and marginal markings are such that students can learn from them and rewrite their papers for a higher grade. (For example, I call attention to inconsistencies in the use of verb tenses and places where subjects and verbs or nouns and pronouns do not agree. It then becomes the student's job to correct the errors. Or, rather than scribble the overused but always vague "awkward," I specify why a sentence or clause needs rewriting. And where a paper is cluttered with unnecessary words, I write the abbreviation "EUW" in the margin next to the offending line, which students are instructed to recognize as "eliminate unnecessary word"; the student must then determine which word may safely be eliminated without altering the meaning. Other abbreviations and notations focus on problems with punctuation, clarity, and choice of words.) Assigned readings and a steady flow of handouts help round out the course, all of which is described in more detail below.

I require that students read for class discussion throughout the course *On Writing Well*, an extremely helpful and readable text by William Zinsser (Harper and Row, 1985). I urge them to make active use of a dictionary and a thesaurus, and I recommend Kate Turabian's *Manual for Writers* and J. Heffernan and J. Lincoln's *Writing: A College Handbook* (which is also required in our university's freshman composition classes). I expose them to other kinds of writing about writing, such as George Orwell's "Politics and the English Language" and Kurt Vonnegut's "How to Write with Style." And I encourage them to learn to recognize, appreciate, and emulate good writing — examples of which I distribute — as an additional route to the goal of improvement.

Before I assign the first paper to be graded, students write two short papers, one an autobiographical essay, the other a review of a film on the revolution in Nicaragua. With these ungraded tasks we go through the motions of what is about to become standard operating procedure. Further, all assignments are explained in detail so there are no misunderstandings (there is always time for questions) and students can budget their time accordingly. Students are also familiarized with a minimum number of editorial markings and instructed in what to look for as they criticize one another's papers. These first two ungraded essays give me a chance to become acquainted with my students so as to anticipate strengths and weaknesses, and it gives them an opportunity to learn how I will respond to their work. In other words, this is good practice for all of us.

In addition, students keep a journal in which they make entries for five to ten minutes at the start of each class. They can write about anything they wish, and I neither grade nor read them. The actual writing is what is important, and at the end of the quarter I have students compare early, midcourse, and late entries to determine if they see any changes. Some observe few differences, but a comment by one student illustrates what I hope most will ultimately realize: "When I began these journal entries, I simply described what I had been doing, but by the end I was writing about what I was thinking."

Since students in the course must be at least juniors, they have usually begun taking courses in their majors. I construct all graded assignments with that in mind.

These include an essay comparing book reviews from a professional journal and the popular press, a review of a book read or being read in a course in the major, an interview in essay form with a professional in the student's field, and an essay analyzing a contemporary issue from the perspective of the student's major. These are the short papers. The longer one, a research paper, is a bibliographic essay, an analytic review of the literature of a subject within the major. A tour of the library, designed to help with assignments, is conducted by a librarian during an early class session; most upper-division students, I have learned, profit from this since few have used the library for more than checking out books.

In addition to detailed explanations for each assignment in the syllabus, I discuss all assignments in class before any work is actually begun, and I distribute handouts that provide supporting information. For example, one handout suggests guidelines for writing summaries and critiques for book reviews. Students read about interview techniques and the use of interviews in their discipline, and they help each other prepare the questions they will ask. Other handouts suggest writing strategies and procedures (including organization and style), alert them to uses and abuses of paraphrasing and the dangers of plagiarism, instruct them in note taking, and call their attention to a host of common writing errors. And they have available, on reserve in the library, samples of successful student papers.

Despite what may sound dry and methodical, to me it is not. I also try to have fun. For example, to demonstrate that even serious subjects can be entertaining, I distribute copies of satirical and humorous writing, including a brief article I wrote on robots and the labor force. Integrating some of my own writing is a convincing demonstration that I practice what I teach; and, not incidentally, my writing has become more precise due to my now keener editorial eye.

But the course can be fun in other ways, especially by looking at the lighter side of writing that is meant to be serious. The *Quarterly Review of Doublespeak* publishes some of the worst misuses of our language. Its editor, William Lutz of Rutgers University, spoke at CSUSB and provided these examples, among others: the military has referred to an invasion as a "predawn vertical insertion"; politicians pledge not to raise taxes but instead vote for "revenue enhancements"; the Environmental Protection Agency tries to pacify us by describing acid rain as "poorly buffered precipitation."

I am always on the lookout in what I read for anything that can help students approach writing more positively. Jack Smith, in his column in the *Los Angeles Times*, ran a series of bloopers collected by teachers (e.g., "When you put Roosevelt and Wilson side by side, you can see that they had few differences but their contrasts weren't that similar." "In the Middle Ages, the Black Pledge was going around."). William Safire's column, "On Language," in the Sunday *New York Times Magazine* frequently is useful. Dear Abby has devoted several columns to word abuse. I even use jokes and cartoons. Comedian Steven Wright says he once went to a place to eat that said "Breakfast Any Time," so he ordered French Toast in the Renaissance.

A *New Yorker* cartoon shows one tycoon sitting by a fireplace at his club saying to another: "Feeling poorly? Thank heaven! I thought you said you were feeling *poor*." Another pictures an elderly couple looking down at a mat in front of an apartment door on which they are about to knock; the mat reads: "Not Unwelcome."

Another instructive technique is to examine the corrected drafts of a professional's writing. Zinsser's book reproduces two pages in manuscript form complete with all word and phrase changes and editorial markings. This is a helpful way for students to see that what appears effortless in print actually took time and concentration. As Samuel Johnson said, "Easy writing makes damned hard reading." Then I circulate a typed copy of a review I wrote for the *American Historical Review* with all my own editorial markings, which collectively represent some eight editing read-throughs. The effect of all this is salutary and enables students to reconceptualize what writing is — that it is a form of thinking, not merely a matter of grammar.

Most of my course time is devoted to evaluating papers. But I do not rewrite or correct spelling and grammar. Instead, as described above, all marginal comments and editorial markings are meant to enable students to make corrections themselves. Thus, I encourage students to eliminate unnecessary words, substitute suspect words with more appropriate ones, rephrase with more feeling or style, use punctuation properly, communicate an idea more effectively, express a view in grammatically correct English, and — most important — rethink their ideas. I might, for example, ask if they have in fact connected evidence and arguments to conclusions. My written comments focus on major problems and strengths, and I do my best to provide encouragement and note improvement, especially since the early going can be difficult, if not depressing, for many students.

The mention of grammar may discourage some readers from considering teaching such a course. A common reaction might be: "I know how to write well enough, and I even know how to spot many grammatical errors, but I am neither trained nor able to teach grammar." Actually, this was my initial response when first asked to teach the course. In fact, I still am not able to teach grammar, nor do I wish to. (The best writers in our English department, I am told, share this view.)

Good writing involves much more than grammar, and that is what I concentrate on. I try to restore life to writing that functions poorly, if at all, and I seek to emancipate energy, imagination, style, creativity, and a feel for a subject when these need an inevitable boost. However, I call attention to grammatical errors and, to help students overcome problems with punctuation, I distribute handouts that provide both rules and specific examples on the use of the comma, semicolon, colon, dash, apostrophe, and hyphen. Further, I schedule two conferences with each student to review graded work, often page by page, and many see me more often.

Finally, some class time is also devoted to the skills involved in writing essay exams. I focus on techniques for brainstorming, the use of notes and outlines, and the value of organization. I stress understanding directive word meanings, analyzing and addressing the question, and keeping within time limits.

I view Social Sciences 495 as I see the history I teach; it is a means to a larger end and serves a higher purpose. Just as history is instructive in the way it illuminates life, writing is both a potent means of communicating a subject such as history and a vehicle for individual development. My ultimate goal in teaching this course is to help students realize their potential as educated human beings through their writing, their thinking, and in finding their own writing voices. I want them to recognize that growth is possible, with effort, and that however much a chore writing may be — and it usually is — it can also be fun and rewarding.

Chapter III:

Test Construction

A Guide to the Skill of
Essay Construction in History

Robert Blackey

(Reprinted from *Social Education*, March 1981)

MANY TEACHERS OF HISTORY, at both secondary and college levels, invariably devote insufficient attention to the essay examinations they prepare for their classes. Typically, on the eve of an examination date, they dash off questions that are believed to deal appropriately with the subject matter they wish tested. Knowing the kinds of responses they expect, the questions seem clear enough; after all, teachers are cognizant of what their questions demand, and therefore they have no difficulty interpreting or seeing the implications of the words they have chosen. Unfortunately, not all students are blessed with such insight, and whether or not they respond as the teacher hopes — assuming they have studied properly — is often a matter of chance. Equally unfortunate is the failure to acknowledge that a student's misinterpretation of an essay question may be the teacher's fault, and thus teachers continue to repeat errors and handicap some among each new wave of students entrusted to their care.

From 1976 to 1980 I was Chief Reader for Advanced Placement European History. In that capacity I served on the committee that wrote the examinations, a process that involved, for each separate test, the deliberations of at least six secondary and college teachers over a period of about a year. I also supervised the annual grading of the thousands of student responses, after which I provided the Educational Testing Service with a report evaluating the performance of the questions. Further, I had access to 25 years of such reports from both European and United States History. What follows, then, represents the collective assessment and reaction of literally hundreds of teachers, all of whom benefited from experience and hindsight. In spite of the fact that a great deal of thought and deliberation have gone into AP essay construction, all too often the best or poorest questions are not discovered until after an examination has been administered and graded. Only then can the least obvious subtleties which determine the success or failure of a question be known. Nevertheless, approaching essay construction with a sense of what has or has not "worked" may help avoid past mistakes; in this fashion we can practice what we teach. (The sample questions included below are from past AP examinations.)

Essay Construction

Goals: All good essay questions, from a grading perspective, should be able to elicit responses of a varied caliber, roughly analogous to students' abilities and preparedness. Questions that can be answered by simple recall of facts should be avoided; they reveal nothing more than a student's skill at memorization. Machines can store and retrieve facts better than we can, so it is pointless to train students to compete with them. Instead, good questions test the student's ability to use historical facts in order to explain and interpret important developments and, by extension, to come to a better understanding of life. For example, the following question offers students an opportunity to exercise historical skills by integrating late medieval developments with those of the Renaissance and Reformation periods, while it also requires them to integrate political and religious forces, as well as to observe national differences as they confront a significant theme: "How did the disintegration of the medieval church and the coming of the Reformation contribute to the development of nation-states in Western Europe between 1450 and 1648?"

Language/Wording: Appropriate language is a vital ingredient in any essay question. Vaguely worded and loose and unstructured items should be avoided. For example, the following question may be provocative, but it deals with concepts that are beyond the capacity of even superior students; moreover, it is poorly constructed and too open-ended: "It has been said that, from 1450 to the present, European life and institutions have been shaped by the existence of a worldwide frontier. Describe the main influence of this 'frontier' on the Europe of two of the following periods: the Elizabethan Era, the Age of Louis XIV, the Age of Reason, the Victorian Age, the period between the two World Wars." Also, by way of example, is the following question, which provided so much scope that it was relatively easy to go off in one direction and write, for instance, only on the revolution with the first clause ignored completely: "'Although the thirteen American colonies were founded at different times by people with different motives and with different forms of colonial charters and political organization, by the Revolution the thirteen colonies had become remarkably similar.' Assess the validity of this statement." It is a useful practice to relate the purpose of a question to the goals of the course in such a way that it can be appreciated by the student and, if necessary, discussed afterwards. Considerable effort should be expended so that questions are well written, uncomplicated, and straightforward. Concepts, terms, and code-words should be used with care, making certain they have been noted in texts or class and, therefore, are familiar to students.

Directions: Statements or quotations followed by the words "discuss" or "assess" (e.g., "The attempt of the Emperor Charles V to achieve the medieval ideal of a

Christian European empire was doomed to failure from the start. Discuss.") usually unintentionally send students off in all directions; words like "discuss" or "assess" by themselves ask for nothing in particular. Make it clear what it is you wish to be discussed or assessed (e.g., "Discuss the origins and evolution of European liberalism as a political movement during the nineteenth century."). Similarly, students need to be led when asked to analyze or evaluate; state clearly what it is you want them to analyze or evaluate.

Questions that ask for the causes of something, or those that request students to explain why something happened, have worked well. Yet, those asking "How do you account for" or "To what extent" frequently elicit vague and weak responses unless the rest of the wording is especially clear and direct. The phrase "In what ways" can be interpreted either as "To what extent" or "How," if, in fact, the former and either of the latter are actually desired, then join them together (e.g., "To what extent and in what ways may the Renaissance be regarded as a turning point in the Western intellectual and cultural tradition?").

Instead of merely asking for the "effects" of something, ask for either the immediate or long-range effects, or both, whichever is desired. In a similar vein, when directing students to "explain and discuss the reasons" for something, and when several kinds of reasons are anticipated, your purposes will be better served if you request them to "explain and discuss the *several* reasons" or "the *variety* of reasons."

Essay questions should be structured so as to encourage or require that students go beyond mere accumulation of facts and textbook knowledge, and that they exercise critical judgment and show thoughtful interpretation.

Students tend to be weak on terminology; if some working definitions are desired, consideration should be given to asking for them as part of the question.

Avoid calling an event successful or unsuccessful (in a question that asks students why an event was or was not successful; e.g., "Why was revolution successful in France in 1789 but unsuccessful in the German states in 1848?") since it tends to stifle creative reflection and original judgment; students might prefer to challenge the assumptions within the question, but hesitate to do so given such wording. It is better to allow students to pass judgment and explain their reasoning. Similarly, when asking for an explanation of the success or failure (or other evaluative terms) of people or events, qualify it by stating the explicit criteria for success or failure, instead of leaving it open.

Finally, it is often wise for some questions to demand "evidence" to support a position or interpretation, even if such an implication is clear to you.

Sequence of Questions: Some attention should be devoted to the sequence of questions on any examination in which a variety of selections is offered. Given the pressure from time limitations, some students might not read all questions carefully and unload on the first one familiar to them. Although little can be done to prevent this, teachers might want to allot more time, offer fewer choices, encourage students to read each question carefully, and/or be certain that all questions are of equal difficulty. Where there is great disparity among questions, students choosing the more difficult ones are at a disadvantage. More specifically, the 1977 AP European History Examination offered two questions, among others, on the decline of the aristocracy in Western Europe and the industrialization of Eastern Europe. They were answered by more students than a traditional one on the origins and evolution of nineteenth-century liberalism. This unexpected result may have been due to the question on liberalism appearing as the last of six choices. Similarly, it has been suggested that had the first and sixth questions on the 1978 examination been reversed, the overall quality of the responses might have been improved. That is, question 1 concerned the Industrial Revolution, a topic which tends to lure less able students and/or result in inferior answers. Question 7 treated the political side of major revolutions, a mainstream subject, with responses being of a high quality. Thus, while both questions were heavily answered, more chose question 1; had their order been reversed, more students might have elected the less troublesome topic. While this is speculation, to be sure, it is worth consideration in order to minimize the number of potential pitfalls.

Breadth versus Specificity: Questions should be constructed so as to be answerable in terms of time allotted and from the standpoint of a reasonable expectation of training for your students.

Questions with compound subjects (i.e., those that treat several variables, such as political, social, and economic factors, or several concepts) may be asking for more than can be reasonably expected; they also encourage students to wander and not focus on the question (e.g., "Estimate the roles of British sea power, French governmental weakness, and Prussian military strength in the relations among states in Europe, 1715-1789."). Similarly, some teachers feel that a broad, generalized question gives students freedom. In practice, however, such questions often force students to use time and energy trying to guess what the teacher really wants.

Avoid questions that are either too general or too specific (or too specialized); a balance between the two should be the aim. Some structure is needed, but room for student initiative should also exist. Questions must be manageable.

Questions within Questions: Multi-part questions (e.g., "Discuss the extent to which early modern European society encouraged education for women. What criteria were used to evaluate women's education or its role, and women's potential for learning? What evolution, if any, can be seen in attitudes toward education for women from the Renaissance through the early eighteenth century?") become unnecessarily complex and should be avoided or kept to a minimum. If used, they should be well thought-out so they elicit only what is desired. Questions asking for too many separate areas to be covered run the risk of some areas being ignored.

Compare and Contrast Questions: Unless phrased very carefully, questions calling upon students to compare and contrast (either explicitly or implicitly) usually, at best, evoke no more than separate listings. Teachers ought to consider offering examples of what they are looking for in such questions, or train their students beforehand in how they should be handled. For example, although the following question may have problems, it instructs students on what it is they should compare, and then on how they should apply that comparison to a broader issue: "Compare the economic, political, and social conditions in Great Britain and in France during the eighteenth century, showing why they favored the Industrial Revolution in Great Britain more so than in France." Comparative analyses are instructive, but even scholars employing such an approach often fail to achieve satisfactory results.

Quotations in Questions: The use of quotations can create unintended and unnecessary pitfalls. Quotations are often interesting, snappy, and clever, but they can deprive students of clear directions: besides, quotations are also frequently subtle, imprecise, and sophisticated, and not necessarily understood or used as hoped. For example, "According to Lord Acton, 'The authentic interpreter of Machiavelli is the whole of later history.' Discuss this statement with reference to the history of modern Europe, concentrating on those periods with which you are most familiar." The Acton quote is indeed provocative, but it is also too cryptic for most students. "Revolt is easier than reform" was the quotation that preceded another question, but such a quote could mean anything and nothing.

Quotations, when used, should not be ambiguous, and the quotation and question must be paired properly: that is, the question should be clearly and directly linked to the quotation. Quotations from historical figures should have the language modernized enough to be understood easily by contemporary students. Metaphors in quotations, like ghosts in old homes, will return to haunt teachers, or else they will be taken at face value.

Dates: Dates should not be chosen arbitrarily since students read significance into them; care should be taken so that dates are used accurately and for specific purposes. When using a set of dates and a question that calls for reference to more than one country, the dates should be equally applicable to each country. The mention of centuries is often not enough to restrict the boundaries of a question, since even the best students occasionally become confused; specific dates should be included (perhaps parenthetically) as well, even though this may be obviously redundant. The use of date-phrases such as "by 1700" or "by the twentieth century" is misleading and should be avoided. "By 1700" can be taken to mean the sixteenth century, only 1700, the beginning of the eighteenth century, or all three. Clear chronological limits are important because they confine responses within reasonable bounds: when it comes to dates, leave no room for doubt or variation.

Words, Concepts, Phrases: Words should be used to express precisely what is meant. Do not introduce unfamiliar words or esoteric concepts on an examination. As a test is being constructed, all words should be scrutinized in an effort to foresee their implications and to determine if they coincide with the intention of the question. The list below does not comprise a collection of prohibitive words; instead, it includes examples that have caused problems for students. As such, it is intended to sensitize teachers and alert them to potential problems.

- *state* (could mean existing government, society, something else, or some combination of things)
- *administration/administrative* (could mean ruler, the government, or more)
- *Central Europe, the West* (these and similar expressions of geography are imprecise unless clearly defined beforehand; list or specify which countries/ states are to be included or excluded)
- *art/literature* (unless it does not matter what type students use, including music and film, specify the type desired)
- *science and philosophy* (questions on intellectual history calling for a discussion of science and philosophy will often result in little or no differentiation between the two)
- *society* (could mean the governed, the government, both or something else)
- *Rationalism, Romanticism* (when these and similar words are used to refer to the societal movements which bear their names, they should be capitalized; otherwise, rationalism emerges as logical, pragmatic, wise, while romanticism is presented as dreaminess, emotion, unclear thinking)
- *social structure* (could be taken to mean any number of different things, including social conditions)
- *liberal, conservative, radical* (these words mean something different to United States and European history, and to different times during those histories)
- *aristocracy/nobility* (students generally see no difference between these words)
- *peasant, working class, middle class* (the first two are often used interchangeably; the latter is broad enough to include a wide range of social classes)
- *culture* (can be used to refer to literary and artistic factors, but also to sociological factors as well)
- *minorities* (can be ethnic, racial, or other)

Right or Wrong Questions: These questions are phrased in such a way that a position is taken or a moral judgment appears to be rendered (e.g., "The European saw himself as a benefactor, carrying the blessings of Western civilization to Asia and Africa. The peoples of these regions viewed the Europeans as disruptive of their own valued traditions. Discuss the conflicting outlooks for the colonized regions of the world from the mid-nineteenth century to 1960."). Such questions encourage ideological rhetoric and, worse, often stifle open inquiry and historical analysis of historical processes. It would be more instructive to focus questions on, say, causation.

Current Events Questions: Questions that deal with or are related to present-day concerns frequently are long on polemics, rhetoric, and emotion, and short on historical analysis. For example, questions on war and military organization, such as the following, attract either military buffs who tend to ignore the question as they expound on their beliefs, or anti-militarists who use the question as a forum from which to make pronouncements about the evils of war: "Write an essay that relates the development of the large conscripted citizen army from its origins in the *levée en masse* to the emergence of the modern nation-state." Questions that deal with minorities and/or toleration tend to generate hot rhetoric about "human beings' inhumanity to other human beings," instead of historical analysis (e.g., "Unpopular minority groups have been a persistent historical dilemma. Explain and discuss the reasons why the Huguenots in seventeenth-century France, the Irish in nineteenth-century Great Britain, and the Jews in twentieth-century Central and Eastern Europe were unpopular with the majority and treated harshly." Or "'The leadership, organization, and programs of ethnic and racial minority movements after 1945 represented a fundamental departure from those which had existed from 1900 to 1945.' Discuss with reference to black Americans or Mexican Americans, giving about equal attention to the periods before and after 1945."). Teachers should be aware of the pitfalls involved, and advise students beforehand of what is expected from them and/or word such questions with care.

Successful Questions for Study

There is no easy road to writing fool-proof essay questions. Each new question has the potential to present a new array of problems. Nevertheless, by employing these guidelines, adapted and modified to suit specific needs, teachers should be able to avoid what have proven to be problems, and use what has worked with a greater degree of success. As a result, students should learn more efficiently and be treated more fairly, and teachers themselves will deserve and earn additional praise. In addition, teachers should consider establishing preliminary expectations or standards for their questions: this can serve the function of a pre-test, and should be pursued, as much as is humanly possible, from the perspective of students so as to anticipate problems. That is, after being written, questions should be screened with regard to intent and the extent that they actually ask what is intended. If there is a colleague with whom you can work to achieve this result, so much the better.

Finally, if studying questions that have been successful (for both students and graders) will aid the reader further, the following are offered from recent AP European and United States History. (It should be noted that United States History AP questions all begin with quotations, whereas only some European History questions are constructed this way.)

1. Discuss the various factors which enabled Europeans to achieve economic and political dominance over many non-European peoples between 1450 and 1750.

2. Explain how economic, technological, political, and religious factors promoted European exploration, from about 1450 to about 1525.

3. In the seventeenth century, England and the Netherlands developed effective capitalist economies, while Spain did not.

   Why did the economies develop so differently in England and the Netherlands, on the one hand, and in Spain, on the other?

4. What political and social changes in Western and Central Europe account for the virtual disappearance of revolutionary outbreaks in the half-century following 1848?

5. Discuss the extent to which nineteenth-century romanticism was or was NOT a conservative cultural and intellectual movement.

6. Assess the nature and importance of economic factors that helped determine the race for empire among the major European powers in the late nineteenth and early twentieth centuries.

7. "Every age projects its own image of man into its art." Assess the validity of this statement with reference to two representative twentieth-century European works in either the visual or literary arts.

8. "The Treaty of Vienna (1815) was a more realistic accommodation to the post-Napoleonic period than was the Versailles settlement (1919) to the post-First World War period."

   Decide the merits of the statement above and in a well-developed argument support your decision with a carefully reasoned analysis of the events mentioned.

9. A favorite device of social critics has been to construct model societies to illuminate the problems and the shortcomings of their times and to project a possible blueprint for the future. Describe and compare the utopias of Jean-Jacques Rousseau and Karl Marx. What were the chief faults they found with their own societies and how were their utopias designed to correct them?

10. "Every successful revolution puts on in time the robes of the tyrant it has deposed." Evaluate this statement with regard to the English Revolution (1640-1660), the French Revolution (1789-1815), and the Russian Revolution (1917-1930).

11. "Both the Jacksonian Democrats during 1824-1840 and the Populists during 1890-1896 attacked and sought to root out special privilege in American life. The Jacksonian Democrats attained power and succeeded; the Populists failed."

    Assess the validity of this view. Give roughly equal attention to the Jacksonian Democrats and the Populists.

12. "Although the United States is widely regarded as the home of free enterprise, business values, and materialism, American fiction since 1865 has generally been critical of business behavior and values."

    Assess the validity of this generalization with reference to the work of at least TWO writers who have treated the behavior and values of businessmen in their fiction since 1865.

13. "Paradoxically, Darwinism provided a justification for both social conservatism and social reform in the period from 1870 to 1915."

    Discuss this statement.

14. "Ironically, popular belief in the 'self-sufficient farmer' and the 'self-made man' increased during the nineteenth century as the reality behind these beliefs faded."

    Assess the validity of this statement.

15. "From 1914 to the present, the main trend in the relationship between the central government and the states has been toward concentration of power in the federal government."

    Discuss with reference to such areas of governmental power as regulation of business, social welfare, and civil rights.

16. "War has frequently had unexpected consequences for United States foreign policy but has seldom resulted in major reorientations of policy."

    Discuss with reference to the First and Second World Wars, giving about equal attention to each.

17. "Between 1776 and 1823 a young and weak United States achieved considerable success in foreign policy when confronted with the two principle European powers, Great Britain and France. Between 1914 and 1950, however, a far more powerful United States was far less successful in achieving its foreign policy objectives in Europe."

    Discuss by comparing United States foreign policy in Europe during the period 1776-1823 with United States policy in Europe during ONE of the following periods: 1914-1932 or 1933-1950.

18. "From 1790 to the 1870s, state and national governments intervened in the American economy mainly to aid private economic interests and promote economic growth. Between 1890 and 1929, however, government intervention was designed primarily to curb and regulate private economic activity in the public interest."

    Assess the validity of this statement, discussing for *each* of these periods at least TWO major areas of public economic policy.

19. "The term 'isolationism' does not adequately describe the reality of either United States foreign policy or America' s relationships with other nations during the period from Washington's farewell address (1796) to 1940."

    Assess the validity of this generalization.

20.   "Presidents who have been notably successful in either foreign affairs or
      domestic affairs have seldom been notably successful in both."

      Assess this statement with reference to TWO presidents, one in the
      nineteenth century and the other in the twentieth century, giving reasons
      for success or failure in each case.

Life Is a Multiple-Choice Question

Ann McCormick Scott

WHEN CHARACTERIZED by felicity of insight, accuracy of detail, and grace of expression, the historical essay is the highest measure of a student's understanding and performance. Eyes closed, silver locks flowing, we teachers hope to orchestrate such essays from the diverse human instruments in front of us. But before Mahler reverberated richly throughout the hall, there were scales and etudes, chords and little memory gems. Multiple-choice questions are the Czerny exercises of history. They offer not only a broad spectrum of learning but also test a variety of skills. They can lead students to see historical relationships they may have missed. Multiple-choice questions underscore the coherence of an essay, for they can test close reading and retention of detail. Well-crafted questions can also elicit responses based on logical sequence, interpretation and application, synthesis, analogy, critical capacity, specialized vocabulary, and general knowledge and awareness. Even writing skills can be tested by recognition and discrimination. To call out all of this requires the maestro to go through step-by-step preparation, and to exercise educated fingers, a willing machine, and plenty of Wite-Out in lonely composition.

To ease the loneliness of composition and minimize problems (for both teachers and students), what follows are five specific and prescriptive steps toward the drafting of a multiple-choice test. The first step provides suggestions to consider before actually beginning and urges us to reexamine the goals and contents of our courses. To the extent that these are already clear on the syllabus, in the daily assignments, and in our heads, we can move along. The second step is general advice on drafting a test: how to outline, set up a stem question, its answer, and the distracters, with some warnings on wording. The third step is the core of the composition, with examples offering a variety of question styles, a menu of samples, and a diversity of tasks; each sample question has been tested in battle. Then the test-maestro is asked to survey the masterpiece for content, skills level, style, appearance, and readability. The finale is close proofreading, accomplished by actually taking the test, ideally a couple of days removed from the original drafting. While that is hardly the sort of advice we want to hear with a test due, thirty-six essays to grade, a soccer game to referee, and a curriculum meeting to live through, push onward. Ultimately the aim is to make the maestro's task easier, and the musicians' response more edifying.

Step I. Establishing the Content and Skills to Be Tested

The worst multiple-choice tests are those canned by committees into text supplements. The second worst are produced by a rushed instructor who races paragraph by paragraph through the required reading and lifts sentences to be completed. The best tests are teacher-made, produced when we have clearly in mind the major content and skills goals of the course and of the unit(s) under study. These should be readily discernible by students via the syllabus and daily assignments, which, when thoughtfully prepared, pay off huge dividends in suggesting the material to be tested. Establishing the content and skills framework of the test can be aided by reviewing these questions to remind us of the major themes, important eras, syntheses, and highlights of learning from the course:

- What are the course objectives? Are these stated in the syllabus?
- What are the expectations of external examinations that may apply to the course, especially the Advanced Placement and Achievement tests?
- What are the content objectives of the unit under study? Are these on the assignment sheet?
- What are the skills objectives of the unit? Are these on the assignment sheet?
- What are the questions assigned to guide students' reading and discussion?
- What are the generally agreed historical highlights of the period under study?
- What historical questions have been subject to controversy or revision?

Decide beforehand which objectives you prefer to test by multiple-choice questions and which you want students to write out as identifications or essays. Balanced coverage of the material to be tested should be the first goal of the testing instrument, not an arbitrary number of questions or points. And points awarded should reflect a balance based on the time to be devoted to each segment of the test, and may also account for differing levels of difficulty.

Length. The course level might well dictate the length of the task you set for students. Most students can answer one multiple-choice question per minute in basic secondary-school courses, grades nine and ten. Intermediate students usually can handle two questions in three minutes (about seventy-five in an hour), and advanced placement candidates can work toward the accomplishment of a hundred questions in an hour.

Wording and structure. 1. Use language that is simple, direct, and free of ambiguity. Do not make a question a test of reading ability unless this is the explicit purpose of the question. Consider underlining key words, such as the term to be defined (socialism) or important instructions (e.g., all of the following except; one of the following is the cause of the others).

2.   Structure the question around one central idea or problem that is clearly presented in the stem and to which all the options relate in the same way.

3.   When several questions are based on a single setting or on stimulus material such as a passage, graphs, or charts, make certain each question is independent of the others in the set. Students should be expected to arrive at an answer from the material provided in the stimulus material, *not* from having correctly answered a previous question in the set. Avoid using distracters in one question that may provide clues for answering another question in the set.

4.   Keep the purpose of each question in mind. That is, if you intend to test factual knowledge, do not "dress up" the question to appear otherwise; if you intend to test critical thinking, be sure the question cannot be answered on the basis of factual information alone.

5.   If you intend a question to be difficult, make certain it is difficult because it requires sophisticated reasoning or understanding of a high-level concept, not because it tests obscure or esoteric subject matter.

6.   Do not use double negatives in a question. If you ask students to answer by identifying an option that is not true, or that is false or incorrect, state the option in positive terms.

Advice. To allow for human fallibility, consider giving students a ten percent margin on teacher-prepared tests. This is the beloved "fudge factor," and it can be provided by writing fifty-five questions for fifty points. The student's errors are then subtracted from the larger number; for example, if the student misses ten questions, the score is 45/50 (fifty-five questions minus ten errors = 45/50 total points). This is not an "extra credit" offer; even a perfect paper would receive fifty points, not fifty-five. But this bit of overkill does give the student fifty-five chances to get those fifty points, while discounting ambiguous questions. And the built-in extras allow the instructor, without guilt, to slip in a few especially challenging questions to stretch the most talented minds.

Step II. Writing the Test: Add Water and Stir

1.   Before composing the test, have before you an outline of the (a) content to be covered; (b) skills to be covered; and (c) types of questions to be considered.

2.   Good assignment sheets pay their dividend in drafting tests. You can go through the unit objectives and discussion-guide questions and use these as opening statements for multiple-choice questions on a unit test. You may not want to be so specific on a cumulative examination, but there will still be generalizations, comparisons, and syntheses you will want to cover. In fact, one way to make a quick rough outline of a multiple-choice test is to go through chapter titles and subtitles, discussion questions, and important objectives. Write an incomplete statement or question for each. Write the correct answer for each. Later you can go back and fill in the "distracters," the incorrect choices.

3.   Generally, good multiple-choice questions require five possible answers, and this is the format students face in both the Advanced Placement and Achievement tests. This does not mean, however, that a teacher-made test cannot offer four to six choices. It is said of those choices that one should be clearly correct and one should be clearly incorrect; the others might be correct answers — but not to your question. In any case, the stem and options should stress real information. They should eschew trickery or entrapment.

4.   Know first the *answer* you want. Write the question or incomplete statement — what is called the "stem" of the question. Then, as the (a) choice, draft the correct answer. Setting out this correct answer first helps you make the distracters parallel in grammar, form, and length. Test coaches advise students that the longest choice is most often the correct choice. Need it be?

For the final presentation of your test, a simple and effective way to scramble the choices you have drafted with the correct answer first is to alphabetize each option by the first word in it. You will see that method used in the samples given below (Step III). But it is surprising how long it takes for students to discover this arrangement.

5.   Use the option "all of the above" with care. Make sure you have not worded the stem with a superlative or first-choice words such as "best," "most," "of highest importance," "initial," or "primary." Do not stick in "all of the above" or its cousin "none of the above" because you cannot think of a fifth distracter. These call for interpretation and therefore the material should be worthy of interpretation. Be sure you see the distinction between "none of the above" and "no exceptions" as options. They call for a different stem and a different task of sorting information. And remember that any of these choices makes the question more difficult.

Step III. Using a Variety of Multiple-Choice Question Styles

The Madeira history department had a satisfying experience in June 1983. Two students sidled up to the United States history instructors after their final examination. One said: "We want to congratulate you for coming up with a creative test." The other chimed in, "It was fun." They were reacting to sixteen pages containing eighty-eight multiple-choice questions (for eighty points), and of course two more pages containing their three (two short, one long) essay requirements. But every other page of the first sixteen had begun with a different sort of multiple-choice question: a cartoon on page 1, a graph on page 3, then document identifications, a map, a drawing, a pair of cartoons from the McCarthy era, and a chronology spread every other page thereafter. Thus the students' tasks were varied and, we think, their senses sharpened. On the final page, a known character made her farewell appearance, testing knowledge of a constitutional provision: "Molly Madeira, obviously a sophisticated Madeira senior, laid down her pen at the end of the United States history exam and called for her lawyer. 'This violates my Eighth Amendment rights! This exam is definitely a case of

_____!'" Naturally, all seemed to know that the answer was option (a): "Cruel and unusual punishment." Therefore, the prescription is: use a variety of multiple-choice stimuli and styles. Students' attention spans will stretch, their interest will rise, and who knows, their performances may improve.

And now, a menu of styles and samples:

1.   Completion

Jim Crowism refers to legislation designed to

(a)   benefit railroad workers
(b)   deny equality to blacks
(c)   increase veteran benefits
(d)   restrict immigration
(e)   sell western lands cheaply

2.   Insertion of correct word or phrase

According to Karl Marx, people act and historical changes occur primarily because of _____ causes.

(a)   cultural
(b)   economic
(c)   humanitarian
(d)   nationalistic
(e)   political

3.   Definition

To British leaders since 1938, the term *appeasement* has most often been equated with

(a)   armistice
(b)   compromise
(c)   negotiation
(d)   surrender
(e)   victory

4.   Match/mismatch

One of the following authors is mismatched with the pivotal work most often associated with that author's name.

(a)   George Kennan — "Sources of Soviet Conduct"
(b)   John Locke — *Of Civil Government*
(c)   Thomas Paine — *Common Sense*
(d)   Upton Sinclair — *The Jungle*
(e)   Harriet Beecher Stowe — *The Red Badge of Courage*

Or a more sophisticated mismatch:

A wise host would not invite one of these pairs to a dinner party:
(a)   Jefferson Davis/John Calhoun
(b)   William Lloyd Garrison/Wendell Phillips
(c)   Thaddeus Stevens/William Seward
(d)   Charles Sumner/Preston Brooks
(e)   Nat Turner/Frederick Douglass

5.   Cause
One of the following was the *cause* of the other three:
(a)   Amendment XII
(b)   Election of 1800
(c)   growth of the two-party system
(d)   Washington's farewell warning against factions

6.   Result
One of the following was the *result* of the other three:
(a)   Chiang Kai-shek becomes Kuomintang leader
(b)   Chinese Communist Party is founded
(c)   May Fourth Movement stirs intellectual China
(d)   Long March sets out

7.   Exclusion
One of the following *does not belong* with the other three:
(a)   John Calhoun
(b)   Alexander Hamilton
(c)   John Marshall
(d)   Daniel Webster

8.   Exception
Examples of powers shared by national and state governments in the United States are all of the following *except*
(a)   administering justice
(b)   borrowing money through bonds
(c)   levying and collecting taxes
(d)   making internal improvements
(e)   regulating foreign commerce
(f)   no exceptions

9.   Step removed
Modern Republicanism, as reflected in the policies of President Eisenhower, encompassed which of the following? 1) economic aid for underdeveloped nations,

2) military aid for United States allies, 3) a moderate extension of some New Deal and Fair Deal programs, 4) support for the United Nations.

(a)   3 only
(b)   1 and 2 only
(c)   1, 2, and 3 only
(d)   2, 3, and 4 only
(e)   1, 2, 3, 4

10.   *Data-based questions*

Stimulus: A table (see Figure 1), a graph, or a growing of nonverbal data.

Types of questions:

(1)   Simple reading of information shown by data.

(2)   Application of data — change, direction; use of percentage of change formula (New value – Original value ÷ Original value x 100 = % change).

(3)   Interpretation of data — meaning, implication, cause, result.

(4)   Misinterpretation of data — to test what cannot be discerned from data, especially to sort out confusion of quantity and percent.

(5)   Verbalizing data — choosing an apt summary or conclusion; choosing appropriate topic sentence or thesis statement as if data were to be summarized verbally.

Figure 1
POPULATION OF EUROPE, 1300-1700
(Estimated in millions)

YEAR	POP.	YEAR	POP.
1300	73	1550	78
1350	51	1600	90
1400	45	1650	103
1450	60	1700	115
1500	69		

Source Shepard B. Clough and Richard T. Rapp, *European Economic History: The Economic Development of Western Civilization*, 3rd ed. (New York: McGraw-Hill, 1975), p. 52.

From 1450 to 1500, the population of Europe increased by

(a)   9%
(b)   15%
(c)   15% per year
(d)   9 million per year
(e)   15 million

The *average rate of growth* of the population of Europe during the worst period of the religious wars, 1550-1650, was nevertheless approximately

(a)   25%
(b)   33%
(c)   25% per year
(d)   2.5% per year
(e)   3.3% per year

Which of the following statements might be the best *topic sentence* for a paragraph summarizing these data?

(a)   After declining to 45 million on account of the Black Death during the 14th century, Europe's population increased steadily by an average of ten million people each fifty years until 1700.

(b)   After 1400, the population of Europe increased steadily, probably due to the improved agricultural techniques.

(c)   The Black Death caused a decline of nearly fifty percent in Europe's population during the 14th century.

(d)   Despite wars and epidemics, the population of Europe grew by more than fifty percent from 1300 until 1700.

(e)   Treasure coming in from the New World caused the dramatic rise in Europe's population in the 16th century.

Figure 2

Source: Herbert Block, *Herblock Special Report* (New York: W.W. Norton, 1974), July 2, 1974.

11.   Cartoon, picture, diagram

Stimulus: Political cartoon (see Fig. 2), historic photo, diagram of a key invention.

Types of questions: Similar to those based on data, especially simple reading or recognition; application; interpretation; implication; verbalization.

The historical issue depicted in the cartoonist's invocation of Orwellian images was

(a)   Abscam
(b)   Civil rights
(c)   Nixon's visit to China
(d)   Vietnamization
(e)   Watergate

Herblock, the author of this cartoon, seems concerned about the basic constitutional principle of
(a)   checks and balances
(b)   federalism
(c)   legislative supremacy
(d)   life tenure of federal judges
(e)   states' rights

12.   Application of historical concepts to more recent situation
The U.S. policy on grain trade with the Soviet Union in recent years reminds
us somewhat of actions taken under _____ during the _____.
(a)   Jefferson, Napoleonic Wars
(b)   Lincoln, Civil War
(c)   Madison, War of 1812
(d)   Monroe, Latin American revolutions
(e)   Polk, Mexican War

13.   Categories: classification by titles, themes, characteristics
Scholars of traditional China recorded details of each imperial dynasty. These
records were then studied during later eras to detect signs of dynastic growth,
strength and decline.

Classify these characteristic situations according to this scheme:
N   =   if the situation was typical of a new, growing dynasty
P   =   if the situation was typical of a dynasty at its peak of power
D   =   if the situation was typical of a dynasty in decline

(1)   A Committee of Regents conducts imperial affairs in the name of an
infant emperor.
(2)   Literature and painting are encouraged by Imperial subsidies.
(3)   Dikes are repaired and irrigation ditches are built.

Or:
Link each of the following statements of political principle with the political
party it most accurately reflects. Use this scheme:
F   =   if principle is largely Federalist (1790-1814)
D   =   if principle is largely Democratic (1790-Civil War)
R   =   if principle is largely Republican (1854-Civil War)

(1)   Both party and president must defend the common man against the
monopolies of the aristocratic and the privileged.
(2)   Governments should attract and serve the interests of the rich, well-born
and able, while avoiding the dangers of excessive democracy.

(3)   The cause of democracy is best served by making the states the repository and guarantor of our rights.

(4)   There is no liberty outside of the Union; to break the Union is to accept anarchy.

14.   *Analogy*
Afganistan : United Nations, 1980 :: _____ : League of Nations, 1935.
(a)   Ethiopia
(b)   Manchuria
(c)   Pearl Harbor
(d)   Saar plebiscite
(e)   Sudetenland

15.   *Chronology*
Place the following pre-World War II events into correct chronological order:
1) annexation of Austria; 2) invasion of Poland; 3) militarization of the Rhineland;
4) occupation of the Sudetenland; 5) takeover of Czechoslovakia.
(a)   1, 4, 5, 2, 3
(b)   3, 1, 5, 4, 2
(c)   3, 1, 4, 5, 2
(d)   4, 3, 1, 5, 2
(e)   4, 1, 3, 5, 2

16.   *Reading question*
Stimulus: A short, relevant passage.
Task: Answer questions on passage that test comprehension; analysis; interpretation; application. Especially good for recognizing point of view, as in this example:

"Each individual, bestowing more time and attention upon the means of preserving and increasing his portion of wealth than is or can be bestowed by government, is likely to take a more effectual course than what, in this instance and on his behalf, would be taken by government."
The quotation above best illustrates
(a)   classical liberalism
(b)   fascism
(c)   mercantilism
(d)   syndicalism
(e)   utopian socialism

17.   *Map*
Stimulus: Outline map, with areas clearly lettered or numbered.
Task: Simple location (least recommended), location by geographical description, or location by historical description.

Some examples of historical description with an appropriate map of Europe, from which the student answers by letter or number of place described:

(1)   The nobles of _____ started the Thirty Years' War by their hostility to the Holy Roman Emperor.

(2)   _____ revolted against its Hapsburg rulers largely because of religious differences, and obtained a *de facto* independence in the 1580s.

(3)   Gustavus Adolphus, leader of the Schmalkaldic League in the Thirty Years' War, called _____ his homeland.

18. *Document recognition, classification, synthesis*
Stimulus: Brief passage from significant, relevant document.
Tasks: Identify by source, title, era, theory advocated, or other classifier.

Or:
Stimulus: Several document excerpts.
Tasks: Match by source, arrange by chronology, synthesize by common theme (religious toleration, growth of parliament, sectionalism).

Match the statements in 1-4 with their most likely speaker, from the list that follows.
(1)   "I did not become the King's First Minister in order to preside over the dissolution of the British Empire."
(2)   It was a Moslem who did it. *"You fool, don't you know it was a Hindu?"*
(3)   "We shall have India divided or we shall have India destroyed."
(4)   "You shall have to divide my body ... before you divide India."

(a)   Clement Attlee
(b)   Winston Churchill
(c)   Mohammed Ali Jinnah
(d)   Mohandas K. Ghandi
(e)   Louis Mountbatten

The basic issue underlying all of the above statements was
(a)   Ghandi's nonviolent resistance
(b)   Indian independence
(c)   Mountbatten's role as viceroy
(d)   Parliament's role in India
(e)   partition of Kashmir

The most logical order in which the above statements were spoken would be
(a)   1, 3, 4, 2
(b)   3, 4, 2, 1

(c)   3, 2, 1, 4
(d)   1, 2, 4, 3
(e)   2, 3, 4, 1

19.   *Writing Skills*

By recognition and discrimination, a student should be able to choose the most apt topic sequence, thesis statement, or logical conclusion from a menu of options. This task might be in combination with questions based on data (see no. 10), or on a cartoon or picture. And you might even test that a student knows what a thesis statement is:

A *thesis statement* differs from a topic sentence, because in a thesis statement the writer
(a)   alludes to the main areas of evidence
(b)   proposes the answer to be supported
(c)   restates the question to be answered
(d)   sets the scene or era of the essay
(e)   traces the roots of an historical event

Which would be the best *thesis statement* for an essay examining the *long-term effects* of Eli Whitney's invention of the cotton gin?
(a)   Cotton culture tended to exhaust soil fertility, and southern technology had not developed to meet this problem.
(b)   The gin was developed in 1793 and ten years later, American cotton production had increased more than ten times.
(c)   Since more labor was needed to cultivate cotton once the crop could be easily cleaned, the South relied more on slave labor and slavery became a more divisive sectional issue.
(d)   Whitney reported that if a man used the gin, he could clean cotton ten times faster than before, but if the invention was used with a horse, then cotton could be cleaned fifty times faster.

20.   *The study of history*

The student may be asked to display all the life skills we have so thoughtfully provided: recognition of primary versus secondary sources; correct citation of sources as notes or in bibliography: most appropriate reference work for a specific task; percentage of change formula; recognition, application to data; national, state, and local government situations; current events; or geographic features and their logical application and interpretation.

21.   *How do you spell relief?*

For psychological uplift, an easy or lighthearted question might be posed. We like this on the bottom of the test's first page — to give a student the courage to move on. You might, depending on your audience, also try for a little levity:

In its first session as part of the Ninety-eighth Congress, the House received a new Equal Rights proposal. What is the final step needed to add such an amendment to the Constitution?

(a)   approval by two-thirds of the Senate
(b)   passage by majorities of both Houses
(c)   ratification by three-fourths of the states
(d)   signature of the President of the United States
(e)   sit-down strikes by American women

Students may never find such relief on a standardized test, but an advantage of the teacher-made test is familiarity and sympathy with the test taker. In any case, the student's task should be varied. Your test will include a wider range of materials and thus enhance the student's ability to handle a wider range of historical sources.

Step IV. Checking the Test

1.   Review your preliminary outline and check for content, skills, and question-style coverage.

2.   Closely examine multiple-choice questions and eliminate wordiness. If most of the options begin with the same phrase, then eliminate those words and add the phrase to the stem:

Wordy:
The members of the Constitutional Convention had a view of human nature that can best be described as

(a)   a belief that people are basically good
(b)   a belief that people are basically irresponsible
(c)   a belief that people are naturally selfish and power-hungry
(d)   a belief that people have never governed themselves well
(e)   a belief that people cannot learn to live together

Better:
The members of the Constitutional Convention had a view of human nature that can best be described as a belief that people are basically

(a)   good and capable of moderation
(b)   incapable of self-government
(c)   irresponsible and disorderly
(d)   selfish and power-hungry
(e)   suspicious of their neighbors

3.   Use "a/an" at the end of an incomplete stem leading to choices beginning with both vowels and consonants. You might also use "(the)" at the end of a stem

to make its use optional in the choices. Keep choices parallel in form. Watch "ing" and "ed" endings. Watch modifier, noun, and verb order.

4.   Check your draft with a view to *appearance* and readability Can you mix questions to provide plenty of white space on the final pages? Are the margins adequate? Is there space between questions? Are the questions varied in length? Are the questions varied in task?

Step V. Final Proofreading

1.   Go through each page and check that question numbers are in order, with no number skipped. Also, scan the answer sheet and check the numerical order of answer blanks.

2.   Go through each page again and check that choices are correctly lettered: a, b, c, d, e.

3.   Finally, here is where your art imitates life. When your complete composition is typed and ready to be reproduced, being careful that your responses will not show up on the students' copies, *take the entire test.*

▼

Finished? Take comfort that the time you devote to write the multiple-choice test returns as time you save to grade it. You have covered more material than essay questions alone permit, and have thus enhanced each student's chance of success. You have objective points against which to weigh the subjective points awarded the facile essay, while giving the less talented writer a chance to achieve. You have a means of gauging a student's strengths and weaknesses: literal reader or selective and focused learner; rote memorizer or critical and synthetic thinker? You may — if everyone misses the map questions — discover a gap in your own teaching; should you roll down "Europe" and use the pointer more often? You have steps to guide your work and ideas to goad your colleagues' efforts. And, maestro, you are fine-tuning young instruments toward a greater understanding of history.

A Multidimensional Multiple-Choice Testing System

Ray W. Karras

MOST TEACHERS OF HISTORY will probably agree with The College Board about the purposes of multiple-choice questions. As stated in its booklet, *Advanced Placement Course Description: History* (May 1984, p. 6): "The questions in the multiple-choice section are designed to test the students' factual knowledge, breadth of preparation, and *knowledge-based analytical skills.*" I have italicized these last words because here is where means fail to serve ends. Few multiple-choice questions asked by The College Board — or by others — actually require students to think critically about their factual knowledge of history.

Neither The College Board nor the Educational Testing Service should be blamed for faulty multiple-choice testing. As a former member of ETS's Advanced Placement Test Development Committee in American History, I can testify that AP multiple-choice questions are designed to reflect, not direct, accepted practices in the country's classrooms. The College Board's *Course Description* is cited here primarily because it reflects standard testing practices. Nevertheless, while AP multiple-choice test makers have good reason to be cautious about radical changes, they also have a commitment to help raise academic standards. The model multidimensional multiple-choice questions offered below represent an approach toward meeting this commitment, as well as the hope that teachers will share in the process of reform.

The following suggestions require systematic classroom instruction. Knowledge-based analytical (i.e., critical thinking) skills call for the explicit teaching of specific processes that can and should be tested. In my own college preparatory courses all work is structured around six specific thinking processes applied to reading and classroom work and is tested in both essay and multiple-choice forms. Rote memorization and straight narrative reporting are discouraged. This approach, it should be stressed, has not prevented students from doing well on traditional multiple-choice tests, nor does it take longer to teach than the conventional variety. I only suggest that narration and rote memorization are inappropriate processes in history courses designed to promote critical thinking through learning knowledge-based analytical skills. The College Board says as much in its advice on AP history courses:

Although there is little to be gained by rote memorization of names and dates on an encyclopedic basis, a student must be able to draw upon a reservoir of systematic factual knowledge in order to exercise analytic skills intelligently. Striking a balance between obtaining a command of systematic factual knowledge and analyzing that knowledge critically is a demanding but crucial task in the design of a successful AP course in history. [*Course Description*, p. 3]

Striking this balance is an equally crucial task for the test maker. What is needed are multiple-choice questions that will at once impose the discipline of objective testing and require critical thinking.

Traditional multiple-choice questions essentially ask for straight recall from text reading or class work. These questions operate on a single level of generalization, asking students to equate one piece of information with another. For example, a *Course Description* sample question asks:

Brown v. Board of Education of Topeka was a Supreme Court decision that
(a) was a forerunner of the Kansas-Nebraska Act.
(b) established free public colleges in the United States.
(c) outlawed racially segregated public schools.
(d) established free public elementary and secondary schools in the United States.
(e) provided for federal support of parochial schools.

No critical analysis is needed to recall the fact that *Brown v. Board of Education* outlawed racially segregated public schools. The same criticism applies to a more sophisticated type of question:

Which of the following was the LEAST important consideration in the United States' decision to drop the atomic bomb on Japan in August, 1945:
(a) Dropping the bomb would give a new and powerful argument to the peace faction in the Japanese government.
(b) Dropping the bomb would presumably shorten the war and therefore save the lives of American soldiers that would be lost in the invasion of the Japanese homeland.
(c) Scientists could propose no acceptable technical demonstration of the bomb likely to convince Japan that further fighting was futile.
(d) Scientists wished to demonstrate to Congress that the $2 billion spent, after long debate, on the six-year Manhattan Project had not been wasted.
(e) The President and the State Department hoped to end the war in the Far East without Russian assistance.

Such a question asks for the recall of a hypothesis (reflected in choice [d]) claiming that the fear of wasting $2 billion was the least important reason for dropping the bomb. The factual basis for rejecting claim (d) is unsteady: What is "long debate"? Who debated whom? "Recalling" hypotheses seems to be diametrically opposed to critical thinking. This question teaches students that hypotheses should be memorized as facts, that there is one "right" hypothesis explaining the dropping of the bomb, and that whatever teachers may say in classrooms about critical thinking had best be put aside when answering multiple-choice questions. If students are to think critically, they should be expected to test hypotheses against reasoning and evidence; they should not be required — indeed, they should be forbidden — to accept as true what is only claimed. Answer (d) may be the best answer to the question, but this is not the way to ask for it.

How then can multiple-choice questions test knowledge-based critical thinking skills? The answer, I believe, first requires a theory of critical thinking that can be applied to multiple-choice questions. Second, we need to standardize and explicitly teach students certain critical thinking processes. Third, we need to construct appropriate multiple-choice questions.

One aspect of critical thinking is that it is a process of relating elements of learning to each other at different levels of generalization. Critical thinking does not translate into the equation that piece of information "A" equals piece of information "B." Instead, we need questions whose parts move between and among at least three levels of generalization: 1) making factual statements, 2) claiming hypotheses, and 3) claiming reasons for believing hypotheses. Given any one of these elements, students may be asked to supply one or both of the others. This is illustrated in Figure 1.

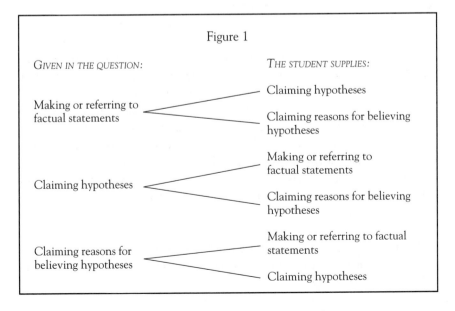

Figure 1

GIVEN IN THE QUESTION: THE STUDENT SUPPLIES:

Making or referring to factual statements
— Claiming hypotheses
— Claiming reasons for believing hypotheses

Claiming hypotheses
— Making or referring to factual statements
— Claiming reasons for believing hypotheses

Claiming reasons for believing hypotheses
— Making or referring to factual statements
— Claiming hypotheses

This theory can be embodied in six specific processes (or steps and operations) which students can be taught to apply to all their reading, writing, and classroom work. These processes ask the student to: 1) raise hypothesis-producing questions, 2) claim controversial hypotheses answering these questions, 3) claim logical reasons for believing the hypotheses, 4) apply factual knowledge as evidence to support the claims, 5) refute opposing claims and evidence, and 6) ask analytical questions for new unknown facts to test the claims the student has made. The student is the active user and developer of these processes. The teacher explains them, provides the historical sources to which they apply, demonstrates and supervises their use in classroom instruction, and evaluates the competence with which they are used.

Defining the terms in the processes is a major teaching task. For example, "claim" — as a verb — is used as "maintaining a position in the face of possible argument" (*American Heritage Dictionary*). As a noun, a claim is a statement of belief about the position taken. Thus, students claim hypotheses and reasons for believing them. Statements of claims are to be sharply distinguished from statements of fact: it is a fact that I arrived late at school; but it is a claim that I could not help arriving late at school. Similar strictures apply to other terms in the processes. Students are guided to these and only to these instructed usages throughout the course.

Arguing historical hypotheses is the centerpiece of this system. By "hypothesis" I mean a value-free controversial claim based on reasons and evidence defended against opposing claims and left open to testing by new and unknown factual knowledge. In this sense, a historical hypothesis is most definitely not a "conclusion." In common usage, "conclusion" may mean "end," yet no historical hypothesis delivers a final end to inquiry. Nor should we accept the meaning of "conclusion" that students bring into our history courses from their mathematics or logic classes. These classes teach, for example, that by deduction, if A = B and B = C, then A = C is a logical conclusion. This is clearly not what historians mean by conclusions. Therefore, it is best to cede the term "conclusion" to other disciplines, and to hold the term "historical hypothesis" for history teaching. We can teach that a hypothesis may claim why historical events happened (e.g., the American Revolution was mainly caused by economic conflict), or what mainly characterizes them (e.g., the Open Door Policy was successful in achieving its aims), or a debatable fact (e.g., Lee Harvey Oswald acted alone in assassinating John F. Kennedy). To be worth studying, historical hypotheses should be controversial.

The following sample questions are taken from final examinations given to college preparatory students in United States history. Each question addresses one of the six processes.

1.   *Raising hypothesis-producing questions.* Here the tester wants students to recognize a question whose answer will claim a hypothesis, and at the same time will be knowledge-based.

Which question will produce a response that is a hypothesis?
(a) Was freedom of speech constitutional between 1776 and 1788?
(b) Was the Sherman Anti-Trust Act constitutional?
(c) Was the *Dred Scott* decision favorable to the Missouri Compromise?
(d) Did the framers of the Constitution intend the Supreme Court to have
     its present powers of judicial review?

In this question choice (a) requires the factual knowledge that there was no constitutional free speech guarantee between 1776 and 1788. It also requires understanding that what is and what is not constitutional is by definition a fact that courts decide. Choice (a)'s answer will be an objective fact, not a claim of a hypothesis. Answer (b) also requires understanding of the concept "constitutional," as well as the knowledge that the Sherman Anti-Trust Act is to this day in effect. Choice (c) requires a simple factual answer, not a hypothesis: *Dred Scott* did declare the Missouri Compromise unconstitutional. Answer (d) is correct. What the framers intended is controversial, as is the nature of judicial review — to which students should remember the Constitution never specifically refers.

2. ***Claiming controversial hypotheses.*** In the following question the student must choose a claim that not only meets the requirements of a controversial hypothesis, but also reflects knowledge of late nineteenth-century history. The correct answer may or may not be a claim developed in class preparation; the student is asked, as in all questions, to analyze and synthesize as the question is answered.

Which of the following is the best historical hypothesis?
(a) Lack of government support mainly caused the relative weakness of the
     labor movement between 1880 and 1900.
(b) The Anti-Imperialist League failed to achieve its goals because it
     opposed Cleveland's policy on Hawaiian annexation.
(c) The Haymarket Square Riot of 1886 resulted in the conviction of eight
     agitators.
(d) The Populist movement shows that farmers cannot compete if they sell
     in an open market.

The correct answer, (a), presents a hypothesis that competes with alternative claims — for example, that ineffective union leadership, or perhaps oppressive employers, were mainly responsible for union weakness. Choice (b), though stated as a hypothesis, is based on factual errors. Cleveland opposed Hawaiian annexation, and the Anti-Imperialist League, of which Cleveland himself was a member, was formed after his administration. Answer (c) merely states a historical fact. Choice (d), stated in the present eternal tense, is not a historical hypothesis, but an economic theory.

3. *Claiming logical reasons for believing hypotheses.* Here the student chooses a set of claims which state reasons that are logically necessary for believing the hypothesis given. At the same time, the correct choice must be supportable by facts. The following example presents a hypothesis and four sets of possible reasons for believing it.

Hypothesis: The United States has consistently maintained the principles of the Monroe Doctrine. Which of the following is the best set of reasons for believing this hypothesis.

(a) I.   Non-interference in Latin American affairs has consistently been upheld in the Roosevelt Corollary.

   II. Non-interference in European affairs has been consistently upheld in the Open Door Policy.

(b) I.   United States reactions to the sinking of the Maine were due mainly to the fear of new European aggression in the Western Hemisphere.

   II. United States policy toward belligerents in Europe in 1916 was due mainly to Wilson's support of the Monroe Doctrine.

(c) I.   The United States rejected the League of Nations.

   II. Lodge's opposition to the League of Nations was due to his desire for a Republican Party victory in the 1920 election.

(d) I.   Non-interference in Latin-American affairs was upheld in Theodore Roosevelt's laissez-faire policy.

   II. Non-interference in Latin-American affairs was upheld in the Roosevelt Corollary.

Choice (a) is incorrect because both its I and II are based on erroneous information. Answer (d) is wrong because the laissez-faire concept is inappropriate in I, and the facts regarding the Roosevelt Corollary eliminate II. Answer (b) is correct. Accurate knowledge of Monroe Doctrine provisions is applied to two episodes. Furthermore, both claims I and II in (b) are controversial at a lower level of generalization than the hypothesis in the question stem; if reasons I and II can be supported, then the hypothesis can be believed. It is not the respectability, but the arguability of hypotheses that students are asked to address.

Erroneous answer (c) illustrates several things about the process. Choice (c)I illustrates the crucial stipulation that a statement of fact is not a claim of belief. It is a fact, not a claim, that the U.S. rejected the League. The statement omits telling why this rejection should be regarded as a reason for believing the hypothesis. Had (c)I said, for example, "United States' rejection of the League of Nations was due mainly to support of the Monroe Doctrine by Wilson's opponents," it would have served as a reason for believing the hypothesis. As it stands, (c)I is only a piece of evidence necessary to support (c)II; taken together, (c)I and (c)II do not give two independent reasons for believing the hypothesis. Even separately, (c)II does not logically support it.

4. *Applying factual knowledge to support claims.* Thus far our questions have explicitly asked students to find relationships between two levels of generalization: between hypotheses and subordinate claims of reasons for believing hypotheses. Implicit has been the third level of generalization, that of knowledge of factual statements. Now we want to make the implicit explicit by testing directly for the relationship between facts and claims. First, however, teachers should clearly teach the characteristics of factual information desired from their students.

When we ask students for facts, we actually ask them for *statements* of facts. We read and write statements of fact; we do not "give" facts — we refer to them. For purposes of instruction it may be said that factual statements tell who, where, when, or what: that they refer to that which can be seen, heard, touched, or counted; and that they include accounts of historical events, statistics, and primary source quotations. For example, it is a statement of fact that Franklin Roosevelt said in 1940: "Your boys are not going to be sent into any foreign wars." But it is a historian's claim, not a fact, that Roosevelt did not intend to send American soldiers into foreign wars in 1940. The nature of statements of fact should be taught explicitly through daily classroom practice.

The question below relates facts to a claim. The factual statements needed are not given in the question; they are instead only referred to.

Claim: Pre-Civil War presidents were more supportive of laissez-faire policies than were post-Civil War presidents. Which pair of statements offers facts that support this claim?
(a) I.   What Thomas Jefferson said about Federalists in his First Inaugural Address
    II. What Woodrow Wilson said about intervention in Europe in 1917
(b) I.   What Grover Cleveland did about Coxey's Army
    II. The reason why Franklin Roosevelt ordered a bank moratorium
(c) I.   What Andrew Jackson did about the Bank of the United States
    II. What Woodrow Wilson did about the Federal Reserve System
(d) I.   What Alexander Hamilton did about the assumption of state debts
    II. What Herbert Hoover said about voluntary self-help in 1930

Choice (a) is incorrect; neither Jefferson nor Wilson discussed laissez-faire in the contexts of the statements. Furthermore, some students mistakenly believe Hamilton was a president; that laissez-faire means any kind of government intervention; and that half a comparison, even with Herbert Hoover in (d), is better than none. Notice too that (b) offers a nonfactual statement of FDR's reasons for the moratorium. Answer (c) is correct because it requires the factual statement that Jackson vetoed one national bank and Wilson signed another into law.

5. *Refuting opposing claims and evidence.* Essentially mirror images of the foregoing processes, refutation elements may be used in multidimensional multiple-choice questions just as supporting elements are used.

6. *Asking analytical questions for new, unknown facts to test claims.*
Students should seek evidence unknown to them that might further support,
weaken, or even upset given claims. The test maker constructs a claim arising from
the assigned reading and then considers facts missing from the assignment that
would further test the claim. For the following example, readings in I. Bartlett, E.
Fenton, et al., *A New History of the United States: an Inquiry Approach* (New York,
1969), were assigned.

> *Claim*: During economic recessions the United States government has
> characteristically attempted to inflate the currency. Which of the following
> is the analytical question that tests this claim?
> (a) What did the Populist Party platform say about ownership of railroads?
> (b) Why did Populists want bimetallism?
> (c) What did the New Deal do about unemployment in 1935?
> (d) What did the Federal Reserve do about the money supply in 1920?

Choices (a) and (c) are irrelevant; besides, the assigned reading already contains
the information asked for here. Choice (b) will yield a claim, not a fact, for an
answer. Correctly choosing (d) shows that the student recognizes an indicator of
evidence not contained in the assignment, that the student knows a function of the
Federal Reserve System, and that 1920 was a year of recession. Finally, further
research into the claim offered would very likely require an answer to the question
asked in (d).

▼

Can students answer the multidimensional questions I suggest? Yes, provided
processes of knowledge-based analytical skills are explicitly, systematically, and
consistently taught and practiced throughout the school year. Ordinarily, twenty-
five multidimensional questions fill a test hour, allowing about two minutes to
think through each question. I have found that at the beginning of the year I can
expect to give passing scaled grades to those who answer at least half correctly; by
year's end the scale tends to move upward. A good way to prepare students is to ask
them to make up their own multidimensional test questions; making these tests is
at least as educative as taking them. For the teacher, constructing a fresh hour test
of twenty-five questions is time-consuming. However, subsequent versions of the
same questions can be quickly constructed by altering one or more elements.

Doubtless, integrating knowledge and critical thinking in its multiple-choice
questions would require a deeper intervention in nationwide history instruction
than The College Board or ETS has yet dared. But there is precedent for such a step.
ETS itself does a marvelous job with similar testing in its *Law School Aptitude Test
Bulletin* — which, oddly, students confront only after they are out of school, indeed,
out of college! Readers familiar with the work of Edwin Fenton at Carnegie-Mellon

University will recognize elements of his inquiry methods in this paper. Perhaps the most striking precedent is found in the essay sections of AP history tests themselves, where students are implicitly invited to use the very processes outlined in this paper.

It is probably true that most history students are unfamiliar with the multidimensional learning and testing system I suggest. Perhaps this is a good reason for teaching them about it.

Chapter IV:

Essay Test Taking Skills

Teaching the Value of Inquiry Through the Essay Question

John C. Bartul

STUDENTS, PARTICULARLY THOSE bright energetic types who take Advanced Placement history courses and, no doubt, their college counterparts, all too often become prisoners of essay questions. In their ambition to complete the tasks they are given, they do not take the time to ask questions about the question. The results of this omission can range from a total misunderstanding of the question posed to a failure to comprehend the many options the question provides to those who thoroughly examine its possibilities.

The problem and the promise can be illustrated with the following essay question taken from Dennis Sherman's, *Study Guide and Readings for the Western Experience, to 1715.* "Protestantism was not simply a single movement away from the Roman Catholic Church; it was a series of separate and often conflicting movements.' Do you agree? Explain."

The question above appears to be rather straightforward. Students are given a statement — "Protestantism was not simply a single movement away from the Roman Catholic Church" — which may or may not be true, but which, with its corollary — "it was a series of separate and often conflicting movements" — governs or sets limits to what they may write about. The next question — "Do you agree"? — and the charge — "Explain" — set additional limits.

On a most general level, students must deal with Protestantism, however defined, and its relationship to the Roman Catholic Church. On this same level, they must either agree or disagree with the statement and its corollary and then, in either case, explain their position. Or must they? Let us come back to that question later.

Before students can even begin to write they must have some comprehension of what the words and terms "Protestantism," "simply," "single movement," "away," "Roman Catholic Church," "series," "separate," "often," and "conflicting movements" mean, and how *each of them* sets limits to what they may write. One way to check this understanding, while exploring alternative possibilities, is to brainstorm by asking questions of the question without being judgmental or censoring the questions asked. The following might begin to clarify this point:

1.   Can one include John Wycliffe or John Huss within the category of Protestant? How about Savanarola? Desiderius Erasmus? Can anyone, including Luther prior to the Diet of Speyer in 1529, be called Protestant? Were the original Protestants men of religion?

2.   What does the adverb "simply" mean? Does it mean alone? merely? solely? singly? barely?

3.   What does "single movement" mean? Doesn't Protestantism have something to do with religion? In what sense is Protestantism, as a religion, a movement? What does it mean to be a "single one"? And who says that Protestantism is "a" religion? What does "movement" mean? Is it a performance? an exercise? an operation? an action? an activity?

4.   What does "Roman Catholic Church" mean? Does it refer to buildings? a group of men holding certain offices? the Pope? belief? practices? or some combination of all of these factors plus others?

5.   What does "series" mean? Does it refer to a particular order, as in the phrase "chronological order"? It appears to be modified by the antecedent word, "Protestantism." Does that change its meaning? Does it mean some sort of organization, i.e., must what you write about be related in some way?

6.   What does "separate" mean? Does it mean alone? singly? without reference to another? unaffected by another? not influenced by? Is the word "separate" modified by the word "series" so that in fact separate cannot be separate?

7.   "Often" is an interesting word. Does its use here mean the movements did not always have to conflict? Or does it mean they did not have to conflict in all respects? Can one conflict in some respects but not conflict generally? or conflict generally but not in some respects?

8.   "Conflicting movements"—for the word "movement" see number three above. But what does "conflicting" mean? and with whom, or between whom is the conflict taking place? Is it between Protestants (whatever they are) themselves? or between Protestants and Catholics? or could it be both of these possibilities?

Let us return to the question raised in the fourth paragraph: "Or must you?" Is it possible to agree with one part and not another? That is to say, for example, that "it" was a series of separate movements but that they did not all conflict? Or that they all conflicted with Roman Catholicism but not with each other? Or that they all conflicted with each other and Roman Catholicism, but did not occur as a series of anything?

The point of all this is that words and questions are not always what they seem. One must ask questions of them, perhaps not as many questions as have been asked here to illustrate the dimensions of the possibilities (and these just skim the surface), but enough to understand the limits, enough to enable one to understand how much leeway one has to control the situation.

Writing is a thought process which, in one sense, is organized and illustrates certain relationships. The organization and the relationships one chooses to illustrate will be governed by one's answers to the questions about the question. Using the same question here are some possibilities:

A.   If Protestantism is not simply (only) a religious movement, or a "series" of religious movements, then might it also be possible to deal with political and social movements? To be more specific, was the decision of Henry VIII of England to assume the role of leader of the Church of England a Protestant movement? Was it a religious movement? Was it a political movement? Was it an economic movement? Was it purely a personal movement leading to his emancipation from Catherine of Aragon? Given Carl G. Gustavson's concept of "multiple causation" in history, could it have been many of these?

B.   If Protestantism is strictly religious, what groups or individuals fall within the category "Protestant"? At what point does Protestantism come into being? Was Luther a Protestant in October 1517? in 1520? in 1521? What is the basis for one's decision? Can one make a case for religious Protestantism beginning around 1400 with the efforts of Wycliffe and Huss?

C.   Can one speak about the Reformation and Protestantism synonymously or are they very different kinds of "things" or "movements"?

Having asked the necessary questions there comes a point where students must choose "a" possibility (meaning one out of many possibilities) and organize their essay in terms of it. Some individuals, perhaps for the sheer intellectual stimulation they get, choose the most remote (outlandish) possibility available. It is recommended that students choose the most obvious possibility or that which is easiest for them to demonstrate because they have the evidence at hand. They ought to prove they can do something relatively simple before delving into something more complex.

In an opening paragraph students should state what they intend to demonstrate. If they can do this they probably have asked some additional questions for which they have found adequate answers, for example:

1.   What evidence exists to illustrate each point made in the opening statement? For example, can one demonstrate that Protestantism was not the name of a single group but one composed of Lutherans or Evangelicals, Calvinists or Reformed, Anglicans or Episcopalians, as well as others too numerous to mention here? On the other hand, can one, at a higher level of abstraction, demonstrate that this umbrella term was appropriate to describe a single movement united in its belief in the authority of the Bible, the central role of Christ as the redeemer, and the overwhelming importance of faith as a means of salvation? In the former case one would argue for separate and often conflicting movements; in the latter, while they might be separate, certain commonalities of belief and practice might be shown to have united them.

2.   Is all the evidence, as outlined, related to the question being answered? Put another way, if one argues for "separate and often conflicting movements," does

the evidence support this position? If one argues for the position that "Protestantism was simply a single movement away from the Roman Catholic Church," does the evidence, the examples one might use, support this position?

If students have not found adequate answers to the questions above, or others similar to them, they should not be writing their opening paragraph. They should be thinking — a process which is a large part of the job of writing — and teachers should consider adding some five to ten minutes to the time allotted for this purpose during examinations.

Given the limited amount of time students have to respond to essay questions on an examination, one would not expect them to ask as many questions as have been asked here. The idea is to establish a mind set, a habit, to help students comprehend the concept that questions need not be prisons if one will but make inquiries of them. To accomplish this goal, teachers can assist students in the practice of asking questions about questions in situations where time constraints do not exist, or where they are very broad.

One might begin, for instance, with the titles of course textbooks. *The Western Experience*, by Mortimer Chambers et alia; *A History of the Modern World* by R. R. Palmer and Joel Colton; and *A History of Civilization: Prehistory to the Present* by Robin W. Winks all imply very different contents. Just the difference in the articles "the" and "a" suggest very different mind sets on the part of the authors. Imagine the possibilities for interpretation in such words as "Western," "experience," "modern," and "civilization." Students and teachers ought not to take these titles for granted. Their possible meanings and the implications of those meanings ought to be explored.

The same process should be followed with chapter headings and subheadings. Using the same texts as above, one finds the appropriate chapter headings on the topic of this essay question to be: "Reformations in Religion 1500-1570," "The Upheaval in Christendom, 1300-1560," and, "The Protestant Reformation." What questions might these titles engender and how different might be the evidence each author would present in support or demonstration of the title? Students who follow the practice of asking questions about such things as chapter headings are also more inclined to become more effective readers because their questions lead them to seek certain kinds of evidence. Note that two of the titles above establish time limits whereas one does not.

To take only the first example, does the time limit "1500-1570" preclude certain efforts toward reformations in religion that might otherwise have to be included, such as the efforts of Savanarola, Wycliffe, or Huss? Would one expect in this case references to the "Babylonian Captivity" of the Roman Catholic Church or the "Great Schism"? Can a case be made for including references to these as causes of "Reformations in Religion 1500-1570"? The possibilities for such questions and the critical reading they require can be enhanced by having students read conflicting points of view. This would be the case, particularly, where the authors use essentially the same evidence while giving their formulations very different perspectives. Such a case would demonstrate the point that one's perspective shapes what one sees. From a macro point of view, Protestantism can be seen as a single movement away from the Roman Catholic Church. From the micro point of view, it is more likely seen as a "series of separate and often conflicting movements."

When students are given essays for homework the only time constraint is that which they place on themselves. One could require them to list the questions they have asked of the question they are responding to and to turn them in along with their outline. When it comes to actual exams, require students to list x number of questions, where x stands for something the teacher thinks is reasonable. Keep in mind that the issue is not the number of questions asked but their quality. In this teacher's experience, students initially resist the process. It takes more of their time. Constant use in the classroom, however, reinforced by frequent reference to items engendered by questions which would not have surfaced without them, demonstrates unequivocally the efficacy of the practice. Within five to ten weeks students should begin to appreciate the value of the process. When transferred to other courses such as literature or to other practices such as newspaper reading, students report increased comprehension. Continued modeling by the teacher will lead students to develop a lifelong habit of inquiry. This behavior pattern will reduce their efforts to seek closure and insure their capacity to view events or experiences from many different perspectives — each giving a possibly different understanding of the world. And that, after all, may be more important than all the factual material we ask them to remember.

No Solo Venture:
Essay Writing in History

Virginia S. Wilson, James A. Litle, and Gerald L. Wilson

ALL TOO OFTEN essay writing is perceived by students in history classes as nothing more than boring, demanding busywork to be endured at best, dreaded at worst, and perhaps, above all, a solitary, even lonely process. The entire essay writing experience can be more profitable if changed from a solo venture to a supportive group process. Essay writing groups of four or six students, carefully and thoughtfully identified by the teacher, can maximize the potential for lively discussion, honest criticism, and mutual cooperation. An even number in each group assures that each student can have a partner within the supportive writing group. This essay writing group concept provides a context in which students assist others, and at the same time, help themselves. Likewise, the peer group approach relieves teachers of the solo burden of generating ideas for papers and reviewing drafts. Students and teachers benefit from the group writing process itself as well as a better finished product.

Fortunately, no setting is more naturally conducive to the development of writing skills than the history class. Natural resources abound. There is a richness of content unequaled by any other discipline. Using the content of history and the methods of historians, students learn to write, and they find the act of writing itself reinforces content. When writing essays, students as "apprentice historians" come to grips with the material and crystallize their own thoughts.

Before each group takes on the writing task itself, these apprentice historians must undertake case study analyses of essays written by professional historians which the teacher has selected relevant to the content under discussion. For example, a teacher might consider selecting essays from *American Heritage* magazine or one of the recent books of readings on United States history. As a homework assignment each student analyzes the selected historical essay. Following this individual reading and analysis, each group during the next regular class period discusses the selected essay. The teacher circulates among the groups to offer assistance as necessary. Incidentally, when the analysis taking place within the group is directed toward a professionally written essay or essays, members of the group tend to be more analytical and critical because no threat is posed to any one of them. This enables apprentice historians to get in the habit of viewing writing analytically.

In analyzing the professionally written essay, the group examines the components of the introduction, the body, and the conclusion. From this examination guidelines emerge for each of these three sections of the essay. For example, in an introduction the group might decide that a time/place setting sentence or two defining the context is appropriate. If historians were writing on the Puritans, they would state who the Puritans were and where they lived, and they would identify the appropriate time period. A second element of an introduction is a statement of a thesis where the writer states the theme and the position being taken on this theme. The third element of an introduction is the identification of the major categories of evidence to be used in support of the thesis. Likewise, the students need to determine the appropriate organization of the body paragraphs and the conclusion. Either during the same class period in which the guidelines are developed by each individual group or the next class meeting, they will be presented to the class as a whole, and from this pool of guidelines those judged essential by the teacher and class members will be copied and placed in students' notebooks for reference as they write their own essays.

Having become familiar with historical essays through case studies, apprentice historians move from the position of critical observers to that of active participants as the group begins the research process. Each group is assigned by the teacher a separate topic based on the content of the current unit of study and asked to research this topic as a means of learning research techniques. For example, in the colonial period such topics as "religious revivalism," "British control of American trade," or the "move toward self-government" might be assigned to a group. Given one of these topics or a similar one, the students in the group in a brainstorming session both narrow the topic and formulate the questions which they hope to answer in their research. The group begins to work on the topic by generating "descriptors." Descriptors are words, events, or people and their synonyms, associated with a topic. If the topic assigned were "religious revivalism," descriptors might include religion, conversion experience, revival, Great Awakening, Jonathan Edwards, George Whitefield, denominations, and United States colonial history. To aid in finding descriptors for any topic, students should consult the Library of Congress Subject Headings Catalogue, an ERIC Thesaurus, or the associated topics in the *Reader's Guide to Periodical Literature*.

Armed with these descriptors, each group meets separately with the librarian for assistance in locating potential resources. The librarian and the teacher explain the research techniques necessary to get maximum benefit from these resources. The group as a whole then prepares a working bibliography, takes notes from the sources and develops an outline. Approximately a week of class and homework time should be devoted to this research process. Since this is the initial research effort, the teacher may wish to have each group present to the class in oral form its research findings following the form of their outline. Just as was the case with evaluating essays written by professional historians, oral presentations often foster a cooperative rather than a competitive attitude within the group.

At this point, the apprentice historian has read and examined the historical essays, participated in the development of guidelines for essay writing, and explored the research process. In addition, essay writing group members have developed a sense of cohesion and comraderie through shared experiences and activities. However, for many students there is a quantum leap between preparation for writing and the actual writing of the essay itself. All members of the class write their first essay on a common topic selected by the teacher. Assuming that the class has moved beyond the colonial period to the period of protest and revolution, the teacher selects a topic such as British reactions to American protests of the Stamp Act. Apprentice historians, using the techniques previously acquired, spend two class periods and a week of homework time researching the topic thoroughly. Upon completing the research process, the individual class members for their homework write an essay introduction, using the already established guidelines. The following day each group combines the introductions written by individuals into a common group effort. Each group's introduction is presented on an overhead to the class for an evaluation. After reviewing each group's introductory paragraphs, the class as a whole writes one introduction.

When writing the body of the essay, a division of labor occurs. If, for example, there are three categories of support for the thesis and six or seven writing groups of four students each in the class, then two/three groups write the body paragraph dealing with the first category of support; two/three more work with the second category and so forth. As a homework assignment, individual members of each group write the appropriate assigned body paragraph. The next day in class every group develops one body paragraph by reworking the group members' individual paragraphs. The two/three groups working on the same category of support then blend their efforts into one clear paragraph to be presented on an overhead to the class. The class evaluates and revises as necessary each supporting paragraph to produce a final draft.

Once the supporting paragraphs are completed and placed in the sequence, the next step is to link them into one cohesive body. To accomplish this, every group as a group writes topic/transition sentences for all the paragraphs of support using connecting thoughts rather than merely connecting words. The teacher presents each group's topic/transition sentences on an overhead. The class discusses them and writes a reworked topic/transition sentence for each body paragraph.

The group process used in writing the introduction is also appropriate for the development of the essay conclusion with its restatement of the thesis, summary of the supporting evidence and explanation of the significance of the topic.

The teacher may wish for students as a group effort to write several essays on a common topic, but at some point, students will need to begin writing their own essays. At this time either a common designated topic may be assigned or students themselves may select topics of high interest to them appropriate to the time period under discussion. Though students are no longer actually writing the essay together, the group support process continues.

First, the group aids its members in generating ideas on topic descriptors, potential resources, tentative theses, and categories for the outline. Following this, students write a rough draft according to the guidelines for historical essays previously developed by the class. At this stage, students serve as critics of their own papers. They check for consistency of support for the stated thesis, accuracy of content, and clarity of expression.

Having completed the process of self-evaluation and rewriting, apprentice historians present their rough drafts to their fellow writing group members with specific written questions that they have on their own drafts. These questions encourage the other group members to take an active role in the evaluation process. The best format for this group feedback is for general responses to be given orally and specific criticisms to be written.

Taking into account the suggestions of the group, apprentice historians rethink their papers. Rewriting at this stage may involve more than just a change of words or corrections of grammar; often it may require a change in the organizational structure. After completing this rewrite, each individual group member trades papers with the assigned group partner. Partners comment on the rewritten sections and check the papers for spelling and mechanical errors. After reviewing the partner's comments, the apprentice historian prepares a final draft which is handed into the teacher along with notes and rough drafts.

In evaluating a student's work, the teacher considers both the process and product, and in the same way that many teachers of mathematics do, gives credit for the steps correctly followed as well as for the final result. The teacher may wish to use an evaluation sheet designed to mirror the class essay guidelines and common elements of style.

The goal of this essay writing process is not to create professional historians (although that could be a delightful by-product) but rather to sharpen essay writing skills so that these apprentice historians can communicate their thoughts more accurately and powerfully. An important part of this group writing process is the requirement of constant rewriting, revising, and editing. Since the process moves in stages over a period of time, the night-before-scissor-and-paste syndrome is eliminated. In addition, since the essay assignments are content-based and unit and topic specific, students actually learn more history in the process of refining their essay writing skills. The learning of history and the development of the craft of writing in a group setting can be exciting, rewarding, and perhaps, even fun.

Bull's-Eye: A Teachers' Guide for Developing Student Skill in Responding to Essay Questions

Robert Blackey

(Reprinted from *Social Education*, October 1988)

ARE YOU A HARDWORKING TEACHER whose students react favorably to what you teach, enjoy time spent in your classroom, and claim to appreciate and learn from your subject matter? Are you also frustrated when students fail to respond on essay exams as you expect? Do their intelligence levels and the quality of their other work suggest that their performance on essay exams does not reflect their abilities? Do your students insist that their essays do not represent their abilities or what they have learned?

If your answer to any of these questions is yes, you are not alone. The problems involved in writing successful essays are not limited to level of teaching or type of student. Graduate students suffer as much as high school students, and gifted students require assistance as well as average students.

Responding effectively to essay questions is not a new problem, but many educators believe it has been aggravated by the erosion of writing and critical thinking skills within our culture as a whole. However serious the problem, I shall contend that it is not irremedial. Persons who seek a solution to the problem may be reminded that a link exists between clear thinking and clear writing, that responding effectively to essay questions is a skill, not an art, and that helping students write essays that reflect their abilities requires extra effort by both teachers and students. It is an effort worth making since skills acquired or perfected by taking essay tests are not replicated by other forms of writing. Essay tests give students practice in writing under pressure and help them learn to create a first draft that communicates clearly, though without the polish of revised and edited prose.

What follows then is a series of suggestions designed to assist teachers and students in developing these skills. Teachers should be aware that what is involved is a process. Just as writing teachers have come to recognize that students improve with instruction in the process of writing (and not merely from more writing, the study of grammar, or the number of the teacher's marks), responses to essay questions can be improved if instruction is understood and presented as a process. Before beginning, however, teachers must prepare the way on their own.

Introspection. The initial step in teaching essay exam writing skills does not involve students. Teachers must take time to reflect upon how courses are organized and determine what students are expected to learn. Much of the factual material that appears in textbooks and fascinates teachers will soon be forgotten. In order to do a service to students and our world, we must therefore teach students to think so as to reflect our discipline's contribution to a broad base of wisdom and understanding. Since most students will be unable to make this discovery without help, they must be shown how to use facts in essay writing and how critical thinking works within a discipline.

Teachers who routinely demonstrate relationships between parts, explain why something is important, examine a range of interpretations, call attention to prejudices (including their own), and draw comparisons and contrasts exemplify what will help students study, take exams, and move beyond mere note taking and regurgitating recitation. Determining, synthesizing, and linking facts, significance, meaning, analysis, and cause and effect are central to virtually all courses. They are also keys to good citizenship and success in life. They must, therefore, be repeatedly demonstrated in class as part of all assignments so as to impress upon students their value over and above course content. For the process to work and improvement to be evident, students must practice constantly — at first orally in class and then on exams.

Question writing. The second step, like the first, also involves teachers working alone — or preferably in consultation with other teachers who review one another's material — because effective student responses on essay exams depend on well-constructed questions. Questions that are awkwardly phrased, carelessly worded, unclearly related to course goals, or vague in the directions provided make the students' task more difficult. Though these concerns are not the focus of this paper, their importance is illustrated by the following question: Were the victorious powers in World War I justified in including a "war guilt clause" in the Treaty of Versailles of 1919 blaming Germany for the war?

If such a question does not explicitly ask that the answer given be justified, yes or no is a complete answer. Although the writer of the question may expect students to address political, social, intellectual, and economic developments in Germany and elsewhere to support the position taken, that intent is not evident in the question. The question would be clearer and much improved by adding the following: "Defend your answer by demonstrating whether conditions in Europe warranted such action."[1]

General directions. Once good questions have been formulated and teachers have demonstrated the thinking of their disciplines, they may provide instructions to assist students in performing their best.

Students should be advised to read the examination directions and then the entire set of questions. If they are to choose from several questions, they should be instructed to select questions they are best prepared for. If several questions are required, time should be budgeted, including setting aside five to ten minutes for proofreading. Teachers should point out that it is better to write something on all required questions and that questions assigned a higher value in points should be answered first. Students should be instructed to respond directly to the question asked, not to different questions that result from their own reformulations. Key words in the instructions may be underscored to make instructions clearer. For example, if part A or part B of a question is to be answered (but not both), 'or' should be underlined and the words 'but not both' added to prevent both parts from being addressed.

Directive words. Good answers to essay questions also depend upon clear understanding of important directive words. Good answers do not require covering the entire territory by writing down everything known; the so-called "shot-gun" approach usually backfires. Essay tests measure students' skill in selecting, organizing, and analyzing material in answering a question. Such words as 'analyze', 'discuss', and 'compare', for example, indicate how material is to be presented.

Though background knowledge is essential, merely to display it is insufficient. If students are asked to compare the constitutions of Britain and the United States, they should receive little credit if they only describe them but fail to indicate similarities or differences. If they are asked to evaluate the causes of the French Revolution, they do not answer the question by listing the causes without ranking them in order of significance and justifying their ranking.

An essay answer is satisfactory if and only if it directly answers the question asked.

Teachers should have their own clear understanding of the directive terms they employ in formulating essay questions, and they should by definition and example clearly and adequately communicate to student examinees the meanings of such frequently occurring directive terms as *analyze, assess, compare, contrast, criticize, define, describe, discuss, enumerate, evaluate, explain, identify, illustrate, interpret, justify, list, prove, summarize,* and *trace.*

Planning and organization. Another important prewriting step involves planning an essay response. Students typically, like race horses reacting to the starter's gun, lunge headlong into their answers, hastily writing down everything of direct or remote relevance they can think of. They should be made aware of the value of organization to clarity. Teachers may wish to establish a "reading period" of five to ten minutes, before students begin writing.

Planning and brainstorming. After choosing the question to be answered and considering the directions, students may use planning time to brainstorm — that is, to prepare a list of major points to be covered. They may jot down, on the test sheet itself or on scrap paper, what comes to mind as they react to the question. This resolves the problem of forgetting points thought of at first but not immediately written about. Students can assess items on the list and expand upon the most important ones, avoiding repetition, addressing elements in order of importance, and grouping them where connections should be made. The list of points resulting from brainstorming need not be complete and additional ones can be incorporated later, but it is an effective way of seeing the components of an answer in perspective. It is also vital for analyzing the question, i.e., for examining it carefully, word for word, to determine precisely what is (and what is not) being asked.

Introduction and thesis. The reading or planning period should be used for outlining and structuring the essay. A well-organized essay, complete with a thematic introduction, body of supporting evidence, and conclusion, will be more favorably received than one that lacks clear structure. Stressing this, the teacher should explain what an introduction is and its role in the essay. Emphasis should be placed on the role and value of a thesis statement that answers the question directly, shows that thought informed the response, and points out the direction the paper will take. A thesis statement should state a brief answer to the question, as if a sentence or two would suffice (supporting evidence follows); it should not merely describe the scheme of organization. In other words, instruct students, instead of stating what they will discuss, to state the meaning and significance of what they will discuss. Time should not be spent repeating or paraphrasing the question.

Historical setting. History students should be instructed how to establish a historical setting for their responses; what happened before the subject of the question and what resulted afterward should be considered in planning a complete essay. This helps students think historically and encourages them to understand the significance of an event in the broader context of what preceded and followed it. Teachers of other disciplines can provide instructions that reflect the characteristics of their fields.

Body and thesis. The body of an essay should not consist only or primarily of factual information. Answers are stronger if historical (literary, scientific, etc.) analysis or argument is provided. Students should be encouraged to express opinions, but such thinking should show use of material to arrive at an understanding of the question. Arguments should be sound and their conclusions based on facts presented; examples should be relevant to the question. Instruct students to use evidence to substantiate all generalizations and to draw generalizations and conclusions from factual material presented. As the body of the essay is developed, the thesis must be kept in mind and even modified if warranted by the evidence adduced. Time is limited, so students must guard against being distracted by tangential issues. Everything contained in the essay, including the conclusion, should support the thesis and be relevant to answering the question.

Conclusion. In addition, the differences between a conclusion and a summary require explanation and examples. Students typically understand a conclusion as primarily a repetition of the main points (that is, a summary), but they better demonstrate thinking skills if they determine significance, meaning, or results — that is, a conclusion — as well.

Proofreading. Several minutes for proofreading should be scheduled in the time allotted for the examination. It is common to misspell even simple words, omit letters or words, or transpose numbers when writing under pressure. Students should be alerted to reread their essays to confirm that the words they use convey the meaning they intend. Although unity, organization, and development are most important to communicate clearly in an essay examination, correct spelling and grammar improve the quality of every essay.

In-class practice. All these suggestions will have minimal effect if they are only cited orally or in writing. The most effective way to ensure that students both understand and know how to implement them is to devote class time to practicing what is preached, to going through the essential steps of responding to essay questions.

Teachers should outline on the chalkboard an effective answer to a sample essay question, thinking aloud as they proceed step-by-step, showing how to analyze a question, brainstorm, formulate an introduction and thesis, provide supporting evidence, and finally draw a conclusion implied by the evidence that answers the question and incorporates the thesis. Students can then, orally and as a class, practice the same exercise, with as many students as possible contributing while the teacher outlines their collective answer on the chalkboard. Students can also gain appreciation for effective responses when they create their own essay questions and respond to those of their classmates, evaluating others' answers in a constructive learning experience.

Model and practice essays. Whenever possible, model essays — good and poor — should be distributed and reviewed by the class, with the teacher highlighting positive and negative characteristics. After students see these differences and internalize the process of essay writing, they should be given practice essay questions to answer.

Teacher comments. When the practice essays are completed, two important steps that remain are (1) teachers' writing comments and (2) students' rewriting their practice essays. Most teachers, at best, make only a few general comments, like captions to cartoons, along with the essay grade — for example, "well done," "good evidence but weak conclusion," "the question is answered only indirectly." Most do not ordinarily allow students to rewrite their answers. General comments, however, are inadequate constructive direction. To improve students' essay-writing skills, extensive teacher comments and student rewriting are necessary. If students are not shown a better way, they will perpetuate their mistakes rather than learn from them.[2]

In marginal and in general comments on student essays, teachers should explain what students do well or poorly and why. Comments are most effective when they lead students themselves to make the corrections or improvements — for example: "Introduction provides general information only and lacks a thesis or point of view relevant to the question; try using enough of that information to whet the reader's appetite and then lead into a thesis based directly on the question." "How is this material relevant to your answer? You leave it to the reader to make the connection when you should be doing the work, and the thinking." "This is a summary of earlier points, not a conclusion. A proper conclusion should answer the question by amplifying on the thesis and demonstrating what is important about the subject based on the evidence you have provided." The more specific the comments, the better, and they may be in the form of statements or questions.

Teacher comments should focus on written expression as well as content. Emphasis on content alone does not enable students to appreciate the link between knowledge and expression, between information and communication. (An alternative approach, albeit a less personal one, for those teachers who recognize the value of such comments but find it difficult to allot the time to write as many as are necessary, would be to prepare a checklist of commonly used comments. Such a list, appropriately marked and returned to students, could be an effective compromise between individualized notations and doing little or nothing; it could be to teachers what proofreaders' symbols are to editors. Still another time-saving alternative would be to require students to submit a blank cassette tape with each exam. Teachers could then read and react audibly, connecting specific comments and suggestions to particular pages and paragraphs. This would enable teachers to be more thorough with limited time, and it could also be used to help students develop an "ear" for the sound of good writing [e.g., "John, listen to what you wrote! ... How does that sound compared to this? It should sound clearer and more to the point. I want you to try rewriting the following sentences:..."].)

Rewriting. With the benefit of the teacher's pointed comments, students should be asked to respond again to the same question. Experience has shown that with repetition of the process, students show improvement. Teachers should further consider allowing students to earn a higher grade by revising their graded essay exams (also turning in the first response to make grading less time-consuming). Students will thus more likely make an effort to understand and use teacher suggestions. Or, the essay test could serve as a first draft for a brief out-of-class assignment to revise and resubmit the essay. Students would have more time to develop ideas, polish their prose, focus on the shortcomings of their essays, and consider what they might do to improve.

Additional suggestions. A few related suggestions are worth noting. In written and oral comments, it is constructive if teachers make positive comments so as to encourage even the poorest student. If possible, teachers should arrange to meet individually with students to review the essays and the teacher's comments; it is a way to determine whether instruction is understood. Finally, overmarking should be avoided. Just as students will not learn if teachers fail to say anything useful, they may not learn if teachers say so much that they are overwhelmed. Consider two or three major issues and, until rewrites or subsequent papers, ignore the rest.

The above suggestions will consume valuable class time, but developing writing and thinking skills is vital to learning and should not be relegated to English teachers alone. What is sacrificed in subject matter will be offset by what is gained in improved skills and comprehension.

▼

Notes

[1] For more specific direction, see my articles, "A Guide to the Skill of Essay Construction in History," *Social Education* 45, no. 3 (March 1981): 178-82; "How Advanced Placement History Questions Are Prepared — and How Yours Can Be Too," AHA *Perspectives* 20, no. 8 (November 1981): 23-25. Of related value are "Designing Effective Writing Assignments," chap. 6 in *Teaching and Assessing Writing*, ed. Edward M. White (San Francisco: Jossey-Bass, 1985) and J.C. Bean et al., "Microtheme Strategies for Developing Cognitive Skills," in *Teaching Writing in All Disciplines*, ed. C.W. Griffin (San Francisco: Jossey-Bass, 1982).

[2] See my article, "Writing in the Major: A Novel Approach That Works," *Perspectives* 24, no. 5 (May/June 1986): 10-13; and Barbara E. Fassler Walvoord, *Helping Students Write Well: A Guide for Teachers in All Disciplines* (New York: Modern Language Association, 1982).

Chapter V:

Textbooks

Teaching and Textbooks

John A. Garraty

IMPROVING THE LEVEL and quality of textbooks is a subject I have thought about a good deal, both because I have been using textbooks as a teacher for more years than I care to remember, and because I have written textbooks for both the grade school and college level. Since becoming head of the AHA Teaching Division I have learned a great deal about what is going on in the profession where matters related to teaching are concerned, and this too has caused me to give thought to the role of textbooks. What follows are some more or less random reflections on the subject.

As for the level at which textbooks are pitched, one reason history is so fascinating is that it can be studied profitably at so many different levels. In elementary school courses, for example, I believe that it is enough to teach history as a story. Most of the elementary United States history texts that I have seen skimp on the narrative element in history. Either they try to avoid being *too* difficult by keeping the number of facts to a minimum, or they focus too much on inculcating values and attitudes through, for example, dragging in references to women, blacks, democracy, and other subjects of contemporary concern at points where they are really not appropriate. I particularly recall, in my perusal of a number of eighth grade texts, material about a black cowboy named Jasper McWhimsey. (All refer to the same cowboy.) None of the accounts has much to say about the man except that he was black; apparently he is included simply so that the book *has* a black cowboy in it. How typical (or atypical) McWhimsey was, or what being a cowboy was like for a black man in late nineteenth-century America, are not discussed.

It is not, of course, the attempt to make young students aware of the important role played by blacks that I question. The heavy-handed way in which the attempt is made and the subordination of historical narrative to the didactic purpose are what seem wrong to me, along with the failure of the authors even to try to make anything significant of the material.

That having been said, I think the level of elementary school texts is much too low. The way to avoid being difficult when telling a story is not to reduce the amount of information but to increase it. Young people do not know much about things they have not experienced, and their experiences have been limited. In telling them about United States history, one needs to provide lots of information that older students may be presumed already to know. Somewhere in any elementary school account of the War of Independence, for example, there should be a description of what it was like to load and fire a musket. More about fewer subjects, not very little about anything, ought to be the guiding principle.

As for the level at which college texts are pitched, most of the ones I am familiar with seem just about right. There are differences in emphasis and approach, but I dare say that 90 percent of what any of the commonly used college texts have to say can be found in all of the others. Texts are relatively less important in these courses to begin with. After all, they represent only part of what the students read, and their teachers are likely to be better informed about the subject than most grade school teachers. Consequently, students are less dependent on the text for their understanding of the subject.

The *quality* of college-level texts is a more complicated matter. Teachers apply different standards than students when estimating quality, yet both sets of standards must be met if a text is to *work*. My uninformed guess about the way most teachers examine new textbooks is that they look first at the handling of something they are especially familiar with. If that section is not up-to-date or if it seems to treat the subject too superficially, most busy teachers are not likely to look much further. But if the treatment is fresh, and if the quotations and factual details are unusual, the book will at least receive their serious consideration.

Students judge a textbook's quality differently. They cannot know (and are unlikely to care) whether the book takes account of the latest scholarship on any particular point. If it uses the same colorful Teddy Roosevelt quote that John D. Hicks or William Underwood Faulkner employed in the 1940s, they are no less likely to be amused, or to learn from reading it. If the material is clearly presented, well organized, not too cluttered with on-the-one-hand and on-the-other-hands, and if the author's opinions seem plausible, they will read the book and probably retain a reasonable proportion of its contents. A text that intrigues teachers may bore or confuse the average student by devoting space to matters of minor importance, or by dealing too much in abstractions, or by spending time explaining why some interpretation of an event is wrong instead of stressing what the author believes to be correct.

I am aware that none of what I have been saying is in any way unusual. Readers will find it no less surprising that I think textbooks are valuable teaching tools. Survey courses can be taught without texts, but most teachers use them. How a teacher uses a text is very much a matter of individual taste. A few, I fear, treat texts almost like scripture, following them almost line by line and holding students responsible for every fact and interpretation. Others prefer to take off from the text, either by elaborating on matters treated in summary fashion or by developing a point of view contrary to that expressed by the author. Still others ignore the text in lectures and discussion, simply telling their students to read the book and use it as a work of reference and in reviewing for examinations. I have no unusual suggestions to make on the subject, but then my own problem is a special one — having put just about everything I know into my text, I find it hard to teach the survey course without repeating myself endlessly.

As for students, however much they may complain about reading textbooks, most of the ones I have questioned agree that texts perform a valuable function. A good text makes it possible for the student to see (or at least sense) the subject whole, from beginning to end in all its aspects. Such a work provides an understanding of the continuity of history, and also of the most fundamental of historical principles, the fact that one thing leads to another, that events have causes, and significance, and results.

Despite what I have just said about the average student's lack of interest in the latest word on this or that historical debate, it is essential that textbooks be kept up-to-date. For an author — or even for the several authors of multiple-author texts — to be familiar with everything that is being written about every subject discussed in a survey of United States history is obviously impossible. But that is not what I mean by being up-to-date. I refer rather to being familiar with what topics are being most affected by recent scholarship and what kinds of history are most relevant for understanding the current concerns of students and teachers alike. I am thinking of such obvious concerns as "grass roots" history, the lives of ordinary people; of the new research into the nature of the family; of the history of women and of various minority groups; of voting behavior; of social and economic mobility; and so on.

It has been pointed out in *Perspectives*, and quite rightly, that current college texts tend to promise more than they provide in these areas. This is not, however, entirely due to the laziness, ignorance, or lack of interest on the part of textbook writers. When new fields are being developed, our reach tends to exceed our grasp. The pieces of the new puzzles are scattered and many of them are missing. I recall that when the interest in black history expanded so rapidly in the late 1960s, the publisher of my college text persuaded a historian who knew a great deal about the topic to criticize the book from that perspective. He pointed out a dozen topics that I had ignored or treated inadequately and suggested many books and articles that I should consult. But at the end of his review he confessed that much of the black history that the authors of college texts should be familiar with had not yet been written.

Furthermore, it is one thing to demand that texts devote more space to aspects of social history and other subjects of current scholarly interest, quite another to give them that space without eliminating material of equal or greater importance. Few historians today would define their subject as "past politics" and nothing more, but the very concept, "United States," is a political statement. One cannot get far in understanding our social history, or any of the other areas I have mentioned, without a solid knowledge of United States political (and economic) history.

How then can one make a text up-to-date in the sense I have used the term? I know of no specific way to answer this question; certainly I have not been able to answer it in my own work in a way that I find completely satisfactory. However, if textbook writers are aware of what scholars are doing and alert to opportunities to use the new material scholars are bringing to light, their books will probably transmit some feeling for the direction in which historiography is moving.

Keeping a text from being out-of-date as distinct from making it up-to-date is equally important and fortunately easier to accomplish. I dare say that large parts of the leading texts of the 1940s read as fresh today as they did four decades ago. But many parts — those dealing or for that matter not dealing with blacks and women, to cite two obvious examples — would seem hopelessly old-fashioned and in many cases positively offensive. A text that is not constantly being rethought, rephrased, reproportioned, and otherwise modified will soon strike even the least sophisticated student as at best old hat. What is involved is principally the kinds of topics stressed and the viewpoint of the authors.

In order for a text to be effective, it ought to avoid unsupported generalizations of all kinds. Statements such as "slaves were often mistreated" and "Andrew Jackson had a hot temper" may or may not be accurate, but they are so abstract that they do not tell the reader much about the subject and, when buried in a long narrative, they are not easy to remember. Students complain about being asked to memorize too many dates and too many details, as well they may. But properly chosen facts — lots of them — make history interesting and, in both senses of the word, memorable. Examples of how slaves were mistreated will make the point clear and incidentally illustrate what the author means by "mistreated." An anecdote or an apt quotation of something Jackson said will serve similar functions. Details are keys, triggers, and sparks that unlock, release, and ignite our recollections of large and important matters. And, of course, details make things specific and thus keep related events and similar ideas separate and distinct in our minds. "Unimportant" facts can be used to remind the reader of larger matters.

I first became aware of how this process works many years ago while lecturing to a freshman class on the events leading to the Civil War. I was talking about the four parties that ran presidential candidates in 1860. In trying to explain the position of the Constitutional Union Party, which sought to avoid rather than confront the divisive issues of the day, I said quite spontaneously that its symbol should have been an ostrich with its head buried in the sand.

I thought no more about the matter until, when given an examination question on the election, a substantial number of students wrote about the ostrich as though it had in fact been the symbol of the party like our Democratic donkey and Republican elephant. I resolved to be more careful about my spontaneous thoughts in future lectures until it dawned on me that every student who mentioned the ostrich also understood what the Constitutional Union Party stood for and why it took the position it did. The picture it evoked reminded them of the ideas and reasons that had made me think of the ostrich while lecturing.

I am not of course suggesting that texts should contain incorrect information or imaginary facts, no matter how striking the effects they might produce. When in my own text I got to the Constitutional Union Party, I confined myself to saying that "ostrich-like," its members tried to ignore the divisive issues of the day. But correct facts that make one person or event distinct from others are marvelous teaching devices. Those that relate directly to what is important, such as my imaginary ostrich, are the best, but almost any concrete detail can serve.

I think, for example, that any historical figure worth mentioning more than once or twice in a survey text — or for that matter in class — ought to be somehow made distinct from the hundreds of others who pass through its pages. In a discussion of Robert J. Walker's career as governor of Kansas Territory in the 1850s, I mentioned that he was small, tough-minded, and energetic, much like the major figure Stephen A. Douglas, whom I had already described at length. In discussing Newton D. Baker's role as Secretary of War in 1917-18, I quoted what he is supposed to have said when he was told that Premier Clemenceau had offered to provide French prostitutes for the men of the AEF: "For God's sake, don't show this to the President or he'll stop the war," which tells the student something about President Wilson as well as about Baker's sense of humor.

I offer these examples diffidently; others might well suggest far more telling ways of characterizing Walker and Baker. My point is that the particular material is in this connection relatively unimportant. It does not matter much whether the subject's appearance is described or his personality, or whether the reference takes the form of an anecdote, or whatever.

Trivial details are especially useful in keeping similar and closely related matters straight, and in holding interest and creating a feeling of what it was like at a particular point in the past. Here is a small example. In describing the War of 1812, most United States history texts refer to the three naval battles won by American frigates early in the war. These engagements were not strategically important, but the fact that they occurred is, and the books mention them. If they are to be mentioned, each, in my opinion, ought to be sharply distinguished from the others. Such details as where in the Atlantic each clash took place, or the number of guns on each ship, or what damage was done to the vanquished, or even the name of the British captain will serve to keep one engagement separate from the others in students' minds.

It is my experience that students do not complain about details such as these. They know that they will not be expected to remember the name of the captain of *USS Constitution*. As a matter of fact, they probably *won't* remember the captain's name, or the number of guns on Old Ironsides, or any particular small detail. But any detail that does come to mind will remind them about the battles, and then, presumably, about their significance or, in this case, their lack of significance.

Small details are especially important when dealing with the great men and women of history. With minor figures, as I have suggested, details help students to keep each individual separate and to remind them of the reasons why the subjects are worth remembering. With our Washingtons and Lincolns, and also with our Frederick Douglasses, Eleanor Roosevelts, and Andrew Carnegies and a hundred others of their stature, details can serve a somewhat different function. They can humanize these monuments, perhaps by showing their quirks and failings, or by describing their non-public interests, or otherwise reducing them to the size of the ordinary human beings they were.

It may well be argued that the points I have been making are of at best marginal significance. If, as I have said, most of the material in any text can be found in any of the others, how important can such matters be? If the chief function of a text is to be a work of reference that students can turn to for this or that fact or in reviewing for an examination, then the things I have been discussing are no more than motivational devices. Is it not the responsibility of classroom teachers to stimulate interest and to focus their students' attention on the particular events and ideas that they as teachers want to stress? But whether marginal or of central importance, texts are part of the educational process. And beyond this obvious fact, being books, texts greatly influence how beginning students react to the subject as distinct from what they learn, or what they like or dislike about a particular class. If our object is to interest students in history rather than merely to teach them certain facts, how history is presented is of vital importance. How they react to their textbooks will, I believe, have much to do with whether or not they read other historical works when their college days are over.

There Is Another Way:
United States History Texts
and the Search for Alternatives

John Anthony Scott

A SCORE OF U.S. HISTORY and social studies texts dominate the high school market; they constitute required reading for millions of young people from the upper-elementary level to the twelfth grade. There is among the American public a developing consensus with respect to these texts, thanks especially to the publication of Frances FitzGerald's *America Revised* in 1979.

Texts, FitzGerald pointed out, are supposed to provide students with historical truth; but this requirement not infrequently collides with a publisher's need to make a profit. Resolution of this conflict of interest is achieved through the elimination of subject matter which might arouse the ire of special interest groups and thus have a negative impact upon adoptions and sales. Censorship, therefore, accompanies the production of these books, and historical truth becomes the victim. The realities of slavery, for example, or the wiping out of Native American peoples are muted. The result is often a pallid, lifeless presentation.

The lack of vitality characterizing these books is accentuated by the failure to base them squarely upon the original sources which alone provide the historian with the means to illuminate history. Textbook writers typically and perhaps of necessity put together their material by relying heavily upon monographic literature — not to mention other textbooks. They tell of events that they have only read about in the works of others, but that they themselves for the most part have not studied from original sources . Books such as this are unsatisfactory.

There is, however, another way to go. Over the past thirty years teachers, historians, and publishers have begun providing some of the literature we seek. This work is characterized by, though not limited to, an effort to make original sources available to students in many varied forms. Such sources include artworks and artifacts; published and unpublished journals, reports, correspondence, and autobiographies; newspapers; folk songs, legends, and oral testimony. This new literature is still in a relatively early stage of development, but it thrives in some schools, especially where it is used by college-bound students. It exists side by side with the textbook leviathan.

Some readers may contemplate this alternative with skepticism: "Isn't it going to be terribly expensive to publish all this material for large numbers of students?"

The answer is, yes and no. A school system that starts collecting documents needs only one camera-ready copy of each item in order to produce all the copies it wishes at trifling cost. The investment is cumulative. If steps are taken to make the material available — and this will be addressed in a moment — a first-class history archive ought to lie within reach of any school system that wants it, at a fraction of the sum that the taxpayer is obliged to pay each year for texts. This is the reason commercial publishers are not interested in promoting the sale of original source materials: there simply isn't enough money in it.

To provide original sources cheaply for school use teachers will need to develop publishing and research arrangements of their own. This may be accomplished by setting up nonprofit educational centers in every region of the country. These centers would be staffed by teachers and students, some professional, some volunteer. Part of the expense would be covered by sales of materials, part by funds from state education budgets, federal grants, and private contributions. One example of a nonprofit institution of this type is the National Center for Curriculum in the Schools, in Los Angeles.

To deprive students of source materials makes it impossible for them to have direct access to our past. Young Americans must read historical sources for themselves if they are to begin to know history. American archives and libraries are crammed with sources that await use. This material constitutes a foundation for the education of American youth and introduces them to the cultural legacy that is their birthright. This archival record possesses enormous diversity. There are, for example, dozens of narratives of African-American slaves and many volumes of recollections of life under slavery. There is a largely untapped treasury of the legends and poetry of Native Americans. And there are sources of great value for Jewish history in general and Yiddish culture in particular.

Not infrequently young people themselves have made valuable contributions to the record, as have others who witnessed youth's experience and then wrote down what they saw and heard. The life of child workers in America's mines, mills, and factories has been eloquently documented by Lewis Hine and the accounts of labor organizers like John Spargo. Mention should also be made of records created by battlefield soldiers and frontier women. These writings have a continuing fascination for young people. There is no better way for them to learn the power of historical literature than through the writings of other young people, dead and gone, who helped to make history and also recorded it.

Today's young people continue this tradition. Our schools need to be thought of not only as places where history is taught, but where it is written. Young immigrants in the process of learning English in California schools are writing how and why they came from Vietnam, or Pakistan, or Hong Kong, or the Philippines, and what experiences befell them on the way. Youth archives constitute a special form of the historical record. They need to be constituted, accessioned, and reproduced. In fact, the very concept of the youth archive may be viewed as central to the emergence of a new historical literature for young people.

From earliest times, men, women, and children in America have told the story of their lives and struggles through the medium of song. These songs are historical sources of depth and beauty. They provide evidence for American history throughout its span. The songs offer firsthand accounts of human life, experience, and struggle, and this is reinforced by the power of music. These songs are even studied in schools for the deaf by children with little or no hearing. This is no mean testimony to the human and historical truth conveyed by the lyrics even when divorced from the exquisite melodies to which they are often set.

Folk songs are now beginning to be disseminated to schools all over the country. Members of the Committee on History in the Classroom established, in 1979, a newsletter entitled *Folk Song in the Classroom*. Laurence I. Seidman, a folklorist and professor of education at Post College, New York, helped launch this nonprofit venture. Issued three times a year, *Folk Song in the Classroom* has a circulation of close to 1,500, and it reaches an audience composed primarily of upper elementary, junior high, and high school teachers.

Some of the "new" historical literature for youth created in recent years has been historical narrative; but where this is so the narrative has been based from first to last upon original sources woven into the story. Forms of historical literature based upon such use and mastery of original sources include videotapes and biographies.

The short story was the art form of the nineteenth century; the thirty- or forty-minute videotape may be that of the twenty-first. Numberless episodes in United States history may be enacted through videotape in the form of dramatizations that introduce students to a given topic. Such historical videotapes open limitless horizons for the cooperation of artists, actors, and teachers. They constitute an art form with a future transcending the instructional and documentary mode with which teachers today are familiar. Videotapes may be produced professionally; they may also be prepared in the schools with the participation of students, teachers, filmmakers, and scholars. One example is the tape recently produced by New England and the Constitution (a non-profit educational group) entitled *The Other Boston Tea Party*. Based upon a play by John F. Carroll, this charming one-hour tape is available to schools for $10. The presentation effectively dramatizes the struggle for the ratification of the Constitution.

Biography, many agree, is a highly effective literary form for inspiring young people with a love of the past. Unfortunately, serious biography for young adults is in its infancy; there are gaps on our library shelves where biographies ought to be. Biography awaits exploration as central to the new historical literature being discussed here. At the moment the principal contribution is the *Library of American Biography*, edited by Oscar Handlin. But more than half the books in this series deal with members of the elite — presidents, politicians, and lawyers. Only three women are included (Abigail Adams, Elizabeth Cady Stanton, Eleanor Roosevelt), two black men (Frederick Douglass, Booker T. Washington), and one Native American (Tecumseh). Champions of the cause of labor, with the exception of Samuel Gompers and Walter Reuther, are conspicuous by their absence. There are no more than three writers or journalists — Benjamin Franklin, Henry Adams, and Theodore Roosevelt. There are no explorers or inventors with the exception of Captain John Smith and Eli Whitney. Distinguished artists, musicians, scientists, philosophers, actors, architects, and activists find no place.

Thomas Y. Crowell's *Women of America* series, edited by Milton Meltzer, contains about twenty volumes produced between 1960 and 1980. It includes writers (Pearl Buck, Harriet Beecher Stowe), artists (Mary Cassatt), scientists (Rachel Carson), activists (Lydia Maria Child, Emma Goldman, Mother Jones), singers (Mahalia Jackson, Bessie Smith), populist leaders (Mary Elisabeth Lease), and health workers (Lillian Wald).

This precedent has been followed in the *Makers of America* series, which Facts on File launched in 1988 with the publication of biographies of John Brown, Frederick Douglass, and Amelia Earhart. Lillie Patterson's *Martin Luther King, Jr., and the Freedom Movement*, published in this series in 1989, may be cited as an outstanding example of the kind of young adult biography we need. Ms . Patterson is one of Maryland's leading black authors. *Martin Luther King, Jr., and the Freedom Struggle* won the Coretta Scott King award for 1989's most distinguished contribution to educational literature concerned with the story of black people in America. Patterson's book provides young adults with an introduction not only to Martin Luther King, Jr., but to the whole civil rights movement. Patterson weaves original sources into her narrative; this in no small part is the secret of her success.

Textbooks traditionally have provided students with an overview of the American past. Without texts will students be able to gain an understanding of the American story? Is there no danger that they will be left holding no more than colorful fragments of a jigsaw puzzle?

I think not; here, too, there is another way. It lies in the creation of a modem epic form based upon study of the traditional epics that constitute part of both the Western and the Native American literary heritage. Modern writers presenting reality in fictional form have already explored this path, especially Mikhail Sholokhov in *And Quiet Flows the Don* and John Steinbeck in *The Grapes of Wrath*. Historians have also begun to experiment with epic. John Anthony Caruso's series, *The American Frontier*, is a beautifully written multivolume epic. A few years ago the National Geographic Society assembled a group of historians, geographers, and artists to prepare a lavishly illustrated historical atlas and accompanying text: *The Making of America* was published in 1984. Not least remarkable was the mural that accompanied it — a five foot folk art bas relief expressing a vision of the American past.

Books such as these do not so much instruct students in factual detail as arouse wonder and delight in contemplation of the historical process. The reader is taken to the mountaintop to view the panorama. Then he or she may see the tides that run and the patterns that form and change. What is important here is not "coverage" but communication.

Teachers who use the kind of historical literature under discussion will need, in the fullness of time, to develop a new pedagogy. "Overview" will need to be understood not as something that the text imposes but that emerges from the classroom process itself. The historian possessing his or her own concept of history will provide materials from which both analysis and synthesis can emerge. The students themselves will thus be enabled to begin creating their own vision of the past based upon the evidence that they have examined.

Will history, approached in the ways sketched, leave too many gaps in the historical narrative? I do not think so. There are myriad themes that may be treated in other works — mini-series — prepared for the purpose. One example is Alfred A. Knopf's *Living History Library* (15 vols., 1965-75). These books are studies of periods or topics in American history based from first to last upon original sources (including songs) interwoven into the narrative; they are written by distinguished historians and teachers, including Marion Starkey (known for her work on Daniel Shays's rebellion and the Trail of Tears), James M. McPherson, Douglas Miller, Milton Meltzer, and Laurence I. Seidman. Dozens more such studies await authors.

The forms of historical literature discussed in this article share the same goal: to bring the past to life with the help of testimony enshrined in the enduring record. Let the people, at long last, be heard. Let them speak and sing from the grave; let them use their own words to tell their story and reach out across time's chasm.

▼

Author's Note: Many thanks are due to Professors Robert A. Blackey, Donald S. Detwiler, and Robert H. Ferrell for their help in the writing of this article.

Response to John Anthony Scott's "There is Another Way"

Gary B. Nash

JOHN ANTHONY SCOTT'S THOUGHTS on the teaching of United States history and social studies are a welcome addition to the growing debate on teaching history in the schools. Scott provides a valuable introduction to some of the lesser known materials that are available to teachers, such as the *Folk Song in the Classroom* newsletter and the *Makers of America* series of biographies for young adults. He also makes the case, with which I agree, that we need to weave into the teaching of history far more original source material so that students will hear authentic voices from the past and will grasp some of the drama and tension of different eras of United States history.

As Scott maintains, music, art, cartoons, autobiographies, letters, diaries, newspapers, and pamphlets are all materials that can enrich the teaching of history. Moreover, as he points out, the problems of reproducing such material within a single school may not be as great as it first appears. But the larger question to which his essay is addressed is much more complicated: namely, can we or ought we replace textbooks with such materials?

My answer is an emphatic "No!" My reasons are two: first, the most recent textbooks that are entering the marketplace are much better than Scott would have us believe; and second, a textbook (even an incomplete or unbalanced one) provides an essential integrating and synthesizing function.

Is it true that the new history-social studies textbooks are censored and rendered "pallid" and "lifeless" by "a publisher's need to make a profit?" Scott believes so and identifies the villain as the American publisher. I believe that textbooks are gradually improving and that, in my case, Scott is aiming at the wrong target. Publishers quite sensibly try to follow guidelines set by states, especially large states. When states change their social studies frameworks and insist on better books (carefully specifying *how* they are to be better), then publishers respond. Or at least some do.

Take the case of California. The new History-Social Studies framework promulgated in 1987 called explicitly for presenting history "as an exciting and dramatic series of events in the past that helped to shape the present"; it called for the enrichment of history through the use of literature of and about the period under study and the repeated use of primary source material. "Poetry, novels, plays, essays, documents, inaugural addresses, myths, legends, tall tales, biographies, and religious literature," it demanded, must be used to "help shed light on the life and times of the people." The framework called specifically for a multicultural perspective throughout the curriculum so that students could learn "that the history of community, state, region, nation, and world must reflect the experiences of men and women of different racial, religious, and ethnic groups." It demanded that the textbooks "present controversial issues honestly and accurately within their historical or contemporary context." It acknowledged the importance of religion in human history and called for historical treatment of the major religions and ethical traditions in world and United States history.

Scott's argument about publisher timidity gains some support from the fact that many publishers were scared off by California's bold new social studies framework. They worried that if other states did not follow California's lead, particularly in devoting three years to the study of world history and three years to the study of United States history, then books published for the California framework would have little sales potential outside that state. But some publishers did come forward, and their books were assessed at length by evaluation panels composed of teachers and scholars and by a tough-minded curriculum commission. Even many of the books that did not pass muster with these evaluating bodies are a far cry from the books that Frances FitzGerald examined in *America Revised* more than a decade ago. Women's history, the history of racial and ethnic minority groups, and of working people — what some call the "new social history" — is now being carefully woven into the traditional textbook accounts of politics, the economy, diplomacy, and war. What is more, the ugly chapters of our history, including slavery, genocidal Indian policies, class exploitation, and violent race relations, are being addressed much more candidly. Of course each book differs in its effectiveness in overcoming the biases, distortions, and omissions of earlier books. But all, including Scott's new textbook entitled *History of the American People*, have moved a considerable distance from the Eurocentric, male-dominated, and largely celebratory United States history textbooks of previous generations. This is not to deny that many further improvements are needed. But the call for multicultural approaches to history and social studies (and for textbooks that more effectively treat gender, religion, class, and region as well) is having an effect.

We should not regard textbooks, even the best of the new ones, as the sole resource for either student or teacher. Good teachers have known that all along. The textbook is a place to begin, a place to go back to, a place from which to launch a variety of teaching activities. It should be liberally supplemented by the kinds of materials Scott details. But it alone can convey in orderly, chronological sequence, the foundational materials needed for an understanding of how American society changed over centuries and how societies and nations around the world developed over a vast period of time. The kinds of biographies, songs, and primary materials that Scott would have teachers rely on, if used in place of rather than in addition to a textbook, would leave most students with only the sketchiest understanding of the complex interrelationships of economic, political, and social factors that have produced historic transformations in American and other societies.

Moreover, the textbook alone can give new teachers, many of whom have only a few undergraduate history courses as background, a firm footing on which to proceed. It alone, in its teacher editions, can provide the wealth of teaching strategies, suggest a wide range of student activities, provide ideas for connecting historical materials with the arts and sciences, direct teachers to additional resources, and show ways to adapt lesson material to the ability levels of both advanced and sheltered students.

While the textbook should still be regarded as an indispensable tool for teaching the history of the United States, it is almost unthinkable that students or teachers should be deprived of it in world history. Consider again the California case, where the new history-social studies framework calls for three full years of study of world history: the history of the ancient world (sixth grade), the medieval world (seventh grade), and the modern world (tenth grade). Probably not one in twenty-five history-social studies teachers has had even one course in ancient history, defined in most colleges and universities simply as the history of ancient Greece and Rome. Those who have studied ancient China, Japan, India, and other parts of the non-European world are even fewer in number. Now, in the new California curriculum, teachers are required to teach sixth graders not only about prehistorical human-kind, but about ancient Mesopotamia, Egypt, and Kush; about the Indus Valley civilization and the beginning of Buddhism; about the Gupta Empire and early Hinduism; about ancient China, including the age of Confucius and the Han dynasty; about ancient Israel and early Christianity and Judaism. Can teachers really be expected to organize materials on a week-by-week and day-by-day basis for teaching such complex and unfamiliar materials to sixth graders? Can they really come up with the rich materials showing artistic and architectural expression in various societies as the best new textbooks in world history do? Can they ferret out the primary sources and literature selections that illustrate life, religion, and thought among the many societies to be studied? Do seventh grade teachers really have the time, resources, and background to organize materials for studying — to take *a single unit* of what the California framework calls for and has gotten in one new textbook — the empires of Ghana, Mali, and Songhai; the organization of village society in West Africa in the medieval period; the causes and character of the Bantu migration; the rise of the West African coastal trading states and of Zimbabwe and the Kongo kingdom?

In sum, teachers should reject the either-or approach implicit in Scott's argument. They should neither jettison textbooks nor teach entirely from them. They should begin with the best textbook available — and of those teaching

United States history some, perhaps, will choose the one he has published in 1990. They should work outward from that textbook, searching for new materials of many kinds and using these materials to enrich the textbook accounts, to delve into the local significance of large-scale phenomena addressed in the textbook and to fill gaps in the textbook as they identify them.

Chapter VI:

Student Activities

Teaching Undergraduates to Think Like Historians

Vera Blinn Reber

AS AN UNDERGRADUATE math and history major, I remember my math instructor's frustration as he tried to answer a series of my questions relating to solving a particular problem. What is the evidence? Isn't there another way to solve that problem? Why won't this approach work? Finally he said, your problem is that you think like a historian.

Whether one teaches a history course to first-year students or graduates, the problem exists of how to teach individuals to think like historians. To think historically student must be able to collect and evaluate evidence objectively and relate the cause and effect of events within a time perspective. Thinking historically requires the ability to describe, explain, analyze, and weigh a complex series of factors within another culture and time. As in my case, many students learn to think like historians through traditional survey courses, which often use textbooks, discussions, and writing assignments. As historians have become more concerned with improving their teaching, they have sought to refine their approaches or to develop new methods for helping students understand the past. Some professors require their students to read model monographs and to examine collections of primary documents which give students the opportunity to analyze evidence or reconstruct an event. Faculty often share their own research and require students to write term papers. Increasingly, computers and new software applications provide additional approaches to teaching students to think like historians. (For a discussion of various approaches see David C. Lukowitz, "Students as Apprentice Historians," *Teaching History*, Spring 1978; Phyllis Hall, "Using Your Research in the Survey Course," *AHA Perspectives*, December 1988; and David W. Miller, "The Great American History Machine," *Academic Computing*, October 1988.)

Although students gain many skills through traditional means, I have not been completely satisfied. The use of document collections never appealed to me as a student, and although I had liked writing term papers, my students do not. The assumption, often unfounded, behind research papers is that students have the basic skills to do historical analysis.

At Shippensburg University a recent curriculum revision required all first-year students to take six credits of world history. The history department agreed to use the same text and the faculty agreed to add no more than a thousand pages of supplemental reading of their own choice. Each history faculty member assumed the task of teaching two to three world history classes of forty students each semester. We set out to teach our students a common body of knowledge, to improve their writing skills, and to teach them to think like historians. With some success I have modified the traditional approaches to writing in my introductory world history class by introducing the use of the journal and the short paper to encourage learning and analyzing through writing. Both forms of writing, which complement each other, help students to learn about the past and to organize and clarify their thinking.

To assure that students do the required reading and develop analytical and writing skills, I have required them to keep journals. The basis of the journal is three entries a week written outside of class after the completion of the assigned reading. Usually, the students answer a broad analytical question which is given in the syllabus, although occasionally they may choose their journal topic, and are required to draft the beginning paragraphs of their short paper, or review a cultural event which they have attended. In addition, students may be required to answer a question in their journals in class. (Numbers of historians have written on the use of journal. See John R. Breihan, "Prewriting in College History Courses," *AHA Perspectives*, March 1986; and Henry J. Steffens and Mary Jane Dickerson, *Writer's Guide: History*, 1987.)

Although the students complained about the excessive number of journal entries, they found the exercise useful in developing analytical skills and assuring good study habits. A rather typical comment from an anonymous student is the following: "I thought having the journal was a good idea. In the beginning of the course, I didn't think I was going to like that idea, but as the semester went on I began to realize how helpful the journal really was. It allowed us to learn to read something and then have to sit down and write the ideas you got from the reading material. I also think it possibly helped improve some writing skills." Another student wrote, "The journals are useful in forcing us to keep up with assignments and understanding them."

In my opinion, the student evaluation of the journals was an accurate reflection of what was happening and what I hoped would happen. Although the writing was time consuming, the journals assured that the students did much of the reading and understood the material. Further, the journal forced students to select from the text ideas that answered the assigned question and to organize them in a convincing manner. The journals, also, tended to improve examination grades, and I had a much better sense of what students understood.

In addition to the journal, I require each student to write a five-page paper. Since the material the students have to master is large and new, I have not asked them to attempt a standard research paper. Rather, in "World History to 1500," I base the writing assignment on *Tales from the Thousand and One Nights* translated by N.J. Dawood. Students are required to read all the *Tales*. They are to take any aspect of the stories relating to manners, beliefs, customs, economy, government, religion, and society existing in Persia, Arabia, or the Muslim world between 850 and 1450 and develop that topic into a five-page paper. Among the topics students have proposed were the relationship between mothers and sons, the commerce of Baghdad, alms giving, the status of women, the djinn, Islam and prayer, the Arab merchant, predestination and Islam, male and female relations in Islam, and Islamic views of marriage among many other topics.

In order to discourage procrastination and help them learn to define the issues and organize the material, students are required to make three journal entries on the topic. The first is a page-long entry on some aspect of the *Tales*; the second, a week later, is a two-page explanation of why the event, value, or belief was important. The student also notes areas of further research to be pursued. The third entry provides a plan for the five-page paper and a discussion of the accuracy of the tales as related to the topic. The next step is the submission of a typed first draft of a paper to a classmate who reviews the paper.

Students are helped in defining the topics by examples in my syllabus. They are also encouraged to discuss the *Tales* with me during office hours. But it is journal writing itself which is most effective in helping students define their topic. In the process of writing the students are forced to clarify their ideas and evaluate the available sources. As a result about 10 percent of the students will choose new topics. By collecting the journals after the completion of three entries, but before a first draft is written, I can also evaluate the suitability of the topics. Sometimes, for example, students assume they can adequately discuss the beliefs of Islam in five pages.

Once the topic is defined, the student is expected to follow two different lines of thought and research. First, the student evaluates the various tales to find as much material as possible on the topic. Second, the student has to use other sources to see if the material presented in the *Tales* was fact or fiction. Although the students are free to organize the material as they wish, they must include three things. They have to describe the material in the *Tales* relating to the topic chosen, describe the material from other historical sources, and provide an analysis concerning the validity of the information drawn from the *Tales*. Papers are required to have a bibliography but no notes. Secondary sources may be used and the number of sources required is minimal. I place some material on library reserve, and students are encouraged to look beyond these aids.

Since I have as many as 120 journals and papers to grade each semester, I ask each student to help me. Students have the first draft of their paper criticized by another student, who has to follow a set form. The reviewer must indicate points in the draft that are of interest with an explanation of why, note areas in which more information is needed, provide specific suggestions for a clearer development and better organization of the topic, offer suggestions on how to use supporting information more effectively, and make spelling and grammatical corrections. On the due date, students turn in a final typed draft, supported by three journal entries, a first draft, and a classmate's written suggestions for improving the draft. How well the student has followed the reviewer's suggestions is evaluated with the final draft.

The students found writing the short paper more difficult than writing journal essays and were divided as to the usefulness of student comments. One positive anonymous student wrote, "I enjoyed writing and researching the short paper. The paper helped me in learning this culture better. The comments from my classmates were very useful. They pointed out my weak points that I had to work on and my strong points." A contrary comment was, "The paper, I felt, was not as useful as the journal. The classmate's opinions did not help." Although the students generally enjoyed the *Tales* and recommended that I continue to use it, I will be changing to *The Travels of Marco Polo* to limit the possibility of plagiarism.

The short paper encourages students to think clearly. They have to deal with the cause and effect of relationship objectively within a time perspective. As all historians do, they have to define topics, read thoughtfully, obtain relevant information, write coherently, and, in addition, evaluate the research and writing of their peers. In the end, they must decide whether the original source was historically accurate and explain their results in a satisfactory paper. Students have also had to deal objectively with a literary source from another culture. I believe this process successfully helps beginning students to think like historians.

Although both the journal and short paper help to develop the thinking and writing ability of students, they do so in somewhat different ways. The short paper emphasizes in-depth analysis while the journal encourages breadth of knowledge. The paper requires formal writing while the journal follows an informal style. The journal entries define the issue to be examined while the paper requires the student to delineate the problem. The journal describes the sources to be used while the paper necessitates that the sources be found and evaluated.

I have used the journal and the *Tales* for four semesters. While there is no objective way to prove that my students think more like historians because of these writing assignments, an examination of their writing early in the semester and at the end of the course suggests that student writing and thinking improved. More significant is the fact that students themselves concluded that both the short paper and the journal aided their writing, understanding, and thinking.

HELP — New Tricks for Old Dogs

John E. Stovel

HISTORY TEACHERS KNOW they can't cover all they want in a lecture or a course, and when they pack their lectures even more tightly students may not retain those last few facts anyway. Clearly, some history teachers could use HELP so their students can learn more effectively. HELP stands for Highly Efficient Learning Procedures, techniques which don't take very long to demonstrate but nonetheless assist students in retaining what is being taught. When used properly, these techniques can also aid the teacher in keeping track of what students are actually learning.

Not all these techniques will help all students, because students have different learning styles. A few will help some students, while others may have wide appeal. We should not assume that all students learn history alike, or that they learn it as we did. Giving students the opportunity to learn in different ways promotes sound educational practices.

The first bit of HELP is the **Focused Free Write**. This is a bit of writing by the student, about five minutes worth, centered on a relevant course topic for which there is no right or wrong answer. The results do not need to be collected and read, but they should be from time to time. Or they can also be read aloud. Either way, they should not be graded. Their purpose is threefold: they give students practice in writing; they ask students to write about a topic freely so that they may discover what it is that really intrigues them about the topic; and they give the teacher an insight into what is going on in students' minds. They can also serve to start a class discussion.

An example of a topic might be: "What was the most important point in the reading assignment for this class, and why?" A few students could read their responses so that the teacher can get a general idea of what they learned from the reading and see the degree of general agreement. Then the discussion could be continued or the lecture begun. Topics can also be created which are specific to the reading. In a class on the "Reign of Terror" ask students to respond to the question, "What advice would you have given Robespierre?" In a class on the late 1930s, have them write on "What should Wilkie have said to win the 1940 election?" Clearly, some answers will be more appropriate than others, but by pursuing the responses, especially the less appropriate ones, teachers can correct historical lapses or misunderstandings before an exam. Teachers who utilize this technique periodi-cally don't need to spend time discussing the question each time students are asked to write. Sometimes the lecture can begin immediately and students will already have focused their attention on the planned topic. They will have sorted their prior knowledge and maybe even have taken a position.

A related sort of HELP is the **Class Summary Paragraph**, written during the last five minutes of the class. Simply have students write the main points of the class on a sheet of paper. Collect them, let them be anonymous if desired, and see what they have extracted from the lecture. This is also very effective for discussion classes. As a variant, ask them to write three questions they have about the class just ended. These can be reviewed quickly and used to launch the next class. The students are writing, which demands that they commit themselves to paper, and the teacher is learning what they think.

Another technique is to have students **Write Exam Questions**. Ask them to write an essay question which gets at the heart of the material. This is not easy, nor is it necessarily a brief exercise, but don't expect students to spend much time at it. The goal is not finished questions, but to have each of them think through the material and search for critical issues. The process, rather than the result, is what is important. A few can be read aloud, and the class can criticize them, not as finished products, but as to what they reveal about the student's understanding of what should be learned.

One dilemma for history teachers is whether to demand research papers from students. Part of the difficulty is the time devoted to grading. A basketball coach breaks the game into its components: fundamentals such as dribbling, passing, and shooting, and plays for particular situations such as zone or person-to-person defenses. History teachers can break the research paper into its components, too. While certainly no substitute for the entire research paper, a bit of HELP comes in the form of the **Topic Paragraph.** Have students begin as if they were going to write a complete research paper. They should do some preliminary reading, choose a subject, do additional reading, and write a topic or introductory paragraph. This forces them to become familiar with the outlines of the material and think what they want to do with it. By writing only the topic paragraph they don't have to write a full paper, and the teacher doesn't have to read a full paper. Of course there are opportunities for chicanery in what appears to be a flimsy assignment, but since research papers often can be purchased by the page on almost any campus, little would appear to have been lost. The hard part of doing research is conceptualizing the problem, and this is what is being focused on by having them write only the topic paragraph.

If another goal is to prove a thesis, which is different from conceptualizing a problem, try an alternative assignment. Have students select a topic, do the research, and then just **Write an Outline** for a research paper. Again, this is no substitute for the real thing, but it does provide an efficient way of checking on students' ability to organize material in defense of a thesis.

Beginning students frequently have trouble handling sources in research papers. They tend to follow one main source and embellish the paper with tid-bits from others. Some HELP comes in the form of an **Annotated Bibliography.** For this exercise, have students select a topic and go to the library to gather sources. Have them peruse the sources and decide how each could be used in a paper. Ask them to write a paragraph about how they would use each source in a paper. Have them identify its genre (memoir, monograph, polemic, etc.), assess its reliability, and discuss its strengths and weaknesses in terms of the paper topic. Like the preceding bits of HELP, this focuses on one aspect of a complex process, and it enables the instructor to check on the students' mastery of historical skills efficiently.

A technique that is especially useful in preparing Advanced Placement students for the exam's Document-Based Questions (DBQ) is **Paraphrasing in Pairs.** Give students an old DBQ, or any other group of documents assigned. Have them pair up and take a minute each, more or less depending on the length of the document, to paraphrase the document aloud to their partner, but without criticizing each other's paraphrase. Then have them take two more minutes to examine the discrepancies between the two paraphrases. They may be able to account for the differences by themselves, or they may ask for help. Teachers could spend a few minutes with the whole class discussing what happened in a few pairs, or go right on to the material planned for the day.

A related activity deals with **Identifying Bias** in documents or readings. After students have read the piece in question, pair them as before and give them a minute each to tell about the bias they found in the document. Then allow another two minutes to explore any discrepancies. Problems they may have had can be discussed with the whole class.

Some students lack confidence in their writing, so that when an essay question is assigned (e.g., "To what extent is the term 'Renaissance' a valid concept for a distinct period in early modern European history?" [from the 1985 Advanced Placement European History examination]), they tend to say that the concept is either totally valid or invalid. Although we as historians may adhere to one or the other poles, we also know there are valid points on the opposite side, and indeed part of the problem is definitional. We would like our students to be comfortable with the ambiguity of the concept of the Renaissance, and familiar with the historical scholarship which shapes the debate. Our students may know a great deal of what we want them to know, but their lack of confidence in their writing may push them toward an all-or-nothing response. We can help them develop confidence in writing about issues where there is something to be said on each side by using a **Yes ... But ...** question. For example, instead of the above question, ask them to write an essay with the topic sentence, "There are many reasons for thinking of a century or so in early modern European history as a Renaissance, but there are powerful arguments against this interpretation." Yes, there was a Renaissance, but no, there wasn't. Students can be asked to write a conclusion where they state their position. In this kind of question, a student has to handle both sides of the debate and show how the arguments interact. By demanding a personal conclusion, teachers also force them to take a position which arises out of their understanding of the terms of the debate. Students who have been fed on a diet of Yes ... But ... questions won't feel the need to play it safe and take one extreme or the other of an argument.

Essay questions that charge students to "compare and contrast" or "assess the validity" can be rewritten in the Yes ... But ... format. Teachers should be prepared to give additional instructions to students if they want them to practice specific tasks such as to analyze, compare, define, and so on. The following examples, all from the 1988 Advanced Placement European History Examination, show how it can be done. The question, "Describe and analyze the ways in which the development of printing altered both the culture and religion of Europe during the period 1450-1600," can be rewritten by asking students to write an essay with the topic sentence, "The development of printing changed the culture and religion of Europe during the period 1450-1600, but in some ways the culture and religion weren't affected at all by the development of printing." This is, of course, a slightly broader question, and students may not have time to do justice to both parts in the time available, but it illustrates how a question can be rewritten.

Another question began with a statement and then gave a charge to the students: "In the eighteenth century, people turned to the new science for a better understanding of the social and economic problems of the day. Assess the validity of this statement by using specific examples from the Enlightenment era." In the Yes ... But ... format students would be asked to begin with the topic sentence, "In the eighteenth century, many people turned to the new science for a better understanding of the social and economic problems of the day, but many did not."

Some questions do ask students to deal with differences among ostensibly similar events or individuals. The following is an example: "Describe and compare the differences among Utopian socialists, Karl Marx, and Revisionist socialists in their critiques of nineteenth-century European economy and society." The Yes ... But ... approach has students begin with the topic sentence, "Utopian socialists, Karl Marx, and Revisionist socialists agreed in their critiques of nineteenth-century European economy and society, but also disagreed in significant ways." Again, this question asks the student for more information, i.e., what the various socialists agreed upon, than the AP examiners asked for. Two more questions from the 1988 AP European History exam can be revised as follows: "Assess the extent to which the unification of Germany under Bismarck led to authoritarian government there between 1871 and 1914." Yes ... But ... revision: "The unification of Germany under Bismarck led to authoritarian government there between 1871 and 1914, but other factors in German history contributed." AP question: "Analyze the extent to which the First World War accelerated European social change in such areas as work, sex roles, and government involvement in everyday life." Yes ... But ...

revision: "The First World War accelerated European social change in such areas as work, sex roles, and government involvement in everyday life, but these changes had their roots in pre-war events."

A bit of visual HELP for students is the use of two **Overlapping Circles**, which mathematicians call Venn diagrams. Draw on the chalkboard two overlapping circles. Each circle indicates some event. The overlapping section indicates shared characteristics of the two events, while the other parts indicate characteristics which are unique to each event. Have students list the characteristics of each event and fit them into the relevant portions of the two circles. Obviously, some events will overlap quite a bit, like the French and Russian revolutions, while others will not overlap much at all, like the French and Glorious revolutions. Some students will be able to organize what they know far more readily by remembering the overlapping circles than from lecture notes or reading.

Part of the difficulty students have in writing has to do with a limited vocabulary in terms of the task at hand. Teachers like to use works of art in class to illustrate cultural movements and on examinations as a stimulus. Students' working vocabularies can be expanded by a bit of HELP called **Listing Adjectives**. Use a picture that might ordinarily be shown, such as of the statue of David by Michaelangelo, and have members of the class write down the adjectives that come to mind. Then go around the class, or call on students at random, having each state one adjective. Write their responses on the chalk board. Typically, the following adjectives will emerge: strong, powerful, muscular, athletic, vigorous, dynamic, youthful, confident, and so on. Few students will have thought of all of them, but all students will now know of words they might use to describe this statue. If they are confronted with an illustration on a test, they can list the adjectives which come to their mind on scratch paper, and they will have a vocabulary and a technique to make their essay more perceptive. As an added bonus, they now have a list of adjectives which can be applied to the concept of the Renaissance as well.

Some students have delightful wits and excel in making epigrams about historical people or events. Have them make **Bumper Stickers** which encapsulate something studied. Even the silliest ones may be enough to help them remember what is desired. One student drew a sketch of a Oliver Cromwell being smashed in the head with a mace, and wrote "Crown Cromwell" next to it. Another sketched the head of Louis XIV and inscribed the phrase "Use it or Lose it." A variant of this is to have them design **Tee Shirts** or **Posters** about what they have studied. By having the students share these in class, all get the benefit of the wit of a few.

This HELP is just that, help for us and for our students. It won't get them to know all the details which fascinate us as historians, but it will help us in our roles as teacher to make the main outlines of what we are teaching more accessible. When I first began to employ these techniques, one of my students, who was obviously bright but had been struggling, suddenly blossomed. All I had done was draw overlapping circles on the board and have the class fill in events of the French and

American revolutions. She just needed the key to what we were studying, and the course opened up for her. Students still laugh when we talk about how one of them characterized Queen Victoria as "Sticky Vicky." These techniques will help our students focus on the essentials of what we want them to learn, and this is what we, as students and teachers of history, need to do with all the resources we can muster.

Students as Historians:
A Convention

Donald G. Morrison

LISTENING TO A FAVORITE STUDENT present her paper on Virginia Woolf's *Orlando* and its role in twentieth-century European literature, as I sat high up in the back of the high school auditorium, I felt as proud as I have ever felt in my teaching career. She addressed her audience with an understanding of their initial incomprehension, describing Orlando's unlikely sex-change and the swashbuckling of the sixteenth century in wry and witty terms. Her audience of teenagers, dressed from Gucci to dirty Guess, listened as raptly as I to her ten-minute presentation. Applause followed as she concluded with the flourish: "and that, ladies and gentlemen, is Virginia Woolf!" The Westchester (New York) Colloquium for European History at New Rochelle High School had begun.

It hadn't been easy. In the careful, nurturing hands of Ira S. Glick, supervisor in New Rochelle, New York for Social Studies, the idea developed: why not bring Westchester's students together in a circumstance where all would be winners, none would be losers; a gathering where research would be shared for the benefit and pleasure of all.

I loved his idea, although I was aware that it can be disorientating, even threatening, for teachers to come together to compare notes, evaluate each other, and compare students' growth. I was certain that if the emphasis could be placed upon students sharing with students, with teachers merely providing the medium by which to do so, the idea would work.

It was decided that the key to making this idea work would be cooperation, not competition, the leitmotiv a trill of students' voices sounding the themes of modern European history as outlined in the Advanced Placement European History course description, these voices commingled in a harmony of scholarship to become a students' version of an AHA convention. An added benefit, we realized, would be an early preparation and review for the AP Examination, the seven themes of the curriculum being emphasized in our format so that reluctant districts would have a built-in rationale for attending.

Letters were written in early October to every Westchester school district which had — or planned to have — an AP program in European history. The response was almost immediate; within two weeks twelve districts had responded positively (eight eventually came representing nine AP classes accompanied by seven teachers). A date was set for the Wednesday before mid-winter break, carefully chosen for three sound reasons: first, February 12, 1986 would give schools time to prepare papers and several months in which to solve the logistical problems of transportation, substitute teachers, and possible needs for funding; second, to avoid the midwinter doldrums that arrive during the winter solstice in the frigid Northeast; and third, if the idea collapsed or if those supporters of the policies of William III fell to fisticuffs with the partisans of Louis XIV instead of presenting civilized essays in defense of their subject, we all would have the week recess to recover and to reassess. Quickly the paper topics came in:

Rubens as Diplomat
Mary Wollstonecraft and the Rights of Women
Nihilism in Russia
Machiavelli's Mandragola
Expressionism in the Early Twentieth Century
Utopian Socialists Contrasted with Early Utopianism
Beethoven as Revolutionary
Mme. Roland's Journals: Woman as Political Thinker
Individualism in Iceland
Jefferson's View of Louis XVI
Charles I and Henrietta-Marie
John Milton as Politician during the Interregnum
The Strategy of the Invincible Armada
The Miracle at Valmy
Galileo as a Propagandist
Richelieu and the Destruction of La Rochelle
Michelangelo's Poetry
Mme. de Stael, Enemy of Napoleon: Gutsy Lady
Martin Luther as a Nationalist
Botticelli and Salvadore Dali
John Law and the Bubbles

and many more — about 175 in all — including perhaps ten further papers with "...: Hero or Villain?" to which teenagers, however sophisticated, are invariably drawn.

We had asked for an indication of both those students who were willing to present papers from each school district and those students who had written papers in one of the eight general areas of the curriculum and could therefore provide as informed an audience for the presenters as possible. We then divided presenters and audience into eight seminars. Students of all AP teachers had either opted to present or to be the audience for a presenter. The seminars were as follows:

I.   The Renaissance
II.   English Democracy
III. The Age of Louis XIV

IV. The Enlightenment
V. Nationalism
VI. Art
VII. Revolution
VIII. The Modern World

Obviously, it was impossible to dovetail each paper-writer into a perfect category — what to do about the author of "Individualism in Iceland" became a running joke: was he a revolutionary and thus belonging in category VII? nay, surely a nationalist and most comfortably placed in V? an artist longing for VI? definitely enlightened so berthed in IV? Because Icelandic affairs were quite beyond the expertise of anyone I knew, I think we eventually plopped him into the "Modern World," and since there've been no fulminating letters to *The New York Times*, I can only assume the lad was happy.

Each of the seven accompanying teachers was placed into one of the seminars not, for a change, for the purposes of "supervision" (though we remained aware of our Hero-Villain contingent and wondered about the depth of their feelings) but rather as facilitators.

Again, our purpose was to provide a forum for students, not an extra soapbox for teachers to thump for two periods of an hour and a half each on a day off. Indeed, though this will come later under a discussion of the colloquium's successes and failures, one of the few major problems was one teacher who did harangue and cow presenters.

And so the format was set. The logistics alone would prove formidable. How do you bring 150 to 200 young strangers into a fully functioning comprehensive secondary school on an average Wednesday, make them comfortable, feed their adolescent appetites, provide eight small as well as large fori for the exchange of ideas and a speaker of interest to keynote, get them off busses and out of cars, back into vans and mini-wagons, assuage teachers' ever-present egos, and above all provide the "space" so that our scholars could trill forth? Administrators may relax: the facilities are there.

The speaker was easy. Wayne Philip Te Brake from the State University of New York at Purchase accepted quickly and proposed as the topic of his address, "Natalie Davis' *The Return of Martin Guerre*: Women in Early Modern Europe," a choice which proved of interest to everyone. It all began at 9:30 a.m. in the auditorium.

Despite a snow storm and a minor accident (my own kids — "but it was the old car"), the opening proceeded smoothly, the introductions were made, the plenary session buzzed with contained excitement, lunch tickets were given out, room assignments were made, student guides were appointed, and the morning seminar was underway.

Everyone was of course nervous, adults as well as students, but there was a palpable sense from all that this was different, this was special, this should succeed. Kids who spent the night addressing mirrors in sequestered bedrooms as they sweated in terror revealed themselves to be natural orators; kids who had clutched research papers with the tenacity of drowning men trying to use them to stay afloat calmly lay them aside and spoke extemporaneously about topics which, they knew, were intrinsically interesting. Their poise and interest made their subjects exciting, and such excitement became infectious. Some of their unvarnished comments (taken anonymously from a follow-up handout) follow:

"I never thought I could do it."

"It was a real high."

"I never had an audience before except for my dog."

"They were really interested in what I had to say."

"It was over before I thought I opened my mouth — let's do it again."

"I never want to have to go through that again, thought I would faint. I'll tape it next time."

"Maybe we could have it videotaped to show college admissions?"

"Were you watching? I couldn't see you. I couldn't see anything I was sweating so bad."

"I was really terrible, wasn't I?"

From the New York State Education Department Director of Social Studies, Donald Bragaw: "I enthusiastically endorse and encourage your efforts to bolster European History AP programs. The special colloquium for students will certainly provide an incentive to the students attending, and to future students to continue their scholarly interest in this social studies subject.... Probably the most exciting part of the program would be the linkage that could be formed between schools and college/university faculty — an alliance that is long overdue."

The afternoon session, during which most remaining papers were presented, was likewise successful. Some seminars had finished presenting their papers, and it was time for students and teachers to sift through the themes which had emerged from the individual addresses. In my own, one of the largest seminars, we never in fact finished and papers were being presented right up until the session was over. Students were allowed to drift from group to group, looking for friends, participating in discussions, listening, or taking notes.

I am a would-be musician and were I to sum up the entire Westchester European History Colloquium it would be in musical terms: the flurry in the strings at the onset of the overture to *Le Nozze di Figaro* comes to mind, the promise of hours nothing shy of thrilling. Rarely, perhaps never, in my career have I seen such sustained excitement in education before, during, and after what seemed, at first, to be merely an intellectual exercise. In order to achieve these harmonies, one needs first a conductor, such as Ira S. Glick, who is selfless in his desire to bring students together. And I would advise anyone planning such an event to enlist an overseer of significant details with the capacity of Carol Bennett as concert mistress: her title as school aide is as silly as her role as functionaire is extraordinary.

As I sat in the galleries of the high school auditorium that wintry day and saw that favored student open her paper, as if opening a score on the stand before a restive audience, I watched her presence still half-a-hundred adolescents to quiet attention. And I knew it was a Students' Day such as I'd never seen before as she began humbly and with quiet dignity: "Perhaps some of you have wondered who Virginia Woolf is and why she might be important in European history. I certainly did until I read this strange book, which I thought was about Elizabethan England, called Orlando…"

Two Minds, One Thought: The Creation of a Students' History Journal

Charles F. Howlett

WHEN ASKED BY MY DEPARTMENT CHAIR to teach the Advanced Placement United States history course a couple of years ago, my initial response was one of cautious optimism. The opportunity to teach above-average students was welcomed; however, how to motivate them was an altogether different matter. What teaching methods and techniques could I employ to arouse their curiosity? What could the students themselves do to make history come alive? This latter question became the focal point of my course and the guiding light for a students' history journal.

Specifically, I decided to structure the course around the actual publication of a high school history journal. This, I hoped, would clarify my role as an AP history teacher to conduct a course based on historical inquiry, theory and visual contact with primary sources (the last being of utmost importance). I was excited by the possibility of what Jacques Barzun, the noted Columbia University historian and administrator, fittingly coined "two minds sharing one thought" (*Teacher in America*, New York, 1946, chapter 3).

Naturally, this goal is an ideal, but it is one well worth trying to reach. In my case it was the challenging possibility of many minds sharing in the single process of historical creativity. I wanted students to remove themselves from a fact-oriented emphasis commonly found in high schools where students are taught to pass a state or regents test, to a new approach encouraging them to recreate the past through the use of their own inquiring minds. In other words, I wanted them to dig deeper into problem solving — asking the "hows" and "whys" of events, personalities, and actions. For example, instead of just describing the frequently related events leading to the dropping of the atomic bomb over Hiroshima and Nagasaki, I wanted my students to unravel the far more fascinating, political, diplomatic, and moral considerations behind President Truman's decision. My purpose was to encourage students "to understand clearly that history puts its emphasis on 'the facts' not for their own sake but for the sake of the meanings they can actually be seen to carry"

(Paul L. Ward, *Elements of Historical Thinking*, Washington, D.C., 1971 p. 5). In particular, I wanted to impress on them that sound historical scholarship proceeds best with materials that are original sources. For students to reach more sophisticated levels of historical inquiry, a teacher must develop assignments based on primary sources that call attention to areas of controversy and are subject to differing interpretation each calling into play one or more standards of good historical work. It is not enough merely to accept what is found in print; it is also important to examine the way in which historians arrive at their conclusions. It was my hope that if students were asked to research and write creative papers using original sources and supplemented by secondary works, they would not only test their own abilities to make sound historical judgments, but also understand how historians work at deriving answers to questions they raised.

In advancing the method of historical inquiry, students encountered a heavy workload. My enthusiasm was not initially shared by all students in the class; many felt the course requirements were awesome and difficult to handle. Most were accustomed to being totally dependent on a textbook every minute of each class period. This led me to impress on them that the AP course was based on college work in which exams were rigorous and textbooks were often used in conjunction with original sources; I would be doing them a disservice if I failed to demand perseverance and discipline. More important, for purposes of the journal and the promotion of historical inquiry, I informed them that historians who are engaged in research, though they make use of secondary sources, try to reach their conclusions primarily on the basis of original sources.

As a means of developing the historian's skills of diagnosing situations and forming judgments necessary for writing a paper in the history journal, I had each student read the first four chapters of Barzun's *Teacher in America*, which was placed on reserve in the library. Two weeks after the assigned reading I set aside one class period to discuss Barzun's definition of education as "discipline of the individual." They were surprised to find out what Barzun meant by that statement, as well as the significance of the relationship between "discipline" and "attention." I wanted them to know that if they were going to write history for print, they must realize "that good history work embodies a style of intellectual discipline that can correct mistaken understandings and point convincingly toward sounder judgments, however colored these must still be by the special views of their makers" (*Elements of Historical Thinking*, p. 4). Indeed, if my students were to "write" history, they had to discipline themselves to pay attention to three things: 1) assembling and clarifying the evidence, 2) determining how collected evidence tells the story and explains the whole situation, and 3) illuminating the human dimension under investigation. Only in this manner would it be possible for them to realize that the skills required to make the past come alive are similar to those most commonly "used in reaching judgments on complex human situations in life" (ibid.).

Obviously, the most important part of the course was the research paper. Much emphasis was placed on this yearlong project, the purpose of which was to generate historical creativity. In seeking to make history come alive in the students' eyes, I encouraged them during the first week of class to consider the prospect of working mainly with primary sources (e.g., diaries, autobiographies, interviews, letters, oral history memoirs, and published writings) to understand more clearly how our predecessors lived and reacted to particular events and situations during their lifetimes. I wanted my students to gain firsthand experience with original materials, and I wanted them to work with those materials to record their own perceptions of the past. If history is a record of the past, I informed them, then the record — the original sources — must be allowed to speak for itself through the pens of those examining it.

In helping them tackle this project, I recommended they read chapters 1, 2, 4, 6, and 11-16 of Jacques Barzun and Henry F. Graff's *The Modern Researcher* (New York, 1977) as well as William Strunk and E. B. White's *The Elements of Style* (New York, 1959). Both books were purchased by the school district, and copies were made available to each student. I wanted to instill two fundamental ideas in their minds: 1) sound historical scholarship requires careful analysis and reflection, and 2) interesting history demands good writing based on hard editing and revision. Consequently, during the first month of the class I set aside three class periods to discuss the assigned readings from both books. The mechanics of writing a research paper were clearly delineated by Barzun and Graff. Students found this book extremely helpful in terms of defining a topic, taking notes, organizing a paper, and utilizing "practical imagination at work." At the same time, they were equally appreciative of Strunk and White's method of pointing out the rules of usage and the principles of composition most commonly violated. During one class discussion, for example, a student commented that she thought I was a social studies teacher, not an English teacher. I politely responded by reminding all the students that history is also literature, and for history to be read, appreciated, and understood it must be written well. Throughout the course of their research I instructed them to utilize both books as constant reference tools and, most important, when writing their papers *always* to keep their audience in mind — because ultimately, their audience would judge their contribution.

To impress on them further the seriousness of this project, I invited a guest speaker to address the class on historical research and writing. In this case the speaker, Barbara Kelly, an employee of the Suffolk County (N.Y.) Historical Society and doctoral candidate at the State University of New York, Stony Brook, talked about her dissertation on the changing architectural designs of homes in late nineteenth- and early twentieth-century Amityville, New York — which was particularly appropriate since the students live in that community. Armed with photos, census dates, family records, personal accounts by former local village leaders, and newspapers, this budding social historian demonstrated how over a period of time architectural designs were affected by the social and economic changes taking place within the community. During her enlightening presentation, Ms. Kelly emphasized the need for writing original papers that were not simply a summarization of ideas gleaned from secondary works (an altogether common habit among high school — and even college — students). If our journal was to be an original contribution to historical scholarship, she added, it was necessary to work with primary sources. "What neat discoveries can you come up with after examining the materials?" she asked. With all her research materials in front of her, including two boxes of note cards, this proved to be an invaluable lesson — the search for new evidence. The students were impressed by the historian at work, with the tools of the trade, and her attempt to recreate the past in written form through the careful examination of primary sources.

It is extremely important to emphasize the point that this research project was more than just a traditional term paper. Yet how were these students to make the leap from high school to college-level writing based on original sources and insight? My answer was to generate interest in the publication of a high school history journal — something a cut above the average term paper in terms of scholarly research and writing. The incentive, of course, was to emphasize the importance of writing for publication. One must realize, to state the obvious to teachers as well as students, that even very bright students do not possess the maturity and sophistication of scholars whose publications reflect years of research and analysis. But the incentive for visiting a college library — fortunately, our proximity to New York City provided just such an opportunity — searching for primary sources, or writing to an archive for papers in order to write a paper suitable for publication, prompted students to act like historians working at their trade. By encouraging them to move away from dependence on secondary sources to the use of primary sources, moreover, I pointed out that their projects would be more realizable if they wrote biographies of individuals and organizations — that is, smaller, more specialized or focused studies — instead of grand surveys of major events such as the Civil War or World War I. This point was crucial to the success of the journal as well as in terms of helping students pick, choose, and narrow their topics.

To begin with, however, the assignment was presented during the first week of class. A timetable was established in which a comprehensive bibliography had to be submitted during the first week of January, a rough draft turned in the first week of March, and the finished product completed a month later. In helping students select topics, I gave each of them a copy of *The Harvard Guide to American History* (Cambridge, 1974), purchased by the school district as a supplementary text for the course, and showed them how to use it for obtaining materials on their subjects. Furthermore, I instructed them on how to consult the *Union Serial List of Manuscripts* after they selected their topics. In some cases students had to write to various libraries for copies of pertinent papers. And, as mentioned previously, very early in the year we discussed the techniques of taking notes, research and writing aptly described in *The Modern Researcher*.

Once topics were selected, I encouraged students to narrow them. For instance, I did not want another general account of Woodrow Wilson's presidency, but something more specific, such as his relationship with Colonel House or his views on the European diplomats at Versailles. In using this to illustrate how to go about narrowing a topic, I had students search through *The Harvard Guide* to see for themselves how conveniently Wilson's career is categorized, what books he wrote, what books have been written about him, and how many of his personal and presidential papers have been edited to date. Use of the *Guide* was instrumental in helping students decide what particular aspect of their historical research they wanted to investigate. After topics were pared down and appropriate sources located, students visited nearby university libraries, wrote to archives and obtained materials through the public library's Inter-Library Loan Office. For each topic chosen (they selected any aspect or personality in United States history they wanted) I first made sure enough information was available to avoid any embarrassing delays.

The results were impressive. Papers submitted demonstrated scholarly seriousness and historical insight. One student traveled to Massachusetts Institute of Technology to acquire information on the yacht designs of Nathanael Greene Herreshoff, a pioneer Long Island yacht manufacturer. Another student conducted extensive research at the Veterans Administration Hospital in Northport, New York, on the psychological effects of war on Vietnam veterans. Still another student contacted sports figures and social analysts to explain how football affects American social life. And using the collected papers of Booker T. Washington, one student wrote an ideological analysis of his ideas on racism and integration as compared to those of W.E.B. DuBois. Original papers were also submitted on music in colonial America, interwar military technology, and the role of doctors during the Civil War.

Since this was intended to be a student history journal, a student editorial committee was chosen to select the best papers for publication. The committee was selected on the basis of my prior analysis of six critical book reviews completed during the course and consultation with the students' English teachers. Once the committee was established, I set aside three days after school to discuss chapter 16 of *The Modern Researcher* in conjunction with *Historian's Handbook* by Wood Gray et al. (Boston, 1964). Barzun and Graff's "Revising for Printer and Public" is rewarding in its clear presentation of a step-by-step approach to editing written manuscripts. *Historian's Handbook* offers examples of proofreading historical writing as well as the various symbols used in editorial work. Specifically, I wanted the student committee to become familiar with the symbols used in revising and editing works for publication. (I photocopied the back cover of *Historian's Handbook*, containing the symbols used for proofreading, and distributed copies to those students who were asked to revise and retype their articles for the journal). Then, along with the instructor, student editors read the papers and judged them on the basis of content, originality, grammar, historical research, documentation of primary sources, and clearness of presentation. Thirty-six papers were submitted and fourteen were ultimately accepted for publication. All students received a grade reflective of their efforts, and those students whose papers were not accepted were encouraged nonetheless to help in the production of the journal; it is interesting that two of the eight members on the editorial committee did not have their papers accepted for publication. The fourteen papers selected were then returned to their authors with suggested comments and corrections and a request for a complete rewrite. The authors then corrected their papers, retyped them, and returned them to the editorial committee for final proofing, all within a two-week period.

Upon completion of this task, a skilled student typist from the business department was paid by the school district to type the articles in journal form on a word processor. In addition, with the help of the art department an appropriate cover design and illustrations were drawn to complement the various articles printed. Cooperation was secured at the beginning of the year with the departments of business and art. All materials were then collated by the editorial committee and sent to the assistant superintendent for instruction. At that point our assistant superintendent, who was most instrumental in seeing this project through to its conclusion, helped procure the necessary money from the district and contracted publication of the journal to a local printing firm. The end result was the publication of Amityville Memorial High School's history journal, *The Journal of Historical Inquiry*.

This was a tremendous undertaking. Many extra hours were spent helping students organize their ideas, make contacts for appropriate sources, correct rough drafts, and of course, decide which papers were most suitable for publication in the journal. Making sure students kept to the timetable was another constant headache. The additional time devoted to editorial matters should not be overlooked either.

I plan to do three things differently next time around. First, due to rising costs of printing, the school district, rather than an outside printing firm, will be asked to print the journal with the assistance of a copying machine; quality of appearance will be sacrificed in order to reduce costs. Second, the journal will be organized according to specific themes in order to give future issues greater coherence and unity. Third, the project will be assigned, where possible, during the summer before the new school year begins; in this way students will have more time to think about their topics, and the instructor will have a better opportunity to direct students to appropriate sources as a means for narrowing available choices — things should then be less unwieldy during the year. Thus in 1982-83, for example, I organized the journal around the theme of Makers of American Foreign Policy. Future possibilities include plans for students to conduct interviews with local residents who lived during the Great Depression and an oral history compilation of the Amityville social scene during World War II. Such modifications, it is hoped, will give more structure and substance to the journal itself.

Was the journal project worth the effort? Yes indeed! Students involved in writing the articles, working as editors, and drawing illustrations acquired a genuine feel for historical creativity and originality; they were making the past come alive through their own printed words. Most important, in working with primary sources they recognized the often overlooked fact that their subjects were real people and organizations, and that actual events remain an integral part of our history and are not simply "facts" appearing on pages glued together between two cardboard covers. In addition, with our emphasizing the publishing aspect, students took greater care in what they wrote, and they came to appreciate the quoted dictum in Barzun's *Teacher in America:* "The substances of what we think, though born in thought, must live in ink" (p. 8).

With the publication of a students' history journal an attempt has been made to help students overcome the secondary-source syndrome, learn to investigate and analyze historical evidence in a professional manner (this should also, not incidentally, aid them with the document-based question part of the AP exam), write better essays, and appreciate the importance of hard editing necessary for publication. Bearing these ideas in mind, it is quite possible that we did become many minds sharing one thought in recreating our past.

Representations of History: Role-Playing Debates in College History Courses

Eve Kornfeld

FEDERALISTS AND ANTIFEDERALISTS from around the nation debate the worth of the proposed United States Constitution and the meaning of the American Revolution in a Philadelphia tavern in 1787. An awakened Connecticut farmer discusses the nature of virtue and the shape of colonial society and culture with the urbane, enlightened Benjamin Franklin in the mid-eighteenth century — in an open field, of course. Frederick Douglass, Margaret Fuller, Henry David Thoreau, and Ralph Waldo Emerson convene at Walden Pond to consider the need for and proper shape of American reform in the 1840s. Sigmund Freud, V.I. Lenin, Virginia Woolf, Jean-Paul Sartre, and Frantz Fanon debate the causes of the peculiar course of Western civilization in the twentieth century from their sofas in Hell in 1989. These are some of the situations in which my students find themselves as we incorporate role-playing debates once or twice a semester into our weekly discussions of the American Revolution, colonial America, United States history, or Western civilization, for I have found that periodic exercises to promote reflection on the representational character of history add excitement and new levels of meaning to virtually all of my college history courses, whether for freshmen engineers or upper-division history majors and future teachers.

The structure of the exercise is fairly simple. The exercise seems to be most effective toward the end of a coherent section of a course (i.e., colonial political culture and the American Revolution in a U.S. history survey, or the twentieth century in Western civilization), after students have read and discussed a variety of primary sources and historical interpretations of the period, heard the central historical issues discussed in lectures, and achieved a certain level of comfort with the material and their discussion section. (I reserve one fifty- or seventy-five minute class period per week for small-group discussion sections of fifteen to twenty-five students each in all of my undergraduate courses. Since the students rarely know or trust each other initially in these sections of large survey courses, the exercise works best after a few weeks have passed.) The debate serves as both a review of familiar material and an opportunity to juxtapose a wide variety of readings and perspectives directly for the first time. For many students, who simply "get through the reading" from week to week and seldom make connections between readings and lectures, this will be the first realization that historical figures (and historians) are responding to shared situations and to each other. A direct juxtaposition of opposing interpretations of historical "reality" at this point in the learning process can thus bring many students a startling new consciousness of the complex nature of historical interpretation, and of the dynamic creation of meaning by diverse individuals and social groups.

A week before the debate, I present the students with a written study guide that sets the scene and suggests some central questions or issues for consideration. These will vary depending on the level and scope of the course, but will always be designed to draw together several weeks of material. For example, in a U.S. history survey, I might ask Federalists and Antifederalists of 1787 to ponder whether the proposed Constitution fulfills or repudiates the original principles of the American Revolution as they variously understood them; in an upper-level course on the American Revolution, I might also complicate this basic question with reference to distinct positions in 1765-66, 1776, and 1783, and in different regions, classes, or ethnic and religious groups. At this time, students choose sides or characters to represent. Once again the level of the course determines the number of characters and amount of precision; students in a survey would simply choose to take the Federalist or Antifederalist position, while upper-level students would adopt the particular stances of Madison, Hamilton, Mason, Gerry, Paterson, Dickinson, et al. Students sometimes need prompting, but more often they make their choices independently and eagerly.

I also remind students at this point that this exercise, like all class participation, will be graded simply: informed participation will earn a check for the day, and the checks will be added at the end of the semester and translated into a letter grade, to count for 20 or 25 percent of the final course grade (depending on the level of the course). This simple grading scheme frees students to experiment with new or even contrary ideas in the debate — as long as they relate to the readings and issues under discussion — without fear of losing favor or points; it frees me to participate in and guide class discussions without needless concern over whether a particular student's comment is worth an A– or B+.

Over the course of the weeks before the debate, students prepare notes on their characters' concerns, positions, language, and personal styles. These can be drawn from the readings assigned for the course, since at least one primary source (book, essay, speech, letter, journal, or visual source) by each character is included in the syllabus. Some students will do research beyond the assigned reading, but this is not required or even recommended; the object of this exercise is not to teach research methods, but to promote critical and synthetic thinking. Some will consult with me during this week, others will meet in small groups or telephone each other to prepare for the debate.

On the day of the debate, I allow the various groups or sides about ten minutes to caucus and coordinate their presentations in order to promote confidence and prevent "split personalities." (This is especially important in larger sections, where as many as ten students may be sharing a role. While some disagreement among Federalists is authentic and productive, for example, too much incongruity during the debate can be confusing.) During this period of energetic cooperative learning, I circle the room, field questions, and suggest strategies, if necessary. We then begin with a short opening statement from each character (or each participant, in a small class), designed to outline his or her basic position on the central question that I posed in the written study guide. I encourage students to be forthright and contentious here, if it fits their characters. These brief opening statements are followed by a free, and often intense, debate among all of the participants.

I moderate the debate lightly. Always in my role as humble tavernkeeper, woodsman, or doorkeeper to Hell, I respectfully request clarification of differences of opinion, greater precision of expression, or information about neglected issues, from the learned Founding Fathers, American reformers, or European intellectuals gathered before me. At times I must also "direct traffic" and invite quieter students to participate in the debate. But more often, I can simply play my role and enjoy the transformation, as even the normally shy students develop the urge to speak, and the outspoken to listen. Over the years, I have witnessed truly magical moments, as a hushed group listened breathlessly to a quiet black man passionately describe Frederick Douglass' life in slavery, or a timid woman insist tearfully, in Virginia Woolf's voice, on a room of her own. Heated arguments over the nature of terrorists, the role of government in American society, or the relative importance of individual liberty and social justice also frequently occur.

After thirty to forty-five minutes of free debate, we resume our own personae and, for the final twenty minutes of the class period, discuss the issues raised in the debate in our own voices. During this period of reflection on the debate, I guide the discussion somewhat more actively, and I urge students to compare the new perspectives they have briefly inhabited with their own deeply-held beliefs. This would seem to be particularly important for those students who have stretched the most during the debate, but this is not always predictable: while some students experience understandable cognitive dissonance after playing Antifederalists, Lenin, or Fanon, for example, others are startled and disturbed just to hear alternative views expressed and defended vigorously. Perhaps most interesting is the severe tension that men generally feel at representing women during these debates; the reverse does not usually hold. Beyond this exploration of the unusual double-consciousness that the representation and then distancing from a strange voice and position has created, I also use the period of reflection to help students to begin to think critically about the historical interpretations of the period that we have been reading or constructing, especially in light of our new insights into the period and the representational aspects of all historical interpretations. When the role-playing debates and subsequent discussions work well, students are reluctant to leave at the end of class period, and frequently continue the discussion outside of the classroom or over lunch.

Finally, the entire exercise is followed the next week by a writing assignment, either in a paper or an in-class essay, which invites fuller consideration of the issues raised in the debate — and the lectures and readings, of course. This writing assignment might also involve role-playing, with different roles and situations than in the debate itself. For example, those who have represented Federalist or Antifederalist Founders in the oral debate might be asked to write an evaluation of those arguments from the very different perspectives of a backcountry Revolutionary War veteran, a Southern plantation mistress, or a free black in Philadelphia. More often, however, I ask students to formulate and defend their own interpretations of the characters, issues, and period under study. Such essays are graded on relatively clear and simple criteria: how well students articulate their historical interpretations (whatever direction they may take), and how well they support those interpretations with evidence drawn from lectures and readings (particularly the primary sources). If the debate and the writing assignment are skillfully constructed to complement one another and involve multiple perspectives, they can elicit both critical analyses of primary sources and secondary authorities, and creative syntheses of a wide variety of material. They can also generate tremendous excitement about learning history, even in the dreaded Western civilization or U.S. history survey.

Historical role-playing debates can thus serve two distinct sets of purposes in college history courses. First, as a special form of active learning, the debates advance certain pedagogical goals which are hard to achieve through traditional lecture methods. Like most kinds of relatively free group discussion, role-playing debates allow students to develop their powers of oral expression and critical thinking, as they test their understandings of the material they are reading and compare it with what they've "always believed," formulate their own historical interpretations, and work toward linguistic precision and effective argumentation under the questioning of others. As cognitive theory and experience alike have proven, this active learning promotes retention of new material, sparks continued interest in the subject, and allows students to enjoy the learning experience.

Role-playing debates possess certain pedagogical advantages over other forms of group discussion. Assuming another role/voice often frees shy or timid students from their normal inhibitions, and allows them to join a group discussion for the first, but seldom the last, time. Further, the combination of cooperation (within a group/side) and competition (between groups/sides) often changes the group dynamics and stimulates vigorous questions, challenges, and defenses. Finally, the role reversal inherent in a situation where the students represent Founding Fathers and the professor a tavernkeeper, disrupts normal patterns of authority and creates unusual possibilities for free, democratic discussion. Experienced once or twice a semester, these unusual situations can foster group cooperation and active learning over a semester, a year, or even an academic career.

Second, role-playing debates help to awaken students to the complex nature of history and historical interpretation. Students accustomed to a single, linear conception of history (whether presented through an authoritative textbook or a single lecturing voice) are suddenly forced to see American culture or Western civilization as a series of contests or debates over values, ideas, and beliefs, held by a variety of social groups and individuals. Even the "sacred" texts of figures of history become problematic, and the "outsiders" more sympathetic, as some students question and others defend them. The more sophisticated students also become alert to the different forms of discourse and uses of language, through their active assumption of strange stances and languages. Moreover, when students return to their own personae toward the end of the class to consider the issues raised by the debate, they frequently experience a new awareness of the representational character of all historical interpretation: the double-consciousness formed through intimate involvement with an historical position and then deliberate withdrawal to a critical distance from that position, creates both a cognitive tension and an awareness that historical interpretations are constructed and can shift.

Thus, role-playing debates and the subsequent discussion of them can help students to see history in a new way, full of contests over values and ideas, problematic texts and partial resolutions, and forgotten voices and interpretations. Most important, students gain these insights by actively joining a historical debate, and there find their own voices and power to construct and contest meaning in history. In role-playing debates and discussions, students learn to consider and respect the views of others, to articulate and defend their own positions, and to tolerate — and sometimes even enjoy — the fundamental differences among us. Surely these are important lessons for citizens of a pluralistic democracy in a global community in the 1990s.

Chapter VII:

Advanced Placement Teaching

Considerations in Planning and Revising an Advanced Placement or Survey Course

Mildred Alpern

ADVANCED PLACEMENT HISTORY TEACHERS generally disclaim the title of "history specialists," a term usually reserved for practitioners who conduct extensive research on a particular topic. Yet competent AP teachers are specialists of a different breed; their area of expertise is the survey course, a course which demands of them breadth of knowledge, imaginative vision, and a flexible teaching style. To be sure, the survey specialist is not the topical expert; nevertheless, the AP teacher must be familiar with recent scholarship in a wide variety of specialized areas and with general currents in the field. Incontrovertibly, a well-crafted survey is more than a set of chronologically or thematically linked topics. It exhibits some grander form of synthesis upon completion. Like a Brueghel painting with its explicit detail, overarching themes, and human insights, the well-designed survey successfully fuses comparable elements in its narration and interpretation of the past. The result may very well be a work of art.

It is the demanding task of the AP or survey teacher to construct such a course for training students in historical thinking and writing. This can be done, in part, by giving careful attention to the following concerns: first, the selection and editing of primary and secondary materials; secondly, the gender-balancing of materials and interpretations of the past; and finally, the cognitive powers of students who are seriously confronting a vast historical sweep that requires of them far more than memorization of significant dates, names and places. Each of these concerns is vital to the design of a balanced, constructive, and current AP course.

Selection and Editing of Materials

From the perspective of most students, the survey is a shapeless abyss, shored up most obviously with a plethora of names, dates, and events. The key to course success, they believe, lies in accurate memorization of detail. Essays which tell "everything" and ignore the focus of a framed question illustrate this spurious sense of history. Can it be otherwise, even with able and ambitious secondary school students so anxious to perform well on school tests and national examinations? AP teachers face the challenge of paring detail, yet elaborating a conceptual framework that integrates disparate data.

Last year, for example, in my AP European history course, students read primary and secondary source accounts of Russian social developments spanning the reigns between Peter the Great and Nicholas II. Of course names, dates, and events infused the narrative account of uneven efforts to modernize Russia. History unfolds dramatically for students. They are intrigued with such events as Peter the Great's commands to his nobility to cut off their beards, the officially sanctioned beating of former serfs *after* the emancipation edict for failure to understand their new communal obligations to the state, and finally, late nineteenth-century French economic investment in railroad construction across the vast Russian terrain. The earlier history of Western Europe — the Enlightenment, eighteenth- and nineteenth-century revolutions, socialist ideology, industrialization, and clamors for women's social and political freedoms can be reexamined and reviewed in the variant Russian context.

Completing the unit, students wrote essays on the ways and manner in which nineteenth- and twentieth-century Russia had shared in the Western liberal reform movements of the preceding centuries. But then the next day's assignment appeared, at least on the surface, to be a sudden shifting of gears: a reading on Freud, selected to compare his ideas with those of Marx and Darwin, and to examine his influence on early twentieth-century views of human nature.

Unfailingly, students are fascinated by Freud's ideas. They are equally captivated with expressionist and surrealist art as visual illustrations of Freud's wider impact. Class analysis of cosmetic and cigarette advertisements as popular examples underscores the attention the media pay to arousing libidinal desires. Student involvement runs high, provoking unending questions and comments. Thus I was surprised when one student blurted after class, "Just when I finally understand Russia and all those czars, you spring Freud on us. Where does he fit in?"

From her perspective she was right of course. I had sprung Freud on the class when I chose to examine intellectual and scientific history at the turn of the twentieth century as background to the loss-of-innocence theme characteristic of early twentieth-century novels and essays. In teaching the survey I lack the luxury of exclusive focus on one major strand, be it intellectual, diplomatic, or some other. My course must encompass far more than a manageable yet narrow slice of the seamless web. The framework must be commodious enough to accommodate diverse topics and themes, and still make sense to students. I explained to my perplexed student that having traced the course of liberal ideology in the Russian context, we would now examine Freud's critique of one of the basic assumptions of Enlightenment thought — human rationality. Freud's uncovering of the role of irrationality in human behavior, I promised her, would furnish insight into the mass appeal of totalitarian leaders and virulent forms of nationalism.

Clearly, conceptual frameworks in survey courses must be overarching enough to embrace the dominant social institutions and the wide range of values their leaders promote, as well as to highlight the heterodox thinkers who challenge the status quo. More importantly, these frameworks must be presented and explained to students as they work through their own understandings and interpretations of the past. Simple board diagrams help, especially those that clarify interactions between elites and nonelites and comparisons between nations and/or cultures. In any event, disparate pieces must fit somehow, and the pieces must deal with human populations — which introduces my second key concern in constructing an AP course.

Gender-balanced Materials

Professor Gerda Lerner of the University of Wisconsin has perceptively stated that women's history is a misnomer (See her pamphlet, *Teaching Women's History*, AHA, 1981). There is no women's history separate and unconnected from men's history, according to Lerner. There are both men and women in history, and in the best of all worlds one could not write of any period without giving equal attention to the experiences of both sexes. However, Lerner notes, written history has traditionally been the history of men's activities ordered by male values.

An AP course requires integration of men's and women's history. A thoughtfully constructed and balanced survey goes beyond traditional compensatory history which identifies those few women whose political stature rivaled male counterparts, women such as Queen Elizabeth I or Catherine the Great.

As illustration, students studying nineteenth-century Western Europe must inquire whether women also shared in liberal reforms and obtained political, economic, and social rights. Was education easily available? Was it available for all classes of women? And when Freud's views of human nature are integrated into the historical narrative, students may profitably debate whether his dictum that "anatomy is destiny" shaped social prescriptions that narrowly channeled women's social options.

Teaching materials for integrating women's history into traditional survey courses have become widely available during the past several years. Yet the challenge remains for imaginative teachers to frame questions and furnish readings on the role and status of women in history. For example, 1870 is a memorable date in European history, the year of the Franco-Prussian War resulting in German unification under Bismarck. It is also the year in which British married women, under the English Married Women's Property Act, gained legal control over their personal property, earnings, and income. Which event has greater historical significance? From whose perspective? Or, what happens to our conception of the Renaissance when we consider the decline in status of upper-class women? Or, further, what can be learned from early United States history to observe that we have founding fathers but no founding mothers?

Undoubtedly, gender-balanced history increases the complexity of teaching about the past and requires sophisticated understanding; but such history enables half the human population to reclaim its heritage — which brings me to my final concern.

Cognitive Abilities of Secondary School Students

What ideas and understandings can students grasp in an introductory course? What powers of conceptualization and abstraction do they possess? Are they easily able to switch wide-angle and macro lenses in analyzing historical continuity and change? And when a student writes in an essay that Nicholas II made concessions to the liberals and granted them Burma (instead of the Duma), has the student made a careless slip or simply regurgitated misunderstood and inaccurate notes?

William Safire of *The New York Times* has noted the garbled ways the young may interpret spoken sounds in the classroom. Children have interpreted "I pledge allegiance to the flag" to mean "I pledge a legion to the flag," and also "I led the pigeons to the flag." Survey teachers need to consider carefully the ways their words make sense and enhance students' understanding of concepts abstracted from the welter of historical data. Comparison reviews help. It is revealing in studying early modern Russian history for students to contrast the policies of Peter the Great and Catherine the Great with those of the Stuart and Bourbon kings in seventeenth-century England and France, particularly when some time has elapsed between their studies of Western and Eastern European history. So much is forgotten so quickly, a hardly surprising fact. After all, students learn in different ways. Their study of history requires constant restudy, i.e., a process of learning to see relationships, including familiar ones, anew and from different angles of vision. The dialectical interplay of overview and close-up examination deepens their understanding and grasp of significance. And, not incidentally, it helps prepare them to respond effectively to essay questions.

Survey teachers frequently need to incorporate topics and themes studied earlier into the current units of study. Readings, discussions, and tests should incorporate this interplay of past and present, and of continuity and change for students to appreciate and conceptualize historical momentum. As illustration, to argue that Freud was a true son of the Enlightenment at first seems contradictory to students. Yet Freud's confidence in the powers of reason to divest human beings of certain illusions about human behavior justifies such an interpretation. In this instance students must review eighteenth-century Enlightenment values to trace continuities in ideas.

▼

In planning and revising an AP or survey course, teachers clearly have serious concerns. How will the final design of the course appear to students? Will they see it as a blurred canvas, some isolated dioramas, or possibly as a tableaux peopled with both men and women defining and redefining their interpersonal and environmental relationships within a series of successive cultures? The use of history lies in the perspective it affords students to step outside their own time and culture frame, to discover the rich variety of human experience, and to measure the values of their own lives against those of other ages and civilizations. A well-crafted course, designed by a specialist of the survey, will provide them with this opportunity.

AP History in the Small and Rural School

James E. Copple

IN RECENT MONTHS, this column has devoted considerable space to articles that have evaluated the methods and growing significance of Advanced Placement (AP) history. Little attention, however, has been given to what could properly be called an AP explosion and its subsequent impact on the curriculum of the secondary school. The emergence of so many diverse courses has put significant pressure upon secondary schools, particularly smaller institutions.

As AP courses capture the attention of curriculum committees throughout the country, teachers in the various academic disciplines find themselves competing for many of the same students. With the promise of AP examinations in government and economics, teachers in the social sciences hope to attract more students to their courses while not threatening existing enrollments in AP U.S. and European history. Smaller schools are thus presented with an opportunity to offer AP classes that are considerably reduced in size. While academically desirable, this is usually unwelcome by budget-conscious administrators and boards of education.

Acquiring school board approval and maintaining departmental support are preliminary hurdles in developing a meaningful AP program. To sustain district interest and continue attracting students to our program in Garden City, Kansas (population 21,000), we have been forced to be creative in our approach. The creative approaches employed in our AP history program have been the envy of other departments and assure us parental involvement and support. These approaches are to some degree facilitated by the size of our community but, we believe, are applicable to *all* schools offering AP courses in history or government.

Accent Local History

Smaller communities are often mesmerized by their own local history. Many of our citizens may not be able to tell you the significance of the Alien and Sedition Acts, but they can tell you about the great buffalo drive initiated by Buffalo Jones in 1888 to replenish the buffalo population of the Central High Plains, or of the Opera House that once made Garden City the cultural center of Eastern Colorado and Western Kansas. Because of an excellent area studies course offered at our junior high schools, students arrive at the high school already aware of many of these local events. The AP course, utilizing documents provided by the County Historical Society, analyzes local historical events in light of their national setting. This provides students an opportunity to analyze primary sources and apply those sources to a specific writing project. I have also found it excellent preparation for the Document Based Question (DBQ). Students have annually made presentations to service clubs and churches in the community on local history projects. This is rewarding to students and meaningful for the whole community. Often their results have been compiled and catalogued in the city library and the archives of the county museum. Students have been attracted to the AP course because of the diversity of these projects. It gives them community exposure and provides a service to our local historical society.

University Alliance

In recent years, AP conferences have stressed the alliances that should exist between the AP programs in our schools and the history departments of our universities. Many small schools in rural settings suffer the geographical disadvantage of not being close to major universities. But this should not discourage AP teachers or schools that are considering establishing an AP program. We have established three programs that have worked to enhance the alliance and attract students to our courses.

Research Day: Every fall we board an activity bus (i.e., an old commercial bus used for long trips and necessary in rural school districts) and travel to Wichita State University (four hours away) where our students descend on the history collection in the university library; the cost of this trip is budgeted and paid for with district funds. The library staff at Wichita State provides a tour and briefs students on how to use their facility. The staff of the library are prepared to answer research questions and assist in acquiring material and equipment. Our students are permitted to examine and even check out primary and secondary sources, and they are also exposed to a wide variety of available scholarly journals. This trip strengthens their research skills and assists in the research paper that is required the first semester.

Further, this opportunity exposes students to the collection of a major university library, an experience that many undergraduates do not have until their junior or senior year in college. Many of our graduates have remarked that this experience made entering their respective university libraries less intimidating.

In addition, we attempt to schedule these trips at a time when the history or political science departments have scheduled a special speaker. This provides our students an opportunity to hear and see a major historian whose work they may have read. These experiences have done more to convince a potential history major of the excitement of our profession than almost any other single event.

University Weekend: The University of Kansas History Department has a director of undergraduate development, Lloyd Sponholtz, who can assist potential history majors in secondary schools. Lloyd has been receptive to our AP classes coming to the university once a year for the purpose of visiting with the members of the history department and exploring the vast resources of its museums and archives. Students visit history classes and are afforded the opportunity to interview the director of the honors program. Part of the experience includes a panel discussion with historians from various fields who explain their current research projects. Students are permitted to ask questions and inquire about the nature of the profession and the research process. Special tours are arranged, and opportunities are given to AP students for visits with undergraduate majors; this has been useful for both the university and our students. From one experience at KU, five of the eleven students who make the seven-hour drive chose KU as their university. KU has realized the significance of this program for their recruitment, and they pay for the lodging and meals for the two days the students are at KU; the school district pays for the transportation. These experiences have made the AP history course at Garden City High School much more appealing.

History Teaching Alliance: Growing out of the above program is our participation in the History Teaching Alliance sponsored by the American Historical Association, the Organization of American Historians, and the National Council for Social Studies. We recently received a grant that will enable our faculty to study at the University of Kansas for two weeks in the summer of 1986. Their topic will be the Constitution and will be followed by four inservice programs that benefit area social science faculty and students; we anticipate full departmental cooperation and participation.

Continuing education of the AP teacher is essential to solid AP history courses, and neither our geographical disadvantages nor the size of our school has inhibited our commitment to strengthen these courses.

Essential to the continuing education of our faculty is their participation in professional organizations. Currently, the AHA reports a membership of approximately 12,000. Of that number, only 521 are secondary school teachers. If the AP program is to continue having credibility with universities, we must take steps that will convince them we are serious about developing our professional skills.

While professional memberships are not the only solution, they are an indication of our willingness to stay current in our fields. The History Teaching Alliance is to be commended for its efforts to strengthen the programs of the schools by allying secondary school teachers with history faculty at universities. These steps, it is hoped, will strengthen the bond that should exist between the secondary school teacher and the university professor.

Washington Seminar

A third and final program that works exceptionally well in smaller communities is participation in programs such as "The Washington Workshops: A Congressional Seminar." Every year we take our AP U.S. history class to Washington D.C. to participate in this one-week seminar. With the emergence of AP government, these programs will take on even greater significance. Beyond seeing and observing the work of the three branches of government, students work in the Library of Congress, tour the Smithsonian Institution's Museum of American History and, of course, tour the National Archives. The week transforms the historical abstractions of the distant past into realities that students can actually experience.

Financing the program is difficult but accessible in smaller communities. Our city has embraced this program by providing special scholarships. Local civic clubs and patrons of the district take pride in sending their students to Washington. Students get involved in a number of fund-raising projects that enable them to pay for transportation. These community-based projects are more easily accomplished in smaller towns where whole communities can become involved. Our students are not lost in the myriad events and programs that larger cities and school districts must face. A trip to Washington provides an invaluable review of American history, and their incessant questions and excitement make the experience meaningful.

These are only several ideas that have been employed to attract students to the AP history program and the world of the professional historian. And, not insignificantly, they have enhanced the main objective of the course. The teaching of history requires the utilization of diverse methods and an openness to experimentation when applying material. There is nothing more pathetic at the secondary school level than an AP teacher who lives with the fear of students' low test scores. Such fear leads, I expect, to a sterile form of presentation and generally produces mediocre scores. While this is a difficult statement to validate, it has been my observation that when teaching to the test, the test becomes the most meaningful part of the course. The discipline of history will suffer greatly if secondary school teachers see high test scores as their primary objective.

A major objective of teaching history, regardless of the level, should be the translation of historical data into symbols and language that are understandable in the contemporary setting. When the data are internalized into the life and experience of students, we have accomplished a major goal. Students will face the test with the necessary commitment to do well, but will also leave the course with greater curiosity and a more intense desire to apply what they have learned.

Smaller schools, and those specifically in a rural setting, should be encouraged to develop an AP curriculum. There are many advantages to be found in the smaller school. While resources may be limited, teachers can utilize devices not easily employed in larger schools. These devices, if creatively conceived and implemented, will attract curious and bright students.

My experience in the rural and small school has convinced me that there is greater opportunity for departmental cooperation and dialogue in developing curriculum and courses. For example, essays written in AP U.S. history have often been accepted in junior English courses that emphasize American literature. This eliminates pressure from students who are already burdened with excessive amounts of homework. Teaming on these assignments has been to the advantage of everyone concerned. English faculty give attention to style and research methodology, while the history faculty evaluate sources, logic, and historiography. This project is time consuming and requires considerable skill. The team approach allows for several reactions and evaluations of a paper that might normally be graded by one instructor.

Teaching AP in a small school with limited resources forced us to be creative. We are certain others may be doing the same or more. What we have not been able to accomplish, however, is the establishment of a regional forum that will facilitate the sharing of concerns and information. Such forums, where history is the substance of the discussion, are necessary if the content of our AP course is to remain consistent with university expectations. It is the opinion of this AP teacher that the AP history courses we offer will be stronger because of such experiences.

With these considerations, small and rural schools should embrace the AP program in order to properly prepare their students for the rigors of college instruction. While issues related to staffing and student-teacher ratios will remain, smaller schools must seek creative approaches to address these issues. The AP concept and its related goals will be more fully realized if we encourage and assist all schools to participate in the AP program.

Is There Life After AP?

Patricia Matuszewski

FAR TOO OFTEN Advanced Placement teachers are forced by parental expectations, a narrow interpretation of the purpose of the course, and sometimes by evaluation procedures based on past student successes on the AP exam to forego much of the excitement of history in favor of teaching to the test. This is often done by copying the least attractive feature of college teaching: passive learning by means of lecture.

If AP is to be more than a mere service course, life must be infused in it; that is, there can and should be active student involvement in developing the knowledge and abilities that will make history a lifelong interest. Further, there can and should be additional social studies courses to provide students with opportunities to utilize their AP skills — life after AP. Therefore, part of our goal as teachers should be to encourage students both to use and love history, rather then merely to pass exams.

Life in AP

Several years ago, I attended a conference designed to introduce new AP teachers to the goals and purpose of, and to suggest methodology and sources useful in, teaching AP history. During the course of this conference, a number of comments were made concerning the need to make sure that the course was taught on a college level. It quickly became apparent that the consensus was that the way to accomplish this is by "covering the material" and "teaching to the test" by means of daily lectures. What was ignored is that often only a minority of the students enrolled in AP classes take the exam. To be sure, we must meet the needs of this minority, though without neglecting the majority who will not take the exam but who are obviously seeking a challenging college preparatory course. Both groups need to acquire a sound basic knowledge of the facts and major themes in history, and to develop research, writing, comprehension, analytic, and interpretive skills. Since many AP history courses are one-year surveys, lectures and essay exams may at first appear to be the most efficient way of covering so much material and incorporating a plethora of skills. While lecture certainly has its place in college preparatory classes, daily lectures, regardless of how well they are researched or presented, are far too passive a form of learning to be satisfying to most high school students. Knowledge can be acquired not only from lectures but also from such varied sources as: guest speakers, research, oral reports, student-taught classes, interviews, debates, role playing, simulation games, and participation in small group discussions. Such activities are time consuming, but they revitalize the class and create a more efficient and productive learning environment in which students share the excitement of question-oriented learning that challenges rather than stifles curiosity.

Writing skills can also be honed in a variety of ways supplemental to, but less predictable and more enjoyable than the standard historical essay. Whatever format is used for written work, the ability to analyze, interpret, organize, and present data is useful not only in history classes but also is transferable to other academic endeavors as well as to law, business, government, journalism, and other fields.

Clearly, writing is an essential life skill for those headed to college, but how is it best taught? Even in this age of shortcuts, there is only one way to learn to write, and that is to write — every day. A few isolated essays during the marking period will not create a writer. But finding the time to evaluate student writing on a regular basis is difficult since most classes are larger than they should ideally be, and it is a rare teacher who has the extra preparation period the Advanced Placement Program recommends. A system that has worked well for me is to require one-page daily essays related to the subject at hand. Thus, students both review the material and practice writing at the same time. Writing quality improves, fear of writing declines, and knowledge and self-esteem are enhanced.

The first few assignments should be collected and evaluated to make sure students are using proper essay form and to note any serious writing problems. Once the momentum is established, essays can be collected and graded once or twice a marking period. The space limitation of one page a day encourages students because of its brevity, and at the same time forces them to abandon the belief that the only good essay is a long essay.

Writing skills can also be developed in a variety of other ways. For example, students can be asked to create a character and faithfully represent that person's reactions to a major event or events of the day. The essay may thus be creative in nature, yet it must be historically accurate. The character's age, race, sex, religion, social class, educational background, and geographic location must be determined, and the events of the day researched and related to a person possessing those characteristics.

Other useful ways to refine research or writing skills include: letters written as if students were participants in historic events; letters to the editor or to local, state, or national officials; guest editorials; essays on local history; and participation in historical essay contests. Researching, composing, and editing a TV or radio script on a historic theme can serve the same purpose and be presented to the class or videotaped for future use.

Research ability, like writing skill, is useful throughout life; it is not merely a device necessary to pass history courses (i.e., otherwise useless, always frustrating, and usually plagiarized). The type of research assignment is not as important as learning the research process. Once material is located, evaluated, and integrated, the results can be presented in the form of the traditional research paper, or as an article for a magazine, newspaper, or journal. Student work can often be published through a cooperative arrangement with the school print shop. (See Charles B. Howlett, "Two Minds, One Thought: The Creation of a Students' History Journal," November 1983 *Perspectives.*) Students may wish to become involved in oral history projects, propose legislation or write position papers on issues of importance to them. Such exercises involve all the skills we wish to develop and, at the same time, encourage students in the acquisition of those skills by illustrating an immediate use for them. While ideally students learn for the pleasure of learning, realistically the humanities, and history in particular, is increasingly called upon to prove its relevance. Surely history taught as described above is a clear response to contemporary criticism without compromising our profession.

In addition to writing and research skills, students need to be able to comprehend, analyze, and interpret materials. While essay exams serve as one device for determining this ability, debates, roundtable discussions, small group discussions, oral reports, oral summaries, simulation games, and the evaluation of media versions of historic or contemporary events serve as other methods of evaluating these important abilities.

The active learning techniques mentioned above have long been used by exactly the sort of conscientious teacher assigned to teach AP. However, the sheer magnitude of teaching AP or the designation of it as a college-level course intimidates far too many of us into retreating to teaching the way we were taught in college: to learn passively.

Teaching AP by encouraging active student involvement requires careful planning on the part of the teacher so that necessary skills are developed and essential information is imparted. Such planning is more complex and demanding and less predictable in day-to-day progress than a teacher-centered lecture course. It can be frustrating to watch from the sidelines as students laboriously wade through the process of problem-solving or conflict resolution when the teacher could "save time" by quickly listing the options available. Such time saving, while tempting, may be an illusion since covering the material guarantees only that the student has been exposed to it, not that she/he has learned it. There are shortcuts, however, which assure that students are in possession of the necessary facts and still have an opportunity to solve problems. For example, if a debate is scheduled, students can be provided with fact sheets from which they can develop their arguments. Obviously, in the best of all teaching worlds, students would be expected to use their research skills to acquire information as well as to analyze, interpret, and use that information. Since time is a factor, however, this is one way to provide students with the experience of ordering and presenting arguments. If a writing exercise is also based on such work, the assignment reinforces many of the skills we seek to develop. Even so, there are those who will correctly point out that a debate will require at least two days of class time, yet the factual information gained could be covered by lecture in only part of one period. While the observation is undeniably true, students who participate do not merely learn the material; more important, they learn how to learn. Since AP exams emphasize the ability to analyze and interpret information accurately and well in written form, a case can be made for taking the time for activities that teach students to analyze and interpret complex, often contradictory material and to present arguments succinctly, convincingly, and well. It is an old truism, but a truism nonetheless, that learning how to learn, write and think are far more important than the actual facts learned. The facts, while not insignificant, should be merely the core around which other skills can be developed.

Other shortcuts can be used to increase class time as well; for example, some notes can be duplicated for student use so that lecture time can be used more effectively for the interpretations and anecdotes that add color and flavor to the historic pageant. It is more effective and efficient to distribute copies of statistical information to avoid the slow, often painful, process of note-taking from complex data. Students will have sufficient opportunity to practice note-taking skills on other material. Lecture outlines also make note-taking easier and faster. In addition to formal lecture, much factual material can be included by means of short oral reports. Reports planned so they fit into the unit maintain continuity and give students important experience in interpreting, summarizing, and presenting material.

Teaching a class in which students are active participants requires careful planning on the part of the teacher since the goal is not simply the excitement of activities (which can create an illusion of productivity without anything really substantive being achieved), but purposeful, creative, reflective activity dovetailed precisely to attain those informational and skills achievements desired of AP students. That the lessons are absorbed seems to be borne out by those who take the AP exams. In our school, as in many others in which the school board neither pays for nor requires students to take the AP exam, only a minority do so. Of those who do choose to take the exam, nearly all receive scores that make them eligible to receive college credit for the course. For the majority who do not take the exam, student evaluations of the course indicate that they feel that it meets their needs for an advanced-level college preparatory course. A further indication of student acceptance of what is considered one of the hardest courses in the school is that the number of AP sections offered has increased at a time when school enrollment has declined.

Life After AP

Even if the teacher has been innovative and the student a participant rather than a passive receptacle in the learning process, the question remains: Is there life after AP? What can a social studies department do to encourage students to pursue history? Clearly our goal is not to train more professional historians; the field is already overcrowded. Neither should AP courses be viewed solely as a route to college credit, but rather as a source of intellectual stimulation and a way to refine academic skills to be used both in the future and immediately in other programs within the social studies department.

One such program which builds on the academic base of AP history is offered by the social studies department at Franklin High School of Somerset, New Jersey. In this recently introduced, nontraditional independent study program, students investigate eight topics of national or international importance during the year by means of selected readings, seminars, interaction with guest experts, field trips, and creative, analytic, or interpretative projects.

The goals of this after-school seminar program are twofold: to encourage personal intellectual growth and development, and to motivate students to involve themselves in the concerns and interests of the larger society. Traditional social studies courses provide little opportunity for students to affect change, or even to perceive that they are capable of affecting change. Even very able students tend to see themselves as victims rather than potential agents of societal growth and development. It is the premise of this program that individuals are capable of influencing their environment in a positive way, while at the same time recognizing to the fullest their own capabilities and talents.

The year prior to offering Independent Study, AP students were polled to find out what topics they were most interested in having included in the course. Seven of those topics were developed for the course by compiling a bibliography and photocopies of articles. The original seven topics included the following: Energy and the Environment, Technology and the Future, World Economic Interdependence, The Influence of the Media in America, Problems of Development and World Order, Ethics and Politics, and Historic Preservation. An eighth unit, "One Person Can," focuses on individuals who have served as catalysts for positive change; it is designed to provide role models as well as practical advice on how individuals can affect change.

Although any one of the topics could serve as the basis of a year's — or even a lifetime's — study, the AP students polled indicated that they preferred to be introduced to a wide variety of issues rather than focusing on a select few. Since only four to five weeks can be devoted to each topic, reading material is designed to provide students with raw data (facts, statistics, graphs, and charts) to analyze and interpret, materials raising the major questions to be considered in the seminars, and information illustrating conflicting points of view on the issues in question. A bibliography for each unit encourages further research within the parameters of this or some other independent study contract. The program is not designed to provide answers but to raise questions, disseminate information, encourage discovery, and generate higher-level learning through positive and supportive group interaction.

Once students have completed the readings, after-school seminars are held to discuss and analyze the assigned materials. Guest lecturers contribute their expertise and enthusiasm as well as practical advice on how to prepare for a career in the profession, and insight on how their profession has an impact on the problems nations face today. Guest experts have included a Peace Corps volunteer, a representative from the Jamaican mission to the United Nations, a highly placed United States official at the United Nations, local government officials, state assembly members, a local reporter, the legislative counsel to the governor of New Jersey, experts on historic preservation, an official of the Federal Reserve Bank, a chief of prison security, a lawyer, a representative from a nuclear power station, a speaker on solar energy use, a nuclear physicist, an expert in heavy-metals pollution in New Jersey water, and a representative from the Space Studies Institute who discussed the potential for space mining and colonization. To ensure proper scheduling, it is important to contact potential speakers as early as possible, although one month in advance of the speaking date is usually sufficient lead time. Many speakers are acquaintances of teachers, students, or students' parents. Such personal contacts are most helpful in getting quality speakers. All speakers donated their time, efforts, and talent. Several commented that they had been rather unsure of how to speak to a high school group, but had been pleasantly surprised to find how attentive the students were and how thoughtful and insightful their questions were.

Field trips directly related to the topics of study are an important and valuable part of the learning experience. Since a school bus can carry more students than there are in this course, other classes have been invited to join the trips related to their courses. Thus the trips serve more than one class in the department and, for about $1,000 (photocopying and field trips), the Board of Education has been able to provide significant participatory experiences for many students. Field trips have included visits to a high-technology beef cattle-bison breeding farm (genetic engineering), Princeton Plasma Physics (fusion energy), Wall Street (Federal Reserve Bank, Stock Market, Commodities Exchange), and the United Nations, as well as historic tours of Princeton, Trenton, and Franklin Township, a visit to the New Jersey State Assembly, and visits to a radio station and *The New York Times*. These trips are in-depth and behind-the-scenes inspections that challenge students to apply what they have learned in the previous weeks.

In addition to independent reading and participation in seminars and field trips, students are expected to complete a project for each of the eight topics studied. To encourage creative, analytic problem-solving approaches, the range of activities from which projects may be selected is designed to be as broad and open-ended as possible, with group projects encouraged. To promote intellectual exploration, it is expected that different types of activities will be utilized. If a student's main interest is creative writing, half of the projects could involve some aspect of creative writing. Other projects, however, must explore alternative methods of approaching an issue. This encourages not only the development of recognized strengths, but offers an opportunity to discover latent talents and abilities in a nonthreatening environment. Student projects can involve creative writing, research and analytic writing, journalism, art, independent trips, participation in public meetings, conferences, workshops, lectures, leadership and organization activities, or student-proposed projects. Many completed projects have proven to be highly imaginative and creative. Representative examples were published in booklet form and distributed to class members at the end of the year.

Fulfillment of course requirements has not proven to be a problem since the students involved are highly motivated. During the first year of the program, students were carefully screened before being invited to participate. Selection was based on demonstrated performance in previous social studies courses, achievement test scores (reading, language arts, and reference skills), mental ability scores, and teacher recommendation. Parental approval for participation in the program was also required. This year, as an experiment, the course was opened to all students with an average of B or better in AP history or approval of the Independent Study advisor. This has served to make the course less elitist, yet the level of enthusiasm and the quality of those who choose to participate has remained high. Since the class meets after school and much of the work is done independently, the self-selection process seems to produce excellent results and has the advantage of being both simpler and more egalitarian than our original selection process. So far we have not run into a problem of having to turn students away, though some students and parents were disappointed that they or their children were not selected the first year. Last year there were 23 students in the course; this year there are 26.

The class could be run with fewer students or, if more qualified students were interested, two sections could be offered. The financial and operational limit would probably be one school-bus load for field trips. Although the program is still in its infancy, student and community response has been positive. The message that "if you're not part of the solution, you're part of the problem" seems to have been retained by many of last year's students who continue to work to improve local and national conditions. Students have written letters, participated as volunteers in political campaigns, met with the school board, worked on township historic restoration projects, and served as volunteers in conservation projects. These students dare to think in terms of action rather than passive acceptance of the status quo. The type of intellectual and practical involvement provided by the Independent Study program allows students to explore a variety of important issues within the context of a discipline in which they have demonstrated success in the past, and at the same time encourages them to become active participants in improving the quality of life for all.

If students are encouraged not only to participate actively in an AP course, but are also offered enrichment opportunities that allow them to make use of the skills developed, AP history becomes not a dead end, but an opening of new vistas, and we can answer the question posed at the beginning of this article affirmatively: "Yes, there is life after AP!"

Chapter VIII:

Multimedia Approaches

Teaching History with Song and Doggerel

Roderic H. Davison

TEACHERS OF HISTORY look for ways to make history more meaningful to students, and more lively and memorable as well. Songs and rhymes are sometimes helpful; they can enliven both secondary school and college courses. I am thinking here not of the good music or the best poetry of an age, which of course can be incorporated into many kinds of history courses, but rather of the popular, the unartistic, even the corny.

Rhyme and song indigenous to the place and period being studied are naturally the most appropriate to illustrate and to emphasize events and developments. They form part of the social and political fabric of every age. They represent popular aspiration and condemnation, pride, and anguish. They help to recreate for the student not only the meaning of history, but its drama, which teachers have always, in varying fashion, tried to introduce into the classroom. (James Westfall Thompson's practice at the University of Chicago of reenacting the baptism of Clovis with some unsuspecting freshman comes at once to mind.) There are also other forms of ditty and doggerel that can help. They follow, under five categories.

First, there is the rhyme, often crude, that comes from the period under study. Simple examples from United States history would include rhymes from election campaigns. During his unsuccessful bid for reelection in 1840, President Van Buren's opponents shouted: "Van, Van, Van / Is a used up man!" One of the better-known chants is the Democratic one of 1884, portraying the Republican candidate for president as untrustworthy: "Blaine, Blaine, James G. Blaine, / The continental liar from the state of Maine!" Some history teachers will themselves recall the yells of students demonstrating in the later 1960s against the Vietnam War — for instance, "Hell, no / We won't go!" or their bitter protests against the bombing in Vietnam and Cambodia sanctioned by President Lyndon B. Johnson: "Hey, hey, L.B.J., / How many kids did you kill today?"

In European history doggerel abounds also. An old favorite is the popular rhyme complaining that English law allowed common agricultural and grazing lands to be enclosed as private property, a process that accelerated in the later eighteenth century: "The law locks up the man or woman / Who steals the goose from off the common, / But leaves the greater villain loose / Who steals the common from the goose." The familiar Mother Goose rhyme also is usually taken to be a protest, even earlier, against enclosures: "Baa, baa, black sheep, / Have you any wool? / Yes sir, no sir, / Three bags full. / One for my master, / One for his dame, / But none for the little boy / Who cries down the lane." The master represents the king, the dame the well-to-do nobility, and the little boy the common people, left with virtually nothing. Other Mother Goose rhymes have varying political and social origins. From England also comes the *Jingo Song*. I have never found its tune, and so have used it in class as doggerel, illustrating the swell of Russophobia in Britain in 1878 with threats of war to save the Ottoman capital on the Straits: "We don't want to fight, but, by Jingo, if we do / We've got the ships, we've go the men, we've got the money too. / The Rooshun Bear we've thrashed before, and while we're Britons true / The Rooshun shall not have Constantino - o - ople!"

The use of doggerel in language other than English helps to broaden cultural horizons a bit, but is often best limited in American classrooms to short samples that are easily translatable. For example, when one discusses Europe after the Congress of Vienna, one can repeat the popular complaint about the unhealthy state of the German Confederation , that "dog," that collection of 39 states with no real central government: "O Bund, du Hund, / Du bist nicht gesund." Or one can join Metternich in his criticism of the free-wheeling British foreign minister, Palmerston: "Hat der Teufel Einen Sohn / So ist er sicher Palmerston." (If the Devil has a son / He certainly is Palmerston.) The German is almost understandable to those who do not know the language. One can voice again the wry judgment of the French that their premier, Georges Clemenceau, made too many concessions in the Paris Peace Conference of 1919 — that Father Victory, as he had been called, was losing the victory: "Pére la Victoire / Perd la victoire." The pun needs writing out on the blackboard, and explaining, but it is worth doing. Such bits of rhyme, fitted naturally into a discussion or lecture, become signposts to a situation or an event. If students can later repeat the rhyme, they are likely to recall the event or situation in context.

Second, and even better, are songs of a given place or period. One can find a good repertoire to accompany United States history. *Yankee Doodle* is good sung doggerel evoking the Revolutionary age. *The Battle Hymn of the Republic* is poetry of a far higher level; nothing conveys better the idealistic aspect of the Union side in the Civil War. *Dixie* is perhaps its best Confederate counterpart. *Tenting Tonight in the Old Camp Ground* gives voice to some of the human sadness of the war. Aspects of economic history attach to *Erie Canal* ("I've got a mule, her name is Sal / Fifteen miles on the Erie Canal"), to *Waiting for the Robert E. Lee* (the Mississippi steamer), to *The Wreck of the Old 97* and other railroad songs, to *Joe Hill* (the Wobbly song), and to many others. George M. Cohan's *Over There* ("The Yanks are Coming! ") blasts forth the youthful, vigorous American participation in the war to make the world safe for democracy. Popular songs of the Great Depression of the 1930s echo the despair and the hope — *Brother, Can You Spare a Dime?* or *Just Around the Corner, There' s a Rainbow in the Sky*, or FDR's campaign song, *Happy Days are Here Again!* The tunes are catchy. Each song, further, nestles in a rich historical background, and represents an integral part of our nation's past. Teachers of United States history can extend this list almost indefinitely.

Songs are even more abundant in European history, given the variety of cultures and languages; they may also, for that reason, be somewhat harder for the American student to comprehend. But many lines or stanzas are easy to translate. They can convey to students something of the emotion inherent in an event or a situation; the actors of the past are, like them, real people with real feelings. The Don Cossack rebel against Moscovy, Stenka Razin, apostrophizes the great Volga River as he sacrifices to her waters his Persian princess, proving to his followers that he had not forsaken them for a life of pleasure: "Volga, Volga, mat' rodnaia / Volga, russkaia reka" (Volga, Volga, our own mother / Volga, Russian river). The song, like the event of the seventeenth century, is stirring. The German student fraternities (Burschenschaften), suppressed by Metternichean conservatives for their nationalism and liberalism, are lamented in the nostalgic song: "O alte Burschenherrlichkeit / Wohin bist du verschwunden?" (Oh, old student splendor / Whither have you disappeared?).

The nationalist Garibaldian anthem of the nineteenth century warning foreigners (especially Austrians) to get out of Italy — "Va fuori d'Italia / Va fuori, O stranier!" — remained popular into the twentieth, powerfully sung by Enrico Caruso. In a different vein, Frenchmen in 1881 at the time of the great anticlerical campaign sang new words to the *Marseillaise* tune: "Aux urnes, citoyens! Contre les clericaux! / Votons! votons! et que nos voix / Dispersent les corbeaux" (To the ballot boxes, citizens! Against the clericals! / Let's vote! Let's vote! and may our votes / Scatter the black crows.). And the British, in World War II, sang new words to the tune of the World War I hit, *Pack Up Your Troubles in Your Old Kit Bag and Smile, Smile, Smile!*: "What's the use of Goering? / He never was worthwhile — So / Pack up your Goebbels in your old kit bag / and Heil! Heil! Heil!" Perhaps too many songs that relate to specific historical events come from wartime, in both European and United States history; one must strive for balance.

What can one do with songs, these and others? The teacher can play one or more occasionally in class, using records or cassettes. Better yet, one can sing. Not all history teachers sing, but many certainly do. Many probably play a guitar, harmonica, accordion, recorder, violin, or other portable instrument. And students can surprise themselves by singing in class, with encouragement. I have sometimes, after discussing the Russo-Turkish War of 1877-78 (the *Jingo Song* war), given out sheets with the words of that epic ballad, *Abdul the Bulbul Amir*, a reflection of that war. The students have sung it and enjoyed it. They recapture some flavor of that era when the daily newspaper flourished, carrying telegraphic war dispatches, and Europe lived on quotidian accounts of that conflict.

The teacher can sometimes give a solo rendition. Former AHA President Professor Gordon Craig sang Bunny Berrigan's *I Can't Get Started* in a lecture on the 1930s at Stanford University. Professor Carl Schorske has been known to break into a Wagner aria while discussing German culture in class at the University of California, Berkeley. Professor Peter Sugar of the University of Washington has related how, when he was a graduate student, his professor, Lewis Thomas, motioned to him to rise in the back of the classroom. *Partant pour la Syrie*, Thomas announced, and together the two sang to the class the song of the French force going off to quell the disorders in Lebanon in 1860. More than one student may know relevant songs, and some can provide instrumental accompaniment, too, if asked beforehand.

A series of songs, as opposed to occasional single songs, can illustrate the long-term development of a people, or some other topic. The teacher can ask students to collect songs representing various periods of American, French, German, or any national history; they can be ordered in class and used for discussion. Some classes may find it profitable to collect songs (or rhymes and poems, too) to illustrate themes like emigration and immigration, labor, social protest, drinking and temperance, revolutions, war and peace. If songs cannot be played or sung in class, teachers will know that their words may serve well even without music.

Once I experimented with a review theme for a course in modern European history, at the end of a semester. The music department had put a piano in the classroom, which prompted me to play fourteen or fifteen songs (my playing is amateur) and ask for identification and historical context. It was surprising how many students in a class of seventy or eighty of the rock generation could identify various songs, and even sing some. The pieces began with *Madame Veto avait promis* (*Dansons la Carmognole*) from the French Revolution. No one could identify that from the tune alone, but singing the words made its origin clear to some. Among the sequels were the *Marseillaise*, known to many students, *Die Wacht am Rhein*, expressing German nationalist feeling in the 1840 crisis with France, Kipling's *On the Road to Mandalay* and *Recessional* of the age of imperialism, the *Russian Imperial Hymn* (*God the All-Terrible* or *God the Omnipotent* in American hymnals), *It' s a Long Way to Tipperary* from the Great War, *Giovinezza* of the Italian Fascists (a tune stolen in part from a Swiss Alpine melody), *Lili Marlene* from World War II, and others. The exercise is beneficial. Quite a few students commented afterward on the historical significance of one or another of the songs, or supplied other songs just as appropriate. The piano was a help, but the songs could have been sung without accompaniment.

Third, apart from doggerel and song from the historical period itself, there is rhyme of later date that encapsulates pieces of history. Some history rhyme, once common, has gone out of fashion; perhaps it could be revived. My grandfather used to chant United States history with his fellows in a one-room schoolhouse in western New York state in the 1860s, beginning: "In fourteen hundred and ninety-two / Columbus sailed the ocean blue." The rhymed couplets went on from there. Each line had almost the same tuneless tune, the accent always on the antepenultimate syllable, as he intoned it to me in the 1920s. English schoolchildren used to recite a rhyming sequence of the kings and queens of England from 1066 on, as I learned from a sister-in-law who learned it from an ancestor: "William the Norman and William his son / Henry, Stephen, and Henry and Richard and John...." It ended, obviously at some date between 1837 and 1901: "Anne, Georges four, and fourth William all passed / And then came Victoria, long may she last!"

No teacher would present such abbreviated chronicle as good history. But all teachers know that mnemonic devices are useful and often interesting. Rhyme helps. To remember the fates of Henry VIII's wives, students have repeated the jingle: "Divorced, beheaded, died / Divorced, beheaded, survived." I have sometimes used a rhyme I made up to remind students of the geographical boundaries that France, in several periods, sought to attain: "The natural borders of France are these — / The Rhine, the Alps, the Pyrenees."

Students can be encouraged to produce doggerel themselves, at least a couplet or a quatrain. Some will try a longer sequence. A senior wrote for me a lively fifty-line ballad on the 1827 battle of Navarino. A junior answered one of my essay questions on a final exam in most presentable iambic pentameter, showing that she was comfortable with the poetic form as well as the subject. Some students might like to devise a rhymed sequence of United States presidents (one ought to exist, though I know none). The first two lines might read: "Washington, Adams, and Jefferson too / And Madison, Monroe, and Adams J.Q...." It is probably worth while to suggest volunteer versification to individual students.

Fourth, students or teachers may be able to compose their own songs on historical subjects, words and tune both. Though it is hard for most, some would enjoy the process and profit from it, and the class may profit too. One has the example of entertainers who do songs commenting on recent history — Mark Russell, for example. Calypso singers of Trinidad have had a tradition of rhyming song about current events. Such was an unpolished but pleasing number on the abdication of Edward VIII so that he could marry Mrs. Simpson: "Tis love, love alone / That caused King Edward to leave the throne...." Or students can look to Hal Lehrer's songs, like "So long Mom, I'm off to drop the bomb / And don't wait up for me," a wry commentary on the advent of the atomic age. Not so many students or teachers may be able to compose tunes, but most can set their own words to a tune already familiar. One colleague did a song on the United Nations Relief and Rehabilitation Administration (UNRRA), the great international post-World War II relief effort, to the tune of *California here I come*. It began: "Cheer up Europe, UNRRA's come / To rescue your residuum / With health there, and welfare, and sanitation / And industrial rehabilitation...." Whimsy is a good ingredient for the home-grown historical ditty.

Finally, as an outgrowth of the preceding sorts of doggerel, there is extended versification in the form of an end-of-semester course summary. Rhyme lends itself well to summation. There are, naturally, other effective varieties of summary. The late Professor E. Harris Harbison of Princeton University created one that became legendary among students, a drama in which his major Ren and Ref characters meet in the Hereafter. Erasmus, Luther, and others participate in a heavy discussion in prose that is sometimes blunt, sometimes elegant. Students appreciate the brief references that jog the memory. They enjoy even more the tone irreverent familiarity with great figures of the past and they like the rhyme and meter.

Teachers inevitably encounter illustrative material for their courses in books and articles, lectures and concerts, broadcasts, and films. They also accumulate rhymes and songs from colleagues and students. There are, additionally, places to look. I discovered recently A Rhymed History of the World by Jack Melone (pseudonym for Winton Meggison, Chicago, 1933). It's corny quatrains carry one from the pterodactyl to Marshal Foch. The Faber Book of Political Verse, edited by Tom Paulin (London, 1986), is of a higher order, including selections from Dante to John Berryman, all in English. S. Blewett's Rhymes of Royalty: The History of England in Verse (London, 1849), runs monarch by monarch, through Victoria: "Long may she reign, till called above / Unrivall'd in her people's love." Poetry of the People, Comprising Poems Illustrative of the History and National Spirit of England, Scotland, Ireland, and America, ed. Charles M. Gayley and Martin C. Flaherty (Boston, 1903), has sections on "Historical and Patriotic" poems. Some of Kipling's poems are almost doggerel, and some have a very modern ring: "When you're wounded and left on Afghanistan's plains / And the women come out to cut up what remains / Just roll to your rifle and blow out your brains / An ' go to your Gawd like a soldier." See Rudyard Kipling's Verse (Definitive Edition, Garden City, NJ, 1940).

Two guides to the historical content of Mother Goose rhymes are Katherine Elwes Thomas' The Real Personages of Mother Goose (Boston, 1930) and William S. and Cecil Baring-Gould's The Annotated Mother Goose (New York, 1962). The two do not always agree and agree even less with Gloria T. Delamar in Mother Goose From Nursery to Literature (Jefferson,NC, 1987).

Of many collections of German poetry Das Oxforder Buch Deutscher Dichtung (ed. H. G. Fielder, Oxford, 1911), and later editions, is the handiest; most of the poems are first-class, not doggerel at all, but many concern historical events. J. G. Legge, Rhyme and Revolution in Germany: A Study in German History, Life, and Character, 1813-1850 (London, 1918) has the advantage of putting its doggerel into English, in the same meter as the German.

It is easier to find American doggerel. Much has been published privately, like E.F. Spicer's Rhymes for the Times (Spokane, 1939), which includes "New Deal Parodies, " quite anti-FDR. Regional versifiers abound, like Wesley Beggs' Rhymes from the Rangeland (Denver, 1912); Farewell, Titanic, Proud Ship of the Sea is included. William O. Thomson, author of Rhymed Americana (Cambridge, 1967), found that "a plethora of posy [sic] flowed from the newly discovered vein" of his rhyming ability as he satirized small town life, Harvard-Yale-Princeton graduates, FDR's campaign against the "nine old men," and WPA shovel-leaners. Examples of similar popular versifying — on immigration, Darwinism, patriotism, pelf, and other themes — salt the scholarly work of Robert H. Walker, *The Poet of the Gilded Age: Social Themes in Late Nineteenth Century American Verse* (Philadelphia, 1963). Some of Robert E. Services' poetry qualifies as doggerel; see his *Collected Poems* (New York, 1952) which includes the moving "Rhymes of a Red Cross Man" from World War I.

Songs offer a double potential for the classroom because they can be used either as song or simply as rhyme. There are hundreds of useful songbooks. Reginald Nettel, *Sing a Song of England: A Social History of Traditional Song* (London, 1954), relates song to politics, religion, and empire. *The Ballad Book*, ed. MacEdward Leach, explains English, Scottish, and American ballads, giving verse only, without music (New York, 1955). Pierre Barbier and France Vernillat, *Histoire de France par les Chansons* (8 vols., Paris, 1959), should be a model for music historians everywhere. Combining music, words, and historical explanation, the survey runs from the Crusades to 1918. *The Gambit Book of French Folk Songs*, ed. Paul Arma et al. (Boston, 1972), has a short section on history, with verses in French and English both.

Deutsche Lieder, ed. Ernst Klusen (Frankfurt, 1980), has a good historical section, words and music both, but no commentary. Similar standard collections, often reprinted, are *Das Grosse Balladenbuch* (Berlin, 1965; 8th ed. 1984), August Linder's *Deutsche Weisen* (Stuttgart; n.d.), and G. W. Fink's *Musikalischer Hausschatz der Deutschen* (Leipzig; n.d.), the latter with over 1,100 songs. A *Russian Song Book*, ed. Rose N. Rubin and Michael Stillman (New York, 1962), furnishes words in Russian and English, music and context for the songs. English and Russian verses also accompany the music in a World War II book, *Songs of New Russia*, ed. Olga Paul and G. Bronsky (New York, 1944[?]). *The Spanish Ballad in English* by Shasta M. Bryant (Lexington, KY, 1973), presents sixteenth- and seventeenth-century ballads with Spanish and English texts without music. Both music and words are in the great compendium of *Irish Emigrant Ballads and Songs*, ed. Robert L. Wright (Bowling Green, OH, 1975).

A good starting place in seeking American songs is John Anthony Scott's *The Ballad of America: The History of the United States in Song and Story* (New York, 1966; reprint Carbondale, IL, 1983). Scott gives introductions, words, and music and adds a long bibliography, including works on how to use song in class. Every song in the book, says Scott, has been sung and in effect selected by secondary school students. Classic collections — each with words, music, and explanations — Carl Sandburg, *The American Songbag* (New York, 1927), John A. and Alan Lomax, *American Ballads and Folk Songs* (New York, 1934), and the work by the son alone, Alan Lomax, *The Folk Songs of North America in the English Language* (New York, 1960). Among the many specialized works are a number on John Henry, the legendary steel-driving man of the 1870s and 1880s; one of the more usable ones is Guy B. Johnson, *John Henry: Tracking Down a Negro Legend* (New York, 1969).

Oscar Brand, *The Ballad Mongers: Rise of the Modern Folk Song* (Westport, CT, 1979; orig. ed. 1962), explains the origins, growth, and use of such songs with nineteenth- and twentieth-century examples; he provides no music, but the words are often fine doggerel. B. Lee Cooper, *Images of American Society in Popular Music: A Guide to Reflective Teaching* (Chicago, 1982), refers to many songs, especially of the post-World War II era, but gives words and music for none; instead, he explores ways of using music in the classroom. Cooper furnishes excellent bibliographies and, like a number of the more recent writers on song, includes an extensive discography.

Finding the Right Film
for the History Classroom

Donald Mattheisen

LIKE MOST OF US who teach history to the television generation, I envy the power of film (and video) to grasp and hold the attention of students. Books and lectures are all very well, but the magical properties of film are too obvious to ignore. By appealing more directly to the imagination or by stirring the emotions, a good film can arouse interest and generate enthusiastic discussion in ways difficult for the classroom teacher to accomplish. According to Daniel J. Perkins, who surveyed a number of history departments, many of us use the occasional film in class because it gives a "feel" or a "feeling" or a "sense" for history. We think that films "convey a reality words cannot," that they "touch the imagination" and involve students "emotionally." We are not always persuaded that these are our highest instructional objectives, only that they are somehow worthwhile. As one of Perkins' respondents put it in "Historians and the Documentary Film: A Survey," "Film just does things that print doesn't. I value those things less than my students [do], but I find it expedient to truckle a little to student tastes."

Our biggest problem is finding the right film for the right occasion. The problem has two aspects. First, a good film — one that is instructive, relevant to the course, and sensitive to historical issues — must be available. Second, we must be able to find it.

Happily, the first aspect of the problem is rapidly being solved for us. Though twenty years ago William H. McNeill could justifiably complain that the films offered for use in history classes were "bits of flotsam and jetsam from the communications world that some bright salesman once figured could be used in schools with little or no adjustment and at minor additional cost," that is no longer entirely true. The selection has gotten much better. There are several reasons for this, but an important one is that historians are now involved in making them. That is not, to be sure, an infallible recipe for success. The enthusiastic band of Yale University historians who made "The Chronicles of America" series in the early 1920s fumbled rather badly. In the often-quoted words of the later critic Paul L. Saettler in A History of Instructional Technology, their project was an artistic and commercial failure because "the films were as dead as the historical detail which characterized them." Obviously, such an undertaking requires cinematic skill as well as scholarly zeal. Not every historian can do it.

But in the past two decades some have acquired the knack. That is in good part a result of the burgeoning of media studies in the 1960s. Film became respectable then, and academics began to pay attention to it. A Historians Film Committee was founded and began its own scholarly journal *Film and History*, in 1970. Both the AHA and the OAH have taken measures to encourage the use of film in history teaching. Individual historians have pioneered efforts to integrate media studies into their graduate programs, and some began to make their own films. Commercial and independent filmmakers have made more and better use of historical advisors, stimulated, among other things, by a policy of the NEH that encouraged historians and filmmakers to work as a team on the historical films it funded. In the end, even some of the commercial and independent filmmakers have acquired an appreciation for historical authenticity, influenced perhaps by the novel attention of the historical profession to the products of their industry.

Taken as a whole, these developments have created an inventory of historical films worth paying attention to, with the promise of more to come. An enumeration would be tedious, but just consider the variety. Most conspicuous are the highly-publicized blockbuster series on topics of broad general interest that usually originate with the larger public television stations, like "The Adams Chronicles," "Eyes on the Prize," and "Vietnam: A Television History." They overshadow a group of similar, if only slightly more esoteric, series and miniseries: "Heritage: Civilization and the Jews," "Roanoak," and "A House Divided," are good examples. Series emanating from the commercial networks, like "Peter the Great" and "North and South", are actually better examples of how *not* to do history, though British commercial firms have given us some gems like the documentary "The World at War" and the fictional "The Jewel in the Crown."

Most instructors, admittedly, would find it tough to schedule an entire film series into a one-semester course (though individual episodes can sometimes stand alone). But historical films generally come one at a time and in copious diversity. There are films about political radicals, *The Wobblies*; about the labor movement, *The Molders of Troy*; about women, *The Life and Times of Rosie the Riveter*; blacks, *The Killing Floor*; Jews, *We Were So Beloved: The German Jews of Washington Heights*; and other ethnics, *Sequin*; about statesmen, *Truman: A Self Portrait*; and politicians, *The Life and Times of Huey Long*; about artists, *Mark Twain: Beneath the Laughter*; and their works, *Isenheim*; about historic cities, *The Isfahan of Shah Abbas*; and their creators, *Architect of the New American Suburb: H. H. Richardson 1838-1886*; about the Middle Ages, *Cathedral*; the Renaissance, *Man in the Renaissance*; the British subjugation of Scotland, *The Battle of Culloden*; the Salem witchcraft trials, *Three Sovereigns for Sarah*; and the American Revolution, *Hard Winter*.

And this is only a small sampling of films made recently for a general audience. It leaves older works out of account — some still good like *Night and Fog*, some now merely interesting as in CBS's "Twentieth Century" series. There are also many old films not originally intended as history but which have themselves become historical artifacts for example, *Triumph of the Will*. It also does not touch on commercial feature films of an historical nature such as *The Return of Martin Guerre*, nor on the large number of films created specifically for the classroom. This latter category includes films made "by historians for historians": some by the British InterUniversity [sic] Film Consortium, *The Munich Crisis*; some done for Britain's Open University televised courses of instruction, "The Historian at Work"; a series by a group of American historians convinced that film art and film instruction are not mutually incompatible, *Goodbye, Billy*; and a film produced by the American Social History Project, *1877: The Grand Army of Starvation*. But mostly it is a vast supply of teaching films intended for various levels of student audience, made with varying degrees of participation by historical advisors and distributed by commercial firms such as Films for the Humanities and The Media Guild. And I have omitted from consideration films made by museums to display or interpret their collections, like the Colonial Williamsburg Foundation, as well as entire fields ancillary to history such as anthropology, archaeology, and ethnography.

I do not make the claim that films can do our teaching for us. On the contrary, the AHA's own pamphlet by John E. O'Connor and Martin A. Jackson, *Teaching History with Film*, stresses throughout that films cannot just be thrown at students without comment, but require classroom discussion to put them into proper context for the course. The second, completely revised, edition of that pamphlet, now called *Teaching History with Film and Television*, 1987, presents a second important caveat: that filmmakers, like writers, are masters of a persuasive craft; their works must be carefully analyzed rather than swallowed whole. Students should be aware of at least some of the tricks of the cinematic trade so they can view films critically or even just intelligently. (My favorite exercise is to show two films on the same subject, and then ask the students what elements in each film — commentary, music, shot selection, show sequence, and so forth conveyed its particular message. Parallel episodes from two very different series on the second world war — *Victory at Sea*, made in the 1950s, and *The World at War*, dating from the 1970s — work very well for this purpose.)

And there is some reason to believe that films are not very good at all at teaching some things — abstract ideas, for example, or the kind of detailed information called for in most multiple-choice tests. Books and lectures may theoretically do a better job of teaching history, although films are usually more interesting and that has advantages for teaching of any sort.

I am sure that a lot of historians are familiar with some of these films and have used them in connection with their courses. I would bet that they discovered them serendipitously: a colleague, or an advertising flyer, or perhaps they saw them on television. I know one method they did not use to find them: they did not conduct a systematic search for just the right film for their class or for their own unique purpose, because there is no way to do that. No such thing as a *Historians Guide to History Films* exists for historians.

There are, to be sure, some useful lists of available films. The latest two-volume edition of R. R. Bowker Company's *Educational Film Locator* of the Consortium of University Film Centers, 1987, catalogs 48,500 items available from the consortium's 52 centers nationwide. More comprehensive is the National Information Center for Educational Media, three-volume *NICEM Film and Video Finder*, from Access Innovation, 1987. It's labelled "first edition" because although NICEM has long published separate catalogs for film and video, this is their first combined list with 90,000 entries. And there is an even bigger on-line version of the latter — called AV-ONLINE — which boasts of 350,000 entries of films, videos, transparencies, filmstrips, etc. So if it is out there, it is probably in one of these catalogs, where you can discover what is available and where to get it.

Other resources historians can use are the electronic clearinghouse, KIDSNET, and the catalog from the National Endowment for the Humanities called *Media Log* which will be updated in the spring of 1990. The *Log* lists over 400 films and radio programs in various disciplines of the humanities.

But to find a film for classroom use you need more than the brief descriptions these lists provide. You need a competent critical evaluation, and that is the problem. It is fortunate that some historical films get reviewed in the following: *Perspectives, The American Historical Review*, the *Journal of American History*, the *OAH Newsletter* and *Magazine of History, Film and History, The History Teacher*, and *Social Education*. A few of them even get extended scholarly treatment there. If you know what you are looking for, you can track down reviews through *Media Review Digest*, 1970ff or *Film Literature Index*, 1973ff, and articles through familiar indexes like *America: History and Life*. Most of us have quite enough research to accomplish in our academic specialties without taking on the responsibility of yet another research project. If you were to embark on such a search, you would still find material on only a tiny portion of the output, for most of the films historians are likely to want — documentaries or films produced for educational purposes — are never reviewed at all. At best they will get a brief notice from a media professional in something like *EFLA Evaluations*, published annually by the Educational Film Library Association, which however, recently changed its name to American Film and Video Association. But such notices are inadequate for our purposes since they do not evaluate the film's approach to historical issues. In any event, they cannot be found through any index. So your systematic search for the right film comes to a quick stop only part way down the road. It is a great pity that so much money and talent go into producing such a wealth of educationally valuable films which then only find their way into the classroom by the occasional fortunate accident of discovery.

However, what a pleasure it would be to teach anthropology, for which Karl G. Heider has provided the requisite film catalog. His *Films for Anthropological Teaching*, American Anthropological Association, 1983, contains 1,575 entries, each one a critical evaluation of some anthropologically useful film or video. In addition, many of the entries provide comments by anthropologists who have used the film for teaching, as well as citations to reviews and other scholarly discussions where appropriate. Historians will never be able to use films in their classroom properly until they have their own version of this work. Somebody ought to do something about it.

Art as Social History in the Western Civilization Survey

Shirley Wilton

HISTORY, SAID VOLTAIRE, is a pack of tricks we play on the dead. The survey course in Western civilization is surely a "pack of tricks" we teachers play on college freshmen, most of whom come into our classrooms thinking they will be learning lists of dates, solid facts, and all the "lessons of the past."

That popularly held view of history as a collection of unchanging dates and unchallenged conclusions, however, is long gone from most college courses. It was, to be sure, the history I studied thirty-five years ago, a history based on a coherent philosophy of nationalism and a sense that what counted were the great leaders and the great states. In today's classroom that confident view of history has been replaced by a conglomeration of topics and viewpoints, most drawn from the perspective on the past that is called social history.

The teaching of history, even at the introductory level, has been affected by the winds of change in the graduate schools and among research-directed historians. In my own classroom the emphasis has shifted in subtle ways, and without conscious planning. The time I once spent on the causes of the fall of Rome is now spent on urban planning in the Empire. Gladstone and Disraeli have been replaced by "Victorian values," and Napoleon III, that "pygmy tyrant of a great people," in Victor Hugo's ringing phrase, has stepped offstage to make way for industrialism. Holy Roman Emperor Henry IV no longer can be seen standing barefoot in the snow at Canossa, and Madame Pompadour's impact on the Diplomatic Revolution no longer seems as important as Mary Wollstonecraft's "Vindication of the Rights of Women."

A lot of good stories are gone, giving up their place to social history, which is neither so easy nor so entertaining. The definition of social history is far from precise and, indeed, its very significance is questioned by many historians. In an article in *History Today* (March, 1985) seven prominent British scholars offered commentaries on "What is Social History?" They agreed, in general, that it involves "major new areas of scholarly inquiry," requires a new methodology which recognizes diverse sources, is largely quantitative, and offers a new approach to the past which de-emphasizes political events and individual action in favor of slow societal change and group experience.

This "new history," which has been so much influenced by the social sciences, is not universally applauded. Jacques Barzun, for example, in a speech given to the Organization of American Historians and published in *The History Teacher* (August, 1986), characterized it as "retrospective sociology," and others have warned that historians have ventured into sociologism. But most historians seem to have found the new history to be the particular pack of tricks of our time, perhaps in the spirit in which Lynn White, Jr. as early as 1963, in an article entitled "The Life of the Silent Majority" (*Medieval Religion, and Technology*, University of California Press, 1978), said that "the novel task of our generation is to create a democratic culture to match our political and economic structures."

In any case, social history is trickling down through all the levels of historical study to the basic survey course. Carolyn Lougee, writing in this column in September, 1986, discussed some of the problems of integrating social history into the introductory course. History seen as experience rather than action, from the viewpoint of society rather than the state, loses the clear periodization of traditional narrative. The subject matter of the course, now ranging from women's history to labor movements and popular culture to army life, appears to the student as "spongy, vague and sprawling," to use Lougee's descriptive phrase. In matters of methodology, students resist attempts to use quantitative data. As Lougee said, they "do not expect numbers in a history course." Other materials used by social historians, such as oral anecdotes, private records, folklore, and items from popular culture, are difficult to find in a format usable in a survey course.

Solutions to the problem of introducing the work of social historians in the survey of Western civilization or the Advanced Placement course in European history range from adopting readings and textbooks oriented toward social history to using computer programs and devising individualized projects. My own modest proposal, faced as I am with five Western civilization classes of thirty-five students each in an open-admissions community college, is to use pictures. I have a sizeable collection of slides, some purchased from commercial sources, some picked up in museum visits, some prepared at my request by the media department. As much as possible I try to use the "masterpieces" of art for the twofold reason that there is more information available on famous paintings, and it serves students better to be given some of the great images from the history of art.

The use of art with history is, of course, not a novel approach. Every textbook is liberally illustrated with paintings, statues, and examples of architecture from every historical period. Commercially prepared filmstrips depend on contemporary prints and paintings, and the close relationship between art and history has long been established.

What is new, however, is that art is being recognized as one of the artifacts available for research in social history. Historians are using works of art not as examples of the culture of a period but as evidence of attitudes and mentalities or as clues to the experience of people in past ages. This seems to be a relatively recent development. Just over ten years ago Merritt Abrash could argue in *The History Teacher* (August 1975) that art is misused in history classes. "First and foremost," he wrote, "a work of art speaks in aesthetic terms ... These considerations are in the domain of art history, which, in fact is a specialization quite outside the education of most [historians]."

Yet, today, many historians are finding works of art very much a part of their own domain. The summer, 1986, issue of *The Journal of Interdisciplinary History* was dedicated to "The Evidence of Art," and contained the work of a number of historians who have used works of art as source material for their research. The influential social historians Fernand Braudel and Philippe Aries have used art works as documentary evidence in their books, and an increasing number of articles in history periodicals incorporate paintings and sculptures as source material.

In the classroom pictures can be a good substitute for the lost stories of traditional political history. A painting can be dramatic, poignant, arresting, or bizarre. The role played by Holbein's portrait of Anne of Cleves in the disastrous one-night marriage of Henry VIII and his fourth wife is a romantic comedy. The involved planning and final composition of David's painting of Napoleon's coronation, as well as the sheer size of the thirty-nine foot canvas, offers a behind-the-scenes example of effective propaganda. Gericault's *Raft of the Medusa*, considered to be the first of the great paintings of the Romantic Movement, is still able to evoke fascination and horror with its scene of agony and death. Salvador Dali's *Premonition of Civil War* is a shocking image of the dismemberment of the Spanish nation.

As teaching tools, art slides have the advantage of being flexible and adaptable. Pictures can be used alone or in various combination, discussed at length if the class responds or quickly dispensed with if time is short or if they fail to meet the objective of the class period. In planning the use of pictures in class, I have found it helpful to think of them in three different groups or categories. The first is made up of slides I have used for a number of years as illustrations of the cultural life of an age, but which can be reinterpreted in the light of recent research in social, technological, or economic history. When these pictures are viewed as artifacts or evidence, new kinds of questions must be asked, such as why the art was commissioned, who viewed it, and what does it tell us about the society that produced it? Content becomes less important than context.

For example, the murals ascribed to Giotto, narrating the life of St. Francis, are an attractive way to introduce an important historical figure, but the famous frescoes in Assisi can also be used to discuss town life in the fourteenth century, changes within the Franciscan order, and the rise of a new, more naturalistic art in response to the popular culture of the time. James H. Stubblebine's *Assisi and the Rise of Vernacular Art* (Harper & Row, 1985) helps place the St. Francis cycle within its social setting and focus attention on the audience rather than the art. Books such as Henry Kraus' *The Living Theatre of Medieval Art* (University of

Pennsylvania Press, 1967) help to interpret stained glass and cathedral sculpture. Thanks to the work of Robert Mark in explaining how medieval cathedrals were constructed ("The Cathedral and The Bridge: Structure and Symbol," with David Billington, *Technology and Culture*, January, 1984), examples of Gothic architecture become more than "Bibles in stone" and can be used to explain the guild system and the transmission of new technologies from town to town. The plates from the great *Encyclopedia of Diderot* show the lifestyles of the rich and famous of the eighteenth century, but they are even more useful as a survey of pre-industrial technology. Brueghel's paintings mirror the lives of ordinary men, women, and children of the sixteenth century.

A second category of slides includes those single, notable paintings so full of information, drama, and clues to social themes that they can be analyzed and discussed in some depth. The use of a single picture is sometimes more effective than a group of slides or a sequence of rapidly changing images. *The Ambassadors* by Holbein, for example, can be discussed on many levels. The two confident young men, standing on either side of a table laden with globes, scientific implements, a lute, an open hymnal, and a rich Turkish carpet, are the yuppies of their age. Politically they represent the development of diplomacy in international affairs. They represent the interests of the King of France in the negotiations by which Henry VIII separated the English church from Rome. Their awareness of voyages of exploration and the new science of their age is demonstrated by the choice of objects displayed between them. The religious tensions of the time are alluded to in the broken string of the lute and the open hymn book. The new interest in optics and the medieval theme of the Dance of Death combine curiously in the distorted "memento mori" of the skull which Holbein imposes on the foreground of the painting. David Piper's *Enjoying Paintings* (Penguin, 1973) is one of a number of sources for information on this painting, and John Berger, in *Ways of Seeing* (Penguin, 1973), offers additional insights into the psychology behind the art.

There are a number of other artworks which, like *The Ambassadors*, seem to represent their age in its social, economic, and political aspects. David's "great and gentle portrait" of the chemist Lavoisier and his wife, painted five years before Lavoisier's death on the guillotine, offers a basis for discussing aspects of the Enlightenment, the role of tax farmers in the pre-Revolutionary French government, and the life of privileged men and women. The *Merode Altarpiece* by Robert Campin is more than a masterpiece of Flemish painting; it is an early example of the change from aristocratic to bourgeois sponsorship of art, a picture of a fifteenth-century town household, and evidence of a change of consciousness in the representation of the Virgin Mary, not as Queen of Heaven, but as a middle-class wife, and in the portrayal of Joseph in his new role as hard-working householder. The publication of Witold Rybczynski's *Home: A Short History of an Idea* (Viking, 1986) brings added appreciation of the kinds of furniture and room arrangements shown in this picture. El Greco's *Dream of Philip II* embodies many aspects of the

Counter Reformation, Ford Madox Brown's *Work* is excellent for discussing some of the assumptions of the Victorian middle class, and Fernard Leger's 1917 revision of Cezanne's *The Card Players* converts the earlier painting into a mechanical representation of machine-men, reflecting Leger's experiences in World War I.

Finally, in addition to re-evaluating familiar art works in the light of new knowledge, or selecting single outstanding paintings for close analysis, a third use of a slide collection is to combine pictures from many periods as a way to present a topic from social history. By grouping pictures from a number of historical periods, the long view of social history can be fitted into the fast-paced narrative of a survey course. At appropriate places in the syllabus, pictures can be shown which demonstrate the duration of certain ideas and institutions, show slow-changing concepts over time, or offer the opportunity to introduce the work of prominent social historians.

For example, a survey of the idea of monarchy through Western history is appropriate at the beginning of the second semester when the Age of Absolutism is the subject. A selection of royal portraits might include the Emperor Justinian wearing the Imperial nimbus as a sign of his divinity, the Holy Roman emperors bearing orb and scepter, the worldly Henry VIII, the majestic Louis XIV, and, finally, the bourgeois and popular monarchs of the modern era.

The history of women can be presented pictorially in many ways, and the nineteenth century, with the changes brought by industrialism, offers an appropriate place to discuss the status of women. I have used Victorian narrative paintings to show the life choices of middle-class women and to contrast the education of boys and girls in their separate roles. Some of the pictures from this era can be used with medieval pictures, such as the Limbourg brothers' *Book of Hours* and Renaissance marriage portraits, to explain changes in the status of women.

Changing concepts of childhood is another topic on which much has been written by social historians, and for which there are illustrations from art history. Pictures of social protest (by Damier, Kollwitz, and Grosz) or containing anti-war statements (by Callot, Goya, and Picasso) can be brought together. A survey of the "faces of Jesus" using concepts from Jaroslav Pelikan's *Jesus Through the Centuries* (Yale University Press, 1985) fits in well with early medieval history. Finally, at the end of the course, a brief reshowing of selected slides serves as a review of the semester's work and, at the same time, can demonstrate the changing role of the artist in Western society.

This article has suggested three ways that art history slides can be used in a survey course in Western civilization or an Advanced Placement course in European history to introduce some of the topics, methods, and conclusions of the new social history while maintaining the traditional narrative structure of the course. It is argued that pictures are more acceptable to students than statistical evidence and may be used to introduce some of the ideas and conclusions of social historians. Using major art works in this way may seem to the specialist or art historian to be a misuse, for the classroom teacher cannot have the expert knowledge of the research scholar. However, if works of art can serve to demonstrate to beginning students, in what may be their only history course, that the study of the past is not limited to a certain body of facts but is composed of a limitless body of questions, those pictures will have been well used.

Some students may conclude, despairingly, that history is indeed a constantly changing pack of tricks played on the dead. On the other hand, some may realize that the study of history is a fascinating search for knowledge through diverse and ingenious means, and may decide to pursue it further. In either case, the survey will have met its purpose as an introduction to the kinds of history being studied and the kinds of questions being asked by historians today.

Chapter IX:

Quantitative History

Teaching Quantitative History with a Database

Lisa Rosner

PROSOPOGRAPHY, or collective biography, has been described by Lawrence Stone, among others, as ideally suited to introducing students to historical research. In a recent seminar I taught students to use computers to create a prosopographical database, with excellent results. I had been interested in doing this for some time, since I use computer databases extensively in my own research and believed that creating one would be an excellent learning tool. In fact, it was—for me as well as my students. Not only did the database turn out to answer interesting questions, but more important, creating it raised a number of fundamental issues of historical research and interpretation.

I organized the seminar around a problem from my own research, the connection between medical education and medical careers in eighteenth- and nineteenth-century Britain. The focus of the seminar was the creation of a joint database, though students also wrote individual research papers on related topics. My intention was to use the seminar to analyze the education and backgrounds of the Fellows of the Royal College of Physicians of London in this period. This was a particularly prominent group of physicians who had the further advantage of being well-documented in the *Dictionary of National Biography* and William Munk's *Roll of the Royal College of Physicians of London*. There were 179 Fellows to divide among seven students, making twenty-five or twenty-six Fellows, which seemed enough for each student to get worthwhile results.

My three main goals for the course were for students to: experience the carrying out of original research; learn quatitative methods in history by actually developing the data to quantify; and acquire enough proficiency in at least creating a computer database to build one in the future.

My first step was to consult with campus computer center personnel about available facilities. I decided to use Ashton-Tate's dBASE III Plus for the course because it is comparatively easy for creating a database, widely available on campus, and amply supported by the computer center. The head of user-support at the computer center provided me with "how-to" guides that she kept for dBASE, and she requested copies of my student instructions so her staff could assist students if necessary.

The next step was in the seminar itself. I spent the first few weeks setting the context for the database because I wanted students to think of quantitative analysis as a way of answering historical questions, rather than as an end in itself. That had been a problem students had in learning quantitative methods from statistics courses: they learned all the mathematical formulas, except how to relate them to historical issues. Furthermore, I knew from experience that research for the database is hard work, and I assumed that students would do it more carefully if they had questions they really wanted answered. In this case, the questions we asked had to do with what sort of factors helped physicians establish successful careers. Was it family background? If so, what kind? Was a physician more likely to become a Fellow if his father was or had been a Fellow? Or was it education that made a difference? Fellowhip, was, for all intents and purposes, restricted to graduates of Oxford and Cambridge Universities; however, many Fellows had also studies for several years at Edinburgh University's renowned medical school. Which, therefore, was the best place to study for a successful medical career? To begin to answer these questions, we read a variety of secondary and primary sources and discussed the arguments proposed by each. At that point I presented the idea of a database. Why not gather as much information as we could on Fellows and see what we could find out?

The students nodded dutifully at this, and they continued nodding after I handed each of them a list of 25 or 26 Fellows with a group of questions to try to answer about each, such as his birthdate, early education, father's occupation, and year of becoming a Fellow. Each student, I explained, would be creating his or her own database, which would then be combined with the others into one large database. Each Fellow would make a separate record in the database, and the students as a group would have to decide how the information could be organized into variables, which dBASE calls "fields." Each individual database had to have the same fields as the others, or they could not be combined at the end to give meaningful results.

The third step was for students, once they had begun their research, to come up with a list of fields. The fields had to have names of no more than ten letters which we would be able to use and remember, such as YOF (year of fellowship) or F_OCC (father's occupation). Students also had to devise a way of standardizing the information they found in their sources so the computer could tabulate it and avoid distortions from oversimplification. For example, a Fellow's father might be variously described in biographical dictionaries as a doctor, physician, MD, or Fellow of the Royal College. Entering the information into the Father's Occupation (F_OCC) category in the database exactly in those words would result in unnecessary proliferation of categories, but subsuming all of them under the category MEDICINE would make it impossible to use the computer to answer one of our most important questions: did Fellows' sons frequently become Fellows in turn? The problem was the basic one of interpretation of primary sources, made more acute by the possibilities and limitations of the computer.

The class periods we spent hammering out the variables, once students had collected information, were not exactly tumultuous but were at least a change from the dutiful nodding of earlier classes. For the first time I saw in my students signs of the creative frustration that always accompanies my own wrestling with this problem when I use computers. I made it clear that I would not simply tell them what variables to create or what values to use in interpreting data, since I had not myself seen the sources. They had to come to some agreement or the database would not work. They did this ultimately outside of class, by dividing the list of questions among themselves, with each student responsible for creating a certain number of variables. We ended with 27 in all, one of which was a COMMENTS variable for information that did not fit any other category. I was encouraged by this sign of cooperation and initiative and moved to the next step: teaching my students how to use dBASE itself.

My goal was to teach students just enough for them to get started entering data, rather than to give them a full course in dBASE. I had written a short manual which I had hoped was completely "user-friendly" and had given a copy to each student as well as to the user-support personnel. Unfortunately, only the best two students found it easy to follow and as with many people who use software frequently, I had neglected to explain many small points. Still with individual coaching, students managed to create their databases and begin entering data. By the end of the week, they had entered all their data and handed me their disks.

At this point, my class schedule fell apart. Unaware of any problems students had encountered with the data entry, I had intended to spend the next class period teaching advanced dBASE techniques for tabulation of data. On seeing the disks, however, I promptly changed my mind. There were too many problems with the research and interpretation of data for us to move on to the next step in computer instruction, and from that point on I made those problems the focus of the course.

The problems were of three types, as I explained to the class the next time we met. The first was simply insufficient research. Many of the students had left out several pieces of easily-obtainable information, such as the year physicians became Fellows. Some had omitted a few physicians entirely. I had some sympathy for this: finding 27 separate pieces of information about 25 different people was a difficult and often tedious task. Each student had done a reasonable job with his or her own database and, presumably, had concluded that just a few missing variables did not matter. Cumulatively, though, the effect was disasterous. I pointed out that their ommissions not only made it impossible to answer any of the questions we had raised, but they also cast doubts on the integrity of the rest of their research. The omitted data had to be found for the project to work.

The second problem, like the first, came from students' forgetting, or perhaps not really believing, that their research was intended for anyone other than themselves. One student, for example, had abbreviated place names so that only she could tell what they were. Another had done an excellent job of printing out her own data, but had created her database using different variables from the rest of the class, so it could not be joined to the others. They had, I said, behaved like soloists rather than an orchestra, as though their individual contributions were more important than the joint final product. They had to remember that data entry was not the end of the project but only the beginning, that the point of the project was not to feed the data into the computer but rather to extract information.

The third problem was the most intriguing. Of the 27 variables, the one students clearly preferred was COMMENTS, because it saved their having to decide, for example, which category to use for Father's Occupation (F_OCC), or whether a Fellow was in Private Practive (PVTPRAC) or was known for his medical writing (abbreviated to Medical Author, field name MEDAUT). In many cases, I found that students had left those variables blank, but included COMMENTS which clearly indicated that, in the above example, a Fellow had been in private practice or was known for his books on medicine. Discussion of this raised an issue that had worried many students. How were they supposed to decide whether a Fellow was in private practice? Their main primary sources were biographical dictionaries, which never simply said, "Dr. So-and-So was in private practice and was also a medical author." Students in the seminar were afraid of being wrong, and as one said, preferred to leave other variables blank and put all the information in COMMENTS.

Difficulty in interpreting sources is a fundamental problem of historical research, and I had naturally encountered it in other history courses. The advantage of the database is that it made clear how necessary interpretation was. I asked students who they expected to make the decision as to whether a Fellow was in private practice. Me? The computer? Some future quantitative historian who had no idea how the information was compiled? The essential task of the historian is to interpret the past based on available sources; we could not cut that out of the course and still call it a history seminar. Given that fact, surely it was best for the person who had actually seen the sources to be the one to interpret them.

As a result of the discussion, even the most worried of my students could see that the decision not to interpret was in fact an interpretation. We had set up fields for variables like private practice (PVTPRAC) so that they either had to be filled in or left blank, and no one wanting to use the database in the future would be able to tell the difference between a variable left blank because a Fellow was not in private practice and one left blank because a student had not done sufficient research or ws afraid to make a decision. Putting the information in the COMMENTS field was no solution, because sooner or later someone was going to have to interpret what all those COMMENTS meant. Let it be sooner, rather than later, I suggested, and returned the disks for revision.

Discussing the problems, as it turned out, was not enough, for many of the gaps and inconsistencies were still there when I recollected the disks. During the class I did what I should have done earlier—I showed students, on the computer, what the combined database actually looked like, and, using dBASE commands like DISPLAY, LIST, COUNT, and AVERAGE, demonstrated why it would not work. We could not find out even a simple piece of information, like the average age physicians became Fellows, because students had still not collected all the data. We could not determine whether Fellows' sons were in fact more likely to become Fellows, because students had not followed the standard categories in entering Father's Occupations (F_OCC). This and other examples had a definite effect on the students. Finally, the database became a tangible reality to the students. For the first time they could literally see what they were creating together, and for the first time could see what they had to do to make it work.

To all this, gratefully, there was a happy ending. The next time I collected disks they did collectively make a workable database, and one which yielded interesting results. Since we had no more time for computer instruction, I tabulated the data myself, rather than teach students how to do it. We then discussed the results in light of the questions raised in the course, such as the impact of fathers' occupations on Fellows' careers, differences between Oxford and Cambridge graduates, etc. I cannot claim that we answered all our questions about the connection between medical education and medical careers in Great Britain, but we certainly did elucidate the issue.

Next time I teach the course I will certainly do some things differently. I will leave more time for computer instruction, and I will rewrite my manual so it is more accessible to students. I will be more prepared and leave more time for the problems of research and interpretation of sources that students will encounter. In addition, I would like to include more explicit discussion of quantitative measures. Having created the database, students could usefully put the data into tables and calculate percentages. The class would also have been an excellent forum for discussing basic statistical concepts like mean, mode, median, correlation, and regression. And I would like to make more explicit connections between evaluation of documents and evaluation of quantitative evidence, perhaps by incorporating both into a final paper.

All in all, I considered the seminar a success which my students were relieved to hear. All said they thought they could use dBASE III Plus again, with some help; one student, in fact, has decided to use it for her senior project to create a database of Jesuit missionaries. All students also believed they had better understanding of quantitative methods in history, including how much work is involved. Most satisfying of all, they were pleased to think they had succeeded in producing something new and original. As one student said, the best part of it was that once we put the data together we could find out all sorts of things we didn't know before.

History by Numbers

R. E. Johnson

"I'VE GOTTA USE WORDS when I talk to you." T. S. Eliot's Sweeny was none too pleased at this obligation, but most historians accept it as a matter of course. Words, written or spoken, are our stock in trade. As researchers and interpreters of the past, we use words to convey our conclusions to others; as educators, we encourage our students to choose words with care and to express themselves with clarity and precision.

From time to time, though, some of us must use numbers along with or instead of words, and here the traditions and conventions of our craft provide less guidance. As recently as ten or fifteen years ago, some members of the historical profession looked upon quantitative history as an unwelcome intruder into the curriculum ("not really history at all," as one colleague put it), an amalgam of sociology and econometrics which really belonged in some other department. Today, the proponents of quantitative methods are regarded with more respect and toleration by their colleagues. Their works have received some of the highest honors the profession can bestow, and whole journals have been created for disseminating the results of their research. Even so, some problems remain.

As a teacher and sometime practitioner of quantitative history I have often encountered a condition that can best be described by the clumsy term *innumeracy*. Despite the awkwardness, its meaning should be clear: If we describe someone who cannot read words as illiterate, there should be an equivalent term for one who cannot understand numbers. To be fair, I must introduce a further neologism and suggest that many of the individuals I have in mind — a substantial majority of the students I encounter, and a somewhat smaller majority of professional colleagues — are actually *seminumerate*. Able to read and write simple numbers, they have considerable difficulty explaining or interpreting numerical information. When they encounter a statistical table in a historical study, they are inclined to turn the page. Reading an author's numerically-based conclusions, they are more likely to "suspend their disbelief," ask fewer questions, and offer less criticism than they would if the author had been using traditional, non-quantitative evidence.

Should this be a cause of concern? The historical profession, like every other branch of academia, has of late shown a tendency towards specialization and subdivision (perhaps, indeed, to subsubsubdivision). Why shouldn't quantitative history follow the same path? Let the quantifiers remain a subdiscipline unto themselves and if, like the fabled Lowells and Cabots, they end up speaking only to one another or to God, will the rest of us be any poorer for that?

The answer, I am afraid, is yes. Regardless of specialization, historians of all lands and centuries are constantly coming up against problems that can only be understood through the use of numbers. To mention but a few examples, how can we hope to interpret elections, famines, or social movements without a clear understanding of numerical evidence? Can we assess the successes and failures of the New Deal, or the horrors of the Middle Passage, or the actual strength of a purported "moral majority" without examining statistics?

I do not mean to suggest that numerical evidence is in any sense superior to the written word, or that it can magically answer all the questions a historian might ask. On the contrary, no historian should ever forget J. H. Hexter's warning, "Few statistics are more pathetic or less useful than the ones that render intelligible a course of events that did not happen." Statistical sources must be scrutinized, criticized, and dissected with no less care than historians would give to memoirs, consular reports, or medieval sermons. My complaint is that at the moment too few historians are making this attempt. Should we, then, be enrolling ourselves or our students in remedial courses in statistics? Not a bad idea, but it may not solve all our problems. What is most needed, as I see it, is not mathematical proficiency but critical judgment. The problems that are likely to prove most vexing to historians, or for that matter to readers of this morning's newspaper, are often arithmetical, requiring simple deductive logic or that old standby, common sense. Before we tackle chi-squares and multiple regressions, we need to learn to think about numbers.

I will go further and suggest that other behavioral scientists might share this problem, might even learn something of worth from historians. In these days of software packages and instant computing, numbers sometimes seem to take on a life of their own. Data can be entered and crunched, and a millisecond later we receive "output" in the form of scores, coefficients, and probability ratings. Unfortunately, such "results" are only as reliable as the original evidence, and statistics, like words, are human artifacts. The numbers that historians (or economists, sociologists, or the rest of the behavioral pack) must use are created and compiled by fallible human beings. They are not a reality in themselves, but a *representation* of reality, and frequently a poor one at that. To find out what they mean we must ask questions, compare one set of numbers with another, introduce hypotheses. We must know who compiled a particular set of statistics, and for what purpose. What is the possibility of error or deliberate fraud? What other conclusions, apart from those of the compiler, can be drawn from a given body of evidence? These are precisely the kinds of questions that historians have been asking about written sources since time immemorial; we must now learn to apply them to numerical evidence.

The questions seem easy and obvious, but not so much so that any beginner will instinctively ask them. To encourage students in this direction I began several years ago to include short statistical assignments in my introductory history courses. For example, a course on the Industrial Revolution, designed for first- and second-year undergraduates, began with a questionnaire asking students to predict the direction of change for a number of social and economic indicators in Britain: the number of workers in cottage industry, 1770-1830; the number of agricultural workers, 1750-1850; the number of draft animals; the size of the average household; the age at marriage; the rate of infant mortality. In most of the examples chosen, available historical evidence runs counter to students' intuitive predictions. (The number of cottage weavers, for example, increased dramatically after the invention of mechanized spinning equipment, and the number of horses used in cartage increased with the growth of railroads.) At intervals throughout the following semester I introduced statistical tables for discussion, encouraging students to read them as critically as they would read other examples of historical evidence, such as parliamentary reports or workers' memoirs. I encouraged them to ask not just "Why did things happen this way?" but "How do we know what happened? What do the numbers mean?"

In one such exercise I distributed two tables showing the occupational break-down of the British workforce between 1801 and 1851 — one giving the absolute numbers of workers in various categories and the other indicating their relative distribution. Students were quick to point out the rapid growth in mining, manufacturing, trade and transport, and the abrupt eclipse of agriculture, whose share of the workforce declined from thirty-six percent to nineteen percent. They barely noticed, however, that the number of workers in agriculture continued to grow throughout this period, from an initial 1.7 million to roughly two million by 1851. Pointing out this apparent anomaly, I asked students to ponder the impli-cations: Could industry be said to have grown at agriculture's expense? How many British workers were forced off the land? What could account for the differences between absolute and relative magnitudes? Could the statistics be misleading? Is the size of the paid workforce an adequate measure of the agricultural population as a whole? Might the definition of an agricultural worker have changed during this period? Do available sources indicate whether family members who were employed on a casual or seasonal basis were counted in the totals? Not all of these questions could be answered from the data at hand, but by asking them the students acquired a different appreciation of the evidence and its problems.

Statistical examples need not be confined to economically-oriented topics. In a course on the Russian Revolution I include a unit on the family backgrounds of party activists; in a modern Europe course I analyze voting trends in Nazi Germany. In each case I try to present the evidence, not in a predigested form with unambiguous conclusions, but as a problem for critical analysis. When preparing examination questions, I always include at least one statistical problem along with more traditional questions; students are asked to interpret a table or diagram, considering its shortcomings as well as its implications.

After a number of experiments along these lines, I have also introduced an undergraduate course entitled, "History By Numbers," the purpose of which is to demystify numbers and enable students to read them intelligently in historical context. The one-semester course concentrates on a series of problems and controversies from several different fields and periods of history: the "Storm over the Gentry" in Tudor and Stuart England; quantitative studies of the standard of living during the Industrial Revolution; *Time on the Cross* and its critics; Peter Laslett and Lutz Berkner on household composition in early modern Europe. [J. H. Hexter "Storm over the Gentry," in his *Reappraisals in History* (London, 1961); E. J. Hobsbawm, "The British Standard of Living, 1750-1850," *Economic History Review*, 2nd series, Vol. X; R. M. Hartwell, "The Rising Standard of Living in England, 1800-1850,: Ibid., Vol. XIII; P. Laslett, "The Structure of the Household in England over Three Centuries," *Population Studies*, 23 (1969); L. Berkner, "The Stem Family and the Developmental Cycle," *American Historical Review*, 77 (1972).] Through a series of exercises based on a single data set, students are introduced to basic vocabulary and techniques of measurement: mean, median, measures of distribution, cross-tabulation. Behind all these tasks is a list of basic themes and questions:

1.   Where do numbers come from? Human fallibility has already been mentioned, and many readers will recall Disraeli's dismissal of "lies, damned lies, and statistics." A careful reader should certainly be on the lookout for bias in numbers, suspicious of data that fit too perfectly with their authors' conclusions. A classic example is wartime casualty figures, which have a tendency, especially when prepared for public consumption, to overstate an adversary's losses and understate one's own. Deliberate exaggeration and misrepresentation are not, however, the only problems a student or researcher will encounter. Information may be gathered or presented in ways that impart a mere subtle and unintentional bias to the results. Statistics on crime or public health, for example, will be affected by the number of police or inspectors who are reporting them, and by the public's disposition to cooperate with authorities; any change in either of these may produce a spurious trend in the data. Historical reports on a country's imports and exports may be distorted by changes in the incidence of smuggling, which in turn may vary with the level of excise taxes. Public opinion polls may be slanted toward one or another segment of a population — subscribers to a particular magazine or newspaper, households with telephones, individuals fluent in the interviewer's language.

2.   Numbers don't speak for themselves. You have to torture them to make them talk. A single set of statistics, manipulated with sufficient ingenuity, can be made to yield answers to many different questions, or even to offer different answers to the same question. A newspaper story last year reported that high school students' use of cocaine had risen by "a mere 1 percent" between 1985 and 1986;

a few days later a reader pointed out that this was actually a rise from 4.8 percent to 5.85 percent of the entire high school population, and that the rate of increase in the number of users was therefore more than twenty percent. Both figures were arithmetically correct, but the urgency of the problem was conveyed quite differently by the reader's addendum. Researchers and readers must learn to live with ambiguity, and to think about the multiple meanings of their data. The problem is not "How to lie with statistics," but how to recognize the multiple truths that statistical evidence may contain. In one of the assignments in my course, students are asked to compare tables from two censuses thirty years apart, showing the age-sex composition of one city's population. Because of changes in in-migration, fertility, and mortality, the overall ratio of women to men in this population changed dramatically during these years, and students are asked to pinpoint the most important trends. The point of the assignment is to see how many different calculations can be made, and how many different conclusions can be supported, using the same body of data.

  3.   You can't always get what you want. Quantitative historians, like others in the profession, are often unable to find a source that directly addresses their topic. Sometimes the object of attention is too broad and vague to be measured (e.g., a standard of living, a revolutionary mood). Sometimes it is a subject the chroniclers of earlier centuries overlooked. In either case we wind up making substitutions, trying to answer our questions with evidence that was compiled for some other purpose. Eric Hobsbawm used statistics on the numbers of animals slaughtered at Smithfield, for example, as an indirect indicator of diet, and hence of well-being, of London's population during the Industrial Revolution. Robert Fogel and Stanley Engerman used probate records of slaveowners' estates as a basis for calculating slave mothers' childbearing patterns. Such ingenuity is commendable but it can also lead a researcher astray. In our eagerness to announce what the data mean, we too easily forget what the sources really *say*. (If the probate records, for example, show a slave mother with children aged nine, seven, and five, does that mean the nine-year old was the woman's first-born ? (R. Fogel and S. Engerman, *Time on the Cross* (Boston, 1974), I:129-38, II:114-15; cf. H. Gutman, *Slavery and the Numbers Game* (Urbana, 1975), 150-52.) If Smithfield's output of beef and sheep did not keep pace with London's population, must we conclude that Londoners were eating less meat?) Here too a careful critic will scrutinize statistics for ambiguity and possible contradictions.

  4.   Even simple effects have multiple causes. The most common problem here is tunnel vision. Preoccupied with our own hypotheses, we may forget the complexity of the real world. When I ask students why, in many populations, the number of widowed females is conspicuously greater than the number of widowed males, the usual response is that women live longer — a correct answer but an incomplete one. Only with considerable prompting do the students remember that widowhood is defined not just by mortality but by remarriage, and hence by social

mores. In most modern societies males have shown a greater propensity to remarry, often to women younger than themselves; as a result the ratio of widows to widowers is often greater than the ratio of elderly women to men. To use numbers intelligently we must try to imagine all the factors, including apparently extraneous ones, that could combine to produce an observed result.

5.   Beware of misleading aggregation. The critical reader will also recognize that multiple causes and trends are more easily forgotten in summary statistics. In particular, the easiest way of summarizing a body of numbers — the "average" or arithmetic mean — often hides more than it reveals. Per capita income can rise, for example, even though most people's wages decline or remain unchanged. All it takes is a sufficiently large increase in a few individuals' earnings.

Some of the most dramatic examples of misleading averages come from the realm of demography. Students are usually astonished to find the death rate (more properly, the Crude Death Rate) in economically less-developed countries to be lower than in industrially-advanced ones. Taiwan's rate in 1966 was 5.36 deaths per 1,000 population, as compared to 11.23 per 1,000 in the United Kingdom. (N. Keyfitz & W. Flieger, *Population: Facts and Methods of Demography* [San Francisco, 1971], 382, 472.) One is tempted to conclude that Taiwanese were twice as healthy as Britons, or lived twice as long, but neither of these hypotheses can be sustained. The essential point is that one number cannot adequately describe an entire population's mortality. Taiwan turns out to have had higher per capita death rates than the United Kingdom in every separate age group. Because of its higher birth rate and rapidly growing population, however, roughly sixty percent of Taiwan's population was between ages five and thirty-five, as compared to forty percent in the U.K., and young Taiwanese do have lower death rates than elderly Britons. The two nations' overall death rates are a reflection, not just of health or longevity, but of the age distribution of their populations.

What should one conclude from this litany of fallacies and potential errors? Some members of the profession will maintain that numerically-minded colleagues are worshipping false idols and forsaking the time-honored principles of historical investigation. My own response is more temperate: I accept the possibility of quantitative research as intellectually sound and rigorous despite the hazards. If the sources are never fully adequate and the conclusions never fully "proven," this hardly sets quantifies apart from fellow historians or from any other students of the human condition.

At the same time, in arguing for a fuller integration of quantitative sources and methods into the history curriculum, I have a broader agenda in mind. I know that few of my students will go on to study history in a systematic way, but I also believe that quantitative reasoning should not be regarded as an esoteric skill. A day does not go by without some journalist or politician bidding for attention or support on the strength of statistical claims or calculations. (As I write these words, residents of my city are being told that freight trains carrying hazardous materials through populated areas are statistically safer if they travel at higher speeds.) I would like my students, as citizens in a democratic polity, to be able to evaluate these claims. Here, surely, is a case where a clearer understanding of the past can promote clearer thinking in the present.

Chapter X:

World History

"The World Outside the West" Course Sequence at Stanford University

James Lance and Richard Roberts

IN AN INCREASINGLY INTERDEPENDENT, multinational, and multicultural world, familiarity with the background, concerns, and problems of societies other than those spawned from the Western tradition has become a present and growing imperative of modern life. Stanford University undergraduates are required to take a year-long Western culture sequence and at least one course on a non-Western culture. This requirement, which was mandated by the Stanford Faculty Senate to take effect in 1980, reintroduced the required "Western culture" after a hiatus of ten years.[1] The non-Western culture requirement — one course as opposed to three quarters for Western culture — reflected faculty concern that if nearly all United States students lack an acquaintance with the Western tradition, their knowledge of the world outside the West is even more limited. The rationale behind the non-Western requirement was clear: five-sixths of the world's population and four-fifths of the world's sovereign nations are located *outside* of Europe and those areas of European settlement considered extensions of the West (the United States, Canada, Australia, and New Zealand). For at least the past forty years, military conflict and economic development in the non-Western world have arguably had a greater impact upon American society than have events taking place in Europe.

Incorporating the non-Western requirement into the existing curriculum presented few difficulties. At Stanford, there are well over 100 humanities and social science faculty specializing in Africa, East Asia, Latin America, and other parts of the non-Western world. Students may satisfy the non-Western requirement by taking any one of about fifty-five designated courses. Most of these courses are designed to introduce students to a particular world area, culture, or society through the perspective of a particular discipline, for example: contemporary African politics, traditional Chinese literature, or the history of colonial Mexico.

In the early 1980s, a group of non-Western area studies faculty proposed a new course sequence, "The World Outside the West." Where this sequence differed from other non-Western courses was in its interdisciplinary and cross-cultural emphasis. The course was to be taught by a team of area specialists — e.g., anthropologists, historians, and political scientists — and would be aimed primarily at sophomores and juniors desirous of fulfilling the non-Western culture requirements.

Those of us proposing this new course were concerned that an unspecified one-quarter, non-Western culture course would not adequately portray the tremendous cultural and social diversity in the non-Western world, and we were dissatisfied with the "high" cultural emphasis implicit in the teaching of the "Western" culture requirement. We proposed, instead, a comparative study of three non-Western cultures over a two-quarter sequence, focusing on a broader definition of "culture." In this course, "culture" was conceived as lived experience, thus emphasizing social history. Since there were no ready-made models for such a course, we spent considerable time exploring alternative ways of conceptualizing and organizing the material we hoped to include in the course and in developing a model of culture which could be used as part of a debate with the proponents of Western "culture" as commonly conceived. We found Fernand Braudel's division of time into natural, social, and eventful time, as developed in his *The Mediterranean and the Mediterranean World of Philip II*, provocative and helpful in shaping the agenda for organizing course materials.

As our thinking evolved, the course came to concentrate on aspects of selected cultures in Asia (China), Africa (Nigeria), and the Americas (Mexico), and was to have a threefold objective: introduce students to a select number of non-Western cultures before and after extensive contact with the West; help students better understand the values, attitudes, and institutions of non-Western peoples in the modern world; and, furnish students with a framework for comparing and contrasting all cultures, including that of the West, thereby heightening students' sensitivity and appreciation of the varieties of human experience.

Students would not be the only beneficiaries of the course. The process of course development would present opportunities for enhanced dialogue among faculty who specialize in the study of non-Western societies. We expected this dialogue to encourage greater sensitivity to the comparative dimension in courses taught in our own fields of specialization and to generate insights into further innovation in the curriculum in regard to introductory courses in specific non-Western areas.

Teaching "The World Outside the West" began in the autumn of 1984-85 with funding from the Mellon Foundation and the National Endowment for the Humanities. From the outset, the faculty team, comprised of two anthropologists, three historians, and a political scientist, had to confront and resolve two critical intellectual problems. One was to see how the various parts of each of the cultures with which they dealt could be presented in such a fashion as to render these parts into an interrelated, coherent, and apprehensible whole. The second problem was to shape the issues of the course — for the peoples of China, Nigeria, and Mexico — into a common and shared discourse. Tackling the first problem required development of intra-cultural understanding; handling the second necessitated trans-cultural comparison.

The faculty involved were convinced that the best way to confront the basic epistemological difficulties of the course was to present an overall and unifying analytic framework which stressed how men and women in different cultural areas responded to common problems relating to human efforts to control both nature and cosmic forces, and how these efforts shaped the society, economy, and polity. Particularly in the first quarter, where these three cultures are studied prior to sustained contact with the "West," we wanted to portray these cultures as dynamic and changing, in order to avoid the stereotype of the "changeless" non-Western world. We paid special attention to the social, economic, political, and intellectual feedback between natural time and social time. Although we began with detailed discussions of physical and human geography, we spent considerable time examining the indigenous world view — the bodies of philosophical, social, and religious thought — in each of the three cultures. The course came to be structured around an examination of what, explicitly, these indigenous bodies of thought express and how they are linked to social, economic, and political organization and change.

The professors' pedagogic goals were to analyze, mediate, and compare these bodies of thought, and to specify how peoples use these bodies of thought to inform, shape, and construct their various cultures. Central to our comparative approach was that these very different cultures were alternative responses to problems all human societies seek to resolve.

This comparative concept — different responses to common problems — helped organize the syllabus, lectures, and reading assignments. The goal here was to get students to appreciate that the great diversity of human cultures reflects the enormous creativity of human beings in their responses to problems and opportunities. We expected that students would come to see that the Western tradition is just one possibility among many. As a result, students would come to adopt a more detached perspective on their own culture.

While none of the faculty agreed on a common definition of culture, there was general concurrence that culture should include the schemes of perception, conception, and social action shared by members of a society in their quest to relate to each other and to make sense out of the universe in which they live. The concept of culture emphasized in the course would include the "Great Traditions" of art, literature, religion, and philosophy, dealing with these not as eternal and immutable verities, but as part of the every day structures of life — including birth, rites of passage, marriage, and death. The course depicted culture as a fluid phenomenon, and solidly rejected the assumption usually made in connection with non-Western societies, that their cultures, once established, remain essentially unchanged thereafter.

Teachers presented both exogenous and endogenous views of the societies being studied in the course. Ethnographies, travelers' accounts, and similar documents imparted a sense of how these societies were viewed by outsiders, while views produced within the cultures themselves, entrenched, for example, in written or oral traditions, imparted a sense of how members of the societies perceived themselves. Faculty considered this emphasis on a dual perspective one of the main tasks of the course, for it would encourage students in the idea that any society can be regarded from a number of viewpoints and that social truth is relative. Regarding non-Western societies only in terms of Western concepts discourages appreciation of many of the cultural nuances essential to those societies and blinds one to their dynamism and creativity.

The faculty believed it imperative to stress in their teaching the immense variety of non-Western societies and cultural traditions. They wanted to sensitize students to the distortions of complex social realities which arise with the use of terms like "non-Western world" or "Third World," which are residual categories indicating not what various cultures are, but what they are not. Such terms not only suggest an unfounded degree of homogeneity in the world outside the West, they have also come to imply backwardness, poverty, and inscrutability. Placing emphasis on the heterogeneity of the non-Western world would indicate the falsification involved in indiscriminate use of such all-encompassing terms like "Third World" and would suggest further why the responses of non-Western peoples to Western intrusion have varied enormously from place to place.

"The World Outside the West" is a two-quarter sequence. The initial segment of the course deals with the societies of China, Mexico, and Nigeria before their enduring contact with an aggressive and interventionist West. The instructors' main objective during the opening quarter is to challenge stereotypical notions of presumably dormant and stagnant non-Western societies which became dynamic only after being energized through contact with the West. The lessons of this part of the course sequence are that many non-Western societies have traditions as complex, and in some cases lengthier, than those of the West and that there are no societies without their own sense of time.

For the instructors involved in the presentation of Chinese society and culture before extensive contact with the West, teaching focuses on some of the major elements which characterized the Chinese outlook, illustrating the ways in which a widely-shared, specifically Chinese world view was manifested in social, economic, and political arenas. Elements stressed include: the absence of a creation myth — that while the emergence of civilized, humane society may need explaining, the world itself simply is and cosmogony is not a serious issue; the view that the cosmos, the human/social realm, and the ordinary world around the Chinese are part of one holistic entity; the closely-related idea that this differentiated and hierarchical whole functions organically, so that conditions on one realm affect what happens in that of another; the emphasis in Chinese thought upon eclecticism, complementarity, and harmony rather than upon exclusivity, contradiction, and struggle; the predilection among Chinese not to divide what one thinks or knows from what one does — knowledge and action are but two sides of the same coin; and, the absence of a self-conscious science, which did not prevent the Chinese from developing a rich tradition of scientific and technological discovery.

Religion receives great emphasis in the examination of the central Mexican Aztec civilization. Teaching centers on the ways in which all aspects of what have been traditionally considered the religious aspects of culture — cosmology, pantheon, priesthood, ritualism, sacrifice, symbolism, sacred sites, architecture, pilgrimages, mythology, divination, magic, and theological and philosophical speculation — were elaborately developed and closely integrated with social and political organization, ethics, art aesthetics, literacy, and daily life. Partly through original documents, students are introduced to the central Mexican world view: they read Aztec philosophical poetry and confront the rudiments of the complicated and sophisticated Aztec calendar. The intimate interweaving of religion with daily life is important for understanding the Spanish conquest of Mexico, for the Aztecs regarded Cortes as a fulfillment of a prophecy which foretold the end of a political-cosmological cycle. Thus, the Aztec defeat cannot be comprehended without reference to Aztec religion and the interaction between Aztec and Spanish world views.

In regard to Nigeria, with the exception of the Islamic tradition to the north, the relatively small scale of most Nigerian societies hindered the development of a professional "intellectual" class. Lacking literacy, precolonial Nigerians did not bequeath to posterity a written corpus of philosophical traditions. The smallness of scale of many of the societies of Nigeria contributed to an intimacy of belief, analysis, and practice. Thus, it becomes extremely difficult, if not impossible, to separate religious thought from ethical behavior, philosophical traditions from political ideas. The Nigerians' complex cosmology, for example, demonstrates their understanding of causality and consequence. Problems of human survival demand a careful and continuous accounting to the spiritual world and the maintenance of balance within it. Examination of the Nigerian life cycle explores the closeness of the past, present, and future in the consciousness of Nigerians and in their religious thought. Throughout the Nigerian segment of the opening quarter, instruction hinges upon this critical sense of intimacy between thought and lived experience.

The second quarter of the course concentrates on the interaction of the three non-Western cultures/societies with the aggressive, curious, expansionist, and interventionist West. In keeping with the religious, philosophical, and cosmological themes of the opening quarter of the sequence, attention is directed toward the response of Christian Europeans (especially missionaries) to the religious ideas and values of the three societies and the responses of the peoples in these societies to the cosmology and ethical norms of the Christians in their midst. The course also addresses questions of how a society like China, with varying degrees of success, maintained its political independence in the face of Western pressure while at the same time it attempted to create new cultural syntheses between Western civilization and its own heritage. In its examination of the range of non-Western reactions to the West, the course reiterates its emphasis on the vast heterogeneity of the world outside the West. Discussion of the reactions of non-Western peoples to the West also reveals their deep ambivalence toward the West, an ambivalence which is one of the inescapable yet most important facts about the contemporary world.

The China portion of the second quarter addresses the issue of how Chinese social and religious thinking did or did not change in response to the intrusion of new modes and models of thought from the West. Lectures and readings cover the missionary movement in China and Chinese reaction to it, the confrontation of traditional ethical systems with rationalistic Western social theories, and the transformation of Marxism into a Maoist synthesis. In general, although the Chinese intelligentsia were exposed to Christianity, they found its message inadequate. They were more accepting of a wide variety of Western secular philosophies, materialist or positivist in character, ranging from Social Darwinism to Marxism-Leninism. Why there was a general embracing of Western secular thought forms one of the principal questions of the second quarter Chinese section. In seeking to find answers to this question, efforts are made to sensitize students to what is universal and what is parochial in Western thought.

The beginning of the second quarter Mexico segment discusses the conquest and colonization of Mexico in terms of the philosophical debates about human nature that the New World inspired in Spanish conquistadores and missionaries. The main subject of debate was whether, and if so to what degree, the indigenous peoples of the New World were fully human, having intellectual capabilities of a level sufficient enough for them to become completely Christian. The enslavers and exploiters argued that Indians, although descendants of Adam and Eve, had devolved to such an extent that they were in essence beasts. Protectors of the Indians argued that they were just like Adam and Eve immediately after expulsion from Paradise and that therefore Indians were ready for full-scale evangelization. From discussions of debates and policies in regard to the Indians, the segment concludes with an examination of the politics, policies, and challenges facing the various Mexican governments during the nineteenth and twentieth centuries.

Second quarter lectures and readings on the peoples of Nigeria concentrate on the quite different responses to Christianity among the followers of Islam and those adhering to "animist" beliefs. The argument presented in the segment is that the many similarities between Islam and Christianity, coupled with the long history of conflict between the two world religions, enabled Muslims to successfully resist the proselytizing efforts of Christian missionaries. The intense linkage of localized animist beliefs with the maintenance of a local small-scale political order, however, created special opportunities for Christian missionary efforts, particularly on the heels of European military conquest. The effects on small-scale Nigerian societies of the confrontation between Christianity and animism are graphically portrayed in Achebe's *Things Fall Apart*. Although rejection or acceptance of Christianity were the most potent alternatives available to Nigerians in their encounter with this aspect of Western intrusion, they were not the only ones. The segment examines instances of syncretic responses to Christianity, such as the Cherubim and Seraphim movement and the efforts of Nigerians to establish an independent Nigerian Christian Church. Studying these syncretic movements accentuates the creativity and dynamism of Nigerian societies in their reactions to the West.

"The World Outside the West" sequence was much neater and tidier on paper than it actually was in the classroom. China, Mexico, and Nigeria were very different cultures, with considerably different historiographical traditions. Moreover, neither Mexico nor Nigeria were recognized precolonial entities. This required that we redefine the units of study: for the first quarter, Mexico was essentially the valley of Mexico; for Nigeria, we had to balance two quite different narratives, one for the northern Muslim Hausa and the other for the acephalous Igbo of the southeast. While the teachers of China and Mexico presented more unitary views of their respective cultures and societies, teachers of Nigeria tried to present the range of diversity in what was to become Nigeria. The Hausa and the Igbo were chosen because they were the principal players in the Nigerian civil war of the late 1960s.

Part of the problem for both teachers and students was the unevenness in the presentations of these regions and in the quality of the literature available. Much more and much better introductory material was available for China and Mexico than for Nigeria. However, the novels and other readings (including Achebe's *Things Fall Apart* and the wonderful autobiography of a Hausa woman, *Baba of Karo*) more than favored the Nigerian side. The course therefore avoided the problems of "equivalences" by acknowledging to students the very different historiographical traditions in the three regions. But other forms of "equivalences" continued to plague the course.

Chronology was one such problem. Events occurred at very different times in each of these areas, as did the point of sustained contact with the West, which was to serve as the transition from the first to the second quarter. Although somewhat awkward for students, we agreed on what we call "conceptual" time, in which comparable events occurred. Thus, the establishment of the Aztec state could be compared to the Ming/Ch'ing transition in China, which was parallel to the consolidation of power by Muslim rulers in Hausaland. Similarly, the transition from the first to the second quarter also followed "conceptual" time, wherein the Spanish conquest of Mexico could be compared to the treaty port system in China and to the British abolition of the slave trade and the beginning of colonial conquest in Nigeria.

The most intractable problem we have faced in five years of teaching "The World Outside the West" has been that of recruiting faculty. This course is extremely labor intensive, involving three faculty for each of two quarters. Thus, finding two faculty for each of the three areas covered — or finding one prepared to teach both quarters — has been a daunting task. Central to the conceptualization of the course, however, was our expectation that the areas included would change over time, but that we would always try to have three different cultures. For the first two years, we included China, Mexico, and Nigeria. The next year, we switched from Mexico to Peru, but retained China and Nigeria. Given faculty leave patterns, we then returned to the original grouping, only to plan for another change for 1989-90 (i.e., Egypt, Japan, and Nigeria as the three cultures "outside the West").

Despite the administrative burdens of long-range planning and the substitution of new areas, these changes have kept the course material fresh. We have to rethink the issues each time we teach, and in the process, we also come a little closer to understanding better the diversity of cultures throughout the world and how to teach about them.

"The World Outside the West" is not designed to be a "world history" course. It is designed to expose students to ranges of diversity in three deeply studied parts of the world and to challenge them to think critically about these areas in relationship to one another and in relationship to the West. The course has a reputation among students as being extremely demanding, but also quite rewarding.

▼

Note

[1] In 1986-87, the Faculty Senate revised its Western culture requirement to reflect demographic and intellectual changes by mandating the inclusion of at least one non-European culture and reducing the significance of the "core"reading list. The collective name of the various tracks was changed to CIV — cultures, ideas, and values. These new courses were introduced first in the fall quarter, 1989-90.

Some Thoughts About the Stanford Course, "The World Outside the West"

Lanny Fields

IN THE PAST FEW DECADES, there has been a concerted effort by American universities to offer courses in non-Western history. This effort is part of a larger perspective made more pressing as a result of U.S. dominance in the world after 1945. The expansion of communism in Eurasia as well as the appearance of trouble spots in Africa, the Americas, and Asia infused this view with urgency. As more experts on non-Western societies appeared, the tendencies to see these areas as mere extensions of the West or as passive receptacles for Western actions or dominations began to be challenged. Yet many Western civilizations texts overemphasized Western societies and experiences and then merely offered a chapter or two on non-Western cultures. In recent years, however, new efforts to correct Eurocentric imbalances in university courses have surfaced.

At Stanford University in the 1980s, the faculty mandated that a variety of non-Western courses be taught. "The World Outside the West" is one of these courses and deserves serious consideration as a model for others.

"The World Outside the West" combines crucial elements needed to teach effectively general education courses: it is cross-culturally centered, interdisciplinary, and team taught.

1.   Cross-cultural courses have the potential to excite students because they examine different cultures and thus expose similarities in the ways problems are approached. Such revelations can affect students in a way comparable to the impact alien cultures had on early explorers. For example, I have noticed how intrigued students can become upon seeing how the Han Chinese and the Romans treated the "barbarians" who threatened their frontiers. Stimulating discussions have been sparked by this and other comparisons.

2.   Interdisciplinary approaches are valuable because they enable students to witness how different academic disciplines regard topics. An economist may stress quite different historical trends or factors than a sociologist or a teacher of literature. I, myself, gained a new appreciation of the Jain tradition of fasting until

death in order to attain an ultimate spiritual realization after I taught with a colleague who specialized in the philosophies of India.

   3.   Team teaching is especially rewarding. Faculty members must discuss (as the Stanford people did at length) a course's educational objectives, conceptual schemes, and analytic modes. Team teaching, of course, often exposes students to varied teaching styles: lecturing, Socratic discussion and discovery, the use of slides, films, or representative artifacts. It has been my experience that interactive teaching is especially rewarding in a team teaching format. In this approach, all faculty members are present at each session and may be expected to interject their perspectives about a given topic. In addition, some classes lend themselves to role playing by the instructors. Perhaps one may become a Japanese politician (Ito Hirobumi) while a second might play an Indian nationalist (Gandhi). These figures could discuss or debate issues as well as interact with students. Used selectively and with careful preparation, such techniques can bring history to life.

   The teachers of "The World Outside the West" also should be commended for interchanging different culture groups beyond Aztec Mexico, Nigeria, and China. This result enabled them to examine new approaches or themes. Replacing China with Japan, for example, might cause them to address the consequences of long-term military rule or the significance of foreign influences. This keeps the course fresh for the instructors, and more importantly, it offers them added and varied insights that inevitably broaden their horizons and improve their ability to teach the course ever more effectively.

   The Stanford team also addressed such problems as staffing difficulties. This is helpful to their peers at other universities who need to learn about the positive and negative aspects of these non-Western courses.

   Evaluation of students, a vital but thorny topic, should also have been considered. Did they employ essay examinations or multiple-choice tests? Were papers assigned? Did they have book quizzes or discussions? How large were the classes? Class size may be a significant determinant of the evaluation measure.

   My major reservation about "The World Outside the West" course is its Eurocentric bias. This is not to say that the Stanford group failed to grapple with the problem. They correctly note that "regarding non-Western societies only in terms of Western concepts discourages appreciation of many of the cultural nuances essential to those societies." I could not agree more, yet the structure of the course sequences themselves reveals Western-derived or baseline expectations.

   The structural orientation of the two-course sequence is Western. Certainly the Stanford team wants to reject stereotypical Western perspectives about these cultures; nevertheless the attempt to show change-driven peoples is clearly Western. Change, dynamic institutions, not to say notions of progress, imply Western orientations. What if a society does not change appreciably over time? What if it views itself as unchanging or stable? If these perspectives shape a culture's self-image, our duty as teachers is to understand them on their own terms, not as we would like them to be. The dynamic, transforming, progressive West seems to be looming in the intellectual background of such courses. Phrases like "absence of a creation myth" or "absence of a self-conscious science" appear in the explication of "The World Outside the West" course. "Absence" implies that the ideal culture must possess a creation myth or a self-conscious science. I begin my World Civilizations courses with a discussion of the biases that inform the study and teaching of such courses. One topic is the Eurocentric world view. We explore terminology (Far East, Middle East), for example, to learn how we in the West look at the world through cultural lenses. One needs to undergo a continual self analysis and a process of introspection along with one's students to rid the curriculum (as far as it is possible) of ideas and terminology that are European-derived. Such an effort, though imperfect, can help us understand the Jains or the Han Chinese on their own terms rather than through a biased viewpoint. Without this awareness and criticism, we are doomed to misunderstanding non-Western peoples.

The second "World Outside the West" sequence necessarily regards each society in the context of its interactive experiences with Western countries. While there is an attempt to examine internal cultural elements and their independent developments (especially with regard to China), the overwhelming thrust of the presentation is to see these cultures through Western prisms. A related and serious problem of this approach is the degree of Western uniformity. How similar or different are Portuguese merchants and British missionaries? Would it not be beneficial for students to examine what the West is? Are there many Wests? Such a discussion about what the "West" means would highlight some problems in teaching and learning when one operates at a dangerous level of generalization.

One interesting practice of the Stanford team is its use of missionary records. This might offer frameworks for comparisons and contrasts with reference to the Westerners and the Aztecs or the Chinese. One might examine the relationship between the political might and ideological mission work. The Chinese often tried to persuade their Muslim subjects about the benefits of Confucianism in a manner not unlike the French Catholics in Southern China. Still, the missionaries' records offer yet another Western framework for misunderstanding non-Western cultures. In this regard, perhaps an examination of the Mayans rather than the Aztecs might offer a less biased view of MesoAmerican society. Perspectives about the Aztecs have often been influenced by sources from Westerners who arrived in the New World after Columbus. Views of the Mayans, on the other hand, have been derived from archaeologists, anthropologists, and linguists who, we might safely presume, are less apt to be prejudiced about their subjects.

The teachers of "The World Outside the West" are sensitive to the problems inherent in offering a non-Western course. Some of these issues are perhaps unresolvable as Westerners learn about non-Westerners; yet it is essential to the learning process that we, students and teachers, seek to know peoples on their own terms rather than as Westerners or as non-Westerners. At least by discussing these concerns with our students we help sensitize them to the severe obstacles as well as to the sublime joys of learning about peoples other than themselves. And the pleasures of learning as seen on students' faces or heard in their voices when they ask questions can offer the teacher a lovely reward which may endure for a day, or perhaps a lifetime.

Teaching World History

William H. McNeill

(Reprinted in *Perspectives*, with the author's permission,
from *Charting a Course: Social Studies for the 21st Century*,
a report from the Curriculum Taskforce of the National Commission
on Social Studies in the Schools (1989).

WHAT CAN A TEACHER DO with the buzzing, blooming confusion that is world history? The problem is two-fold. On the one hand, the subject is infinite. On the other hand, considerable attention must be paid to the heritage of Western Civilization that shaped American institutions and made the country what it is. Mere confusion will inevitably result from an indiscriminate effort to deal with everything we know about the past; and if too little emphasis is placed on the world-transforming character of Western Civilization throughout the past 500 years, then our heritage from that truly remarkable epoch of world history will be inexcusably undervalued. As yet, there are no generally agreed upon models; historians have only recently begun to try to frame a coherent vision of the history of the world.

Yet the imperatives pointing toward a world history are obvious. In the first place, our country has become part of an intensely interactive world system that no longer revolves solely upon events in Europe, as was (or at least seemed to be) the case as recently as the 1930s. To deal effectively with Asians, Africans, Latin Americans and Europeans we need to know how the historical past has shaped their diverse outlooks upon the world. In the second place, migrants from Asia, Africa and Latin America have filled our classrooms with students whose ethnic and cultural background is not "Western." They need a past they can share with Americans of European descent; and equally, Americans of European descent need a past they can share with all their fellow citizens, including the indigenous Indian population that got here before anyone else. World history fits these needs, and only world history can hope to do so.

How then should the history of the human adventure on earth be presented in our classrooms? We need a clear and distinct idea about what matters most. Teachers might rely on a few simple rules of thumb:

1. Human power and wealth have increased through time because people strive for them. People are perpetually on the lookout for new skills or ideas that will increase

their wealth or power. Borrowing interesting new capabilities from strangers may upset existing relationships; it may arouse in some the desire to maintain local practices undefiled, and it may hurt some people while it benefits others. Still, the changeability of human history results from the modification of established ways of thinking and acting provoked most often by contacts with strangers.

2.   People are often unaware of the consequences and implications of particular actions or choices, so that human purposes are a very imperfect guide to what actually occurs. Side effects regularly distort purposes. Multiple causes are everywhere, and so are cross purposes. The open-endedness of human experience needs continual emphasis to counteract the tendency to treat whatever did happen as somehow foreordained.

3.   Students should try to make moral judgments about the past, but only after they have thought about the norms and expectations that prevailed among those being judged. Students need to know that human beings make sense of their lives by striving to conform to the norms of behavior that group membership imposes on them.

These rules of thumb about how to approach human history still do not answer the practical question of how to distribute classroom time among the infinite possibilities that world history offers. Two overarching goals should guide decision making.

First, students need to realize that they share the earth with people whose beliefs and actions are different from their own and arise from divergent cultural heritages. The way to make this clear is to define as fully and richly as possible the distinctive national traditions of the United States, and then to sample other cultural traditions, choosing for closer study those cultures of importance for global affairs in our time. Schools must therefore teach both the national history of the United States and the history of the rest of the world, paying special attention to the principal civilizations of Eurasia (including that of Western Europe) because they shaped the world views of the majority of human beings today. Africa, Latin America, North America as well as Eurasia came to share in the European heritage owing to the same processes of expansion that operated within Eurasia itself.

Second, students need to know that the various cultures and different civilizations that divide humanity are all part of a larger process of historical development whereby successful ideas and skills, wherever initiated, spread from people to people and culture to culture. Elaboration and diffusion of skills are as old as the emergence of humanity, whose distinctive trait is learning how to do things from others. Finds of obsidian and other scarce minerals in places remote from their origin show that Paleolithic hunters communicated across long distances. In subsequent ages, trading and raiding, missionary enterprise, and mere wandering linked communities. This means that the One World of our time is not new. The speed of communication and rapidity of reaction have increased enormously, but the process of innovation and diffusion of skills is age old.

Indeed that is what defines the pattern of world history as distinct from the pattern of more local histories, including the history of separate civilizations. Accordingly, world history ought to be more organized around major breakthroughs in communication that, step by step, intensified interactions within ever larger regions of the earth until instant global communications became the pervasive reality of our own time. By focusing on the pattern of interaction, and showing how borrowed skills and ideas always had to be adapted to fit local geographical and cultural environments, a simple and commonsensical pattern for world history emerges within which detailed study of any chosen time and place will fit smoothly.

The course of study should begin with a sampling of the culture of pre-literate societies. Hunters and gatherers and autonomous villages of food producers prevailed in the distant past. A few such societies survived into modern times, allowing anthropologists to study them with insight and sympathy. That insight can and should be communicated to students just because their lives are set in an utterly different sort of social environment. But this can only be preliminary. The major focus of attention must be upon the major civilization of Eurasia.

Studying European, Chinese, Indian, and Middle Eastern civilizations with sufficient sympathy to be able to present their ideas and institutions, so to speak, "from the inside" is a formidable task. But art and literature — the "classics" of each civilization — are available, and even small excerpts from such classics can convey something of the spirit and distinctive flavor of the civilization in question. Looking at the reproductions of great works of art and reading translations from the world's great literature invites students to react as individuals to the treasures of the human past. That experience ought to be part of every course in world history.

But random sampling of the world classics will only create confusion. Teachers can simplify without unduly distorting the reality of the four principal Eurasian cultural traditions by showing how each was built around a master institution, with a ruling idea to match. For ancient Greece, the territorial state was the ruling institution and the matching idea was natural law, applicable both to humans within the polis and to inanimate nature. For China, the extended family and the notion of decorum played a similar organizing role for the behavior of human beings and of the cosmos. For India, the ruling institution was caste and the organizing idea was transcendentalism, that is, the reality of the spiritual realm above and beyond the illusory world of sense. And for the Middle East, bureaucratic monarchy and monotheism played the same organizing roles.

Obviously, these four separate institutional-and-idea systems mingled through subsequent time. Thus, with the rise of the Roman empire and spread of Christianity, European civilization blended the Middle Eastern and part of the Indian with its Greek heritage. Similarly, China, Japan and the adjacent East Asian peoples borrowed a great deal of the Indian heritage when Buddhism spread to that part of the world. Middle Easterners combined the Greek heritage with their own after Alexander's conquests and borrowed Indian transcendentalism a few centuries later. India, likewise, toyed with Middle Eastern ideas of bureaucratic monarchy as early as the 3rd century B.C., and explored the full complexity of both Middle Eastern and European civilizations after 1000, when first Moslem and then European conquerors intruded upon Hindu society as a new ruling caste.

Since each of the major Eurasian civilizations took form long ago — before 400 B.C. in Western Eurasia and before 100 B.C. in East Asia — a course in world history must devote considerable emphasis to this classical, formative stage. But once a grasp of the enduring character of each civilization has been achieved, emphasis ought to shift to the processes of interaction across civilizational boundaries and the subsequent blending of what had begun as separate traditions.

Main landmarks of that process may be listed as follows:

1.   The rise of cities, writing and occupational specialization, centered initially in the Middle East. The impact of Middle Eastern skills and ideas extended all the way across Eurasia by 1500 B.C., when the Shang dynasty brought chariots and such characteristic ideas as the seven-day week to the valley of the Yellow River.

2.   The opening of regular caravan connections between China and Rome, and between the Middle East and India about 100 B.C. At about the same time, Mediterranean sailors discovered the monsoons of the Indian Ocean and began to participate in a much older sea-borne commercial network uniting the Indian Ocean with the South China Sea. The so-called Silk Road was the most famous overland route, but the caravan world extended north and south of the Silk Road proper, and in common with the navigation of the southern seas, created a slender Eurasian world market for luxury goods that could bear the cost of long distance transport.

3.   The development and spread of the so-called higher religions of Judaism, Buddhism, Christianity and Islam between about 500 B.C. and A.D. 630. These faiths provided a moral universe that countered the injustices and impersonality of urban bureaucratic and hierarchical society by inviting their followers to create communities of believers wherever they found themselves. This stabilized human relations within the expanding Eurasian civilizations, and, through conscious and deliberate missionary activity, attracted neighboring peoples into the widening and ever intensifying circles of interacting civilizations.

4.   The large scale domestication of camels after about A.D. 300. Caravans could now cross hot deserts, with the effect of bringing Arabia and West Africa into the interacting circles of civilizations. The Moslem Middle East became the principal center of the resulting system of trade and transport, and Moslem skills spread in every direction. In particular, Moslem merchants taught the rules of bazaar trading to the nomad world of the Eurasian steppe and also to the Chinese.

5.   Cheap and dependable water transport resulted from technical advances in shipbuilding and, equally important, from the extensive canalization of rivers, especially in China. The horizon point of this development came about A.D. 1000

when long distance trade ceased to be confined to luxuries, and began to alter everyday life for ordinary people because goods of common consumption could now bear the cost of transport across hundreds and even thousands of miles. In many ways, this represents the dawn of the modern age, as much or more than the familiar date of 1500. China was the principal center of the resulting intensification of exchanges and, like the Moslems before them, the Chinese swiftly developed skills superior to the rest of the world.

6.   The establishment of the political unity throughout much of Eurasia by the Mongols in the thirteenth century. This was the principal medium for the diffusion of Chinese skills westward, for as the career of Marco Polo illustrates, the Mongol peace allowed literally thousands of people to move back and forth between China and the rest of the Eurasian world. Chinese skills therefore spread westward — notably gunpowder, printing and the compass, three key technological elements in Europe's subsequent assumption of world leadership.

7.   The familiar opening of the oceans by the Europeans just before and after 1500. European merchants established trading posts on the coasts and islands of the Indian Ocean and played an increasingly active part in the trade and politics of the southern seas and East and West Africa thereafter. In addition, the Americas entered abruptly into the circle of Eurasian interactions, exposing the Amerindians to repeated disease disasters and allowing Europeans to establish thriving colonies in the new World. (From this point onward, the history of the United States becomes part of world history and ought to be treated as such. Some separate treatment of United States history is needed; but world history ought not to omit our national past. Instead, world history courses should put the national past in perspective).

8.   The tapping of mechanical power for industrial production and then for transport and communication, beginning in a dramatic way, about 1750. From this time onward, the three fold structure suggested in our ideal curriculum becomes a practicable guide for directing attention toward the most important traits of the modern age: 1) the democratic revolution in government, 2) the industrial revolution in economics, and 3) the demographic upsurge.

In studying this increasingly far ranging and intensive interaction, the way each step prepared the way for the next, is worth emphasizing. But as always, history is not a simple success story. Costs must be counted as well as gains. The loss of autonomy for local peoples and cultures that resulted from the arrival of powerful strangers in their midst was always the price of admission to the interacting circle of sophisticated skills and exchanges. Exposure to new and lethal infectious diseases was another cost of the civilizing process. Each expansion of the range of communications put new populations at risk, and the resulting die-off from the sudden onset of smallpox and other diseases regularly weakened local peoples and sometimes crippled or even destroyed them. The case of the American Indians is the most dramatic example, but Australians, Polynesians, and peoples of the Siberian forests suffered parallel disease disasters in modern times; and catastrophic disease encounters in earlier ages — the Black Death and the Antonine plagues — are also worth attention.

World history built along these lines can prepare students to live in the interactive world of the twenty-first century more serenely and wisely than would otherwise be possible for them. It would also give appropriate weight and attention to the primacy of Western civilization in the last five hundred years.

Study of world history with the help of simple ideas like these can be an intellectually uplifting experience; it is also an essential preparation for citizenship. World history is therefore very much worth doing, and worth doing well. It belongs with the national history of our country at the core of K-12 social studies.

Teaching the United States in World History

Peter N. Stearns

THE DILEMMA IS OBVIOUS, visible in most history texts and in all but the most experimental curricula: the past is divided into two parts, the United States and whatever else in the world is studied historically or, more simply and obviously, US and THEM. We can modestly rejoice of course, that there is often something beyond the national horizon, as against some teaching traditions that pay little attention to anything save the glories of one's own country and its antecedents (a narrowness true in some school systems here as well). The fact remains that the characteristic split, between purely United States courses and a world or something-else course, not only leaves bridges unbuilt but fosters in many students a truly unfortunate tendency toward historical isolationism, as the complexities and troubles of most of the world's history seem oddly unrelated to the glorious saga of our own ascent.

Students do absorb from school and from the general culture a number of myths and half-truths about America's uniqueness and its separation from most larger world processes. They can discuss these in some detail, despite their ignorance about all sorts of United States history specifics and despite considerable cynicism and intelligence in other respects. It is perpetually amazing to me how many good college freshmen know for certain that the United States has historically offered unparalleled mobility opportunities, unprecedented openness to change and progress, and unique altruism in foreign affairs (this last with specific subsets such as the fact that we "gave" the industrial revolution to Japan after World War II, a hardy perennial in my world history courses until I took firmer steps to hammer home the Meiji era).

The fact that beliefs of this sort are oversimple, verging on outright incorrect, in situating the United States in a larger world and comparative framework, suggests a serious task for world historians in helping students locate what they know or think they know about their own national past in a more general history. For students' beliefs affect not only their perceptions of the United States, but a tendency to downgrade other societies because of an implicit impulse to measure these societies against an unrealistically demanding standard. It is probably true, as

Leften Stavrianos has argued, that the United States has been unusually lucky in its past, compared to other societies, though even this cannot apply to all key groups in American history, but it has obviously not exceeded world norms so blithely as many students — including students who do very well in world history per se — continue to believe.

The task of addressing these issues, of finding ways to integrate the United States to some degree into world history courses, is at least as formidable as it is compelling. World history courses almost by definition have too much to do already. At the same time the habit of assuming that students "get" their United States history in repetitious abundance, and certainly in separate courses in school and college, remains deeply ingrained. It has been undeniably convenient to let the twain not meet, given the traditions of history teaching and the burdens on those of us who foolhardily present the whole rest of the world in a semester or two. Yet the result has been to leave the task of connecting — or more commonly, of failing to connect — to students themselves. This is a conceptually demanding job, when a world history framework is juxtaposed to a usually rigorously national context presented additionally in a separate course taken in a different year. The task is complicated further, as I have suggested, by the biases many students bring to it. The result, in my firm belief, is a need to do more to provide some suggestive guidance to the process of integration, so that students do not emerge with prejudices unchallenged or simply with the sense that God decreed two different histories, one ours and one theirs.

Having said this, admittedly a fairly obvious point save for our curricular traditions, I have no magic formulas that will make the resulting integration easier. I do have some ideas that may stimulate other suggestions and actual curricular experiments, plus further knowledge of experiments already undertaken. The goal, certainly, should be clear: the need to deal with what seems to me a significant challenge in history teaching now that a world framework is increasingly envisaged.

The challenge does not add up to a need to handle a great deal of narrative detail about American history in the world history course. There is no time, and hopefully, given the possibility of cross-referencing to previous work at least in a college-level course, some limits to the necessity. The desirability of sketching key themes in the United States' past, however, and tying them into the world history framework may seem still more difficult than simply designating a few weeks' chunk to American details. It is this approach, however, that I wish particularly to address, not again with complete plans but with some thoughts on how to proceed.

The first distinction is chronological: the issue of handling American history before the 1870s differs markedly from that afterwards. While the North American colonies and the new United States were not without some economic, demographic, and symbolic significance in the wider world before 1870, these points of contact can be fairly quickly evoked and are readily outstripped by the impact of most other inhabited areas including Latin America. After about 1870 this situation changes, among other things as a result of the growing world-scale operations of American agriculture and key corporations such as the Singer sewing machine company. The familiar world political role, becoming visible by the 1890s, followed close on the heels of these earlier contacts and ushered in the overt world power impact with which we still live today, for better or worse. For a world history course that pays serious attention to the later nineteenth and twentieth centuries, then, the claim of United States history for a treatment in detail comparable to that lavished on other major societies, qualified only by a hope of greater student knowledge, is considerable. The suggestion is, then, for a chronological shifting of gears between very broad-brush treatment from the seventeenth to the later nineteenth century, and more meticulous integration over the past 100 years, based on a change in world significance that can be explicitly presented and justified to a world history class.

While detail is not required, for world history purposes, the first long period of United States-in-the-wider-world history should not be entirely neglected. It does help illustrate some themes in world history from the seventeenth century onward, as will be suggested below. It is essential as the basis for understanding later United States patterns when world significance cannot be gainsaid. Just as some sketch, albeit brief, must be offered for Russia before 1480, or Japan before and during civilization's initial advent, not for their own sake so much as in order to set some themes that persist into later periods when the societies occupy a more visible place on a world stage, so a formative United States period — if a long one — should not be entirely ignored. And this is all the more important in that student awareness and some common misconceptions begin to apply to this period, making it essential to establish some links to wider themes even before United States inclusion becomes imperative in world terms outright.

Given inherent lack of time and the need not to exaggerate American themes while paying them some heed, the first three centuries of what became United States history must obviously be inserted in a careful analytical framework, not rehearsed in a narrative for its own sake; and this analytical framework is most logically comparative. Some ingredients of North American history may of course have been developed in discussions of Amerindian societies and the European voyages of discovery; I do not mean that focus on 1600 and after has no preparation. In this treatment, however, the principle contributions of a world history framework are, first, to help students see how landmarks of what became United States history fit into larger world trends in this timespan and, second, to located major features of this history in a comparative context.

The world history course provides an opportunity to ask students — and most of them have never really been presented with questions — what aspects of emerging United States history are truly distinctive, in a comparative framework, and whether indeed the United States was building toward becoming a "civilization" in its own right. Of course the debate about American exceptionalism needs to be framed with care, lest it escape the proper time limitations of a world history course and take on undue significance. In a course, though, that builds on a civilizational approach to some degree, and has already established the importance of careful comparison as one means of gaining intelligibility and managing data, these basic questions about early United States history follow logically. They also allow, again if only briefly, some treatment of certain of the common student misconceptions. I spend at least one session, and it is usually a lively one, talking about the American exceptionalist argument particularly as it applies before 1900. I want students to know in capsule form the latest findings about comparative mobility patterns, which indicate that American mobility culture differed from that of other frontier or early-industrial societies considerably more than the reality of mobility differed, and what this all means about the way we conceive of the United States' past in larger comparative terms. I want them to remember that key distinctive ingredients of the United States' past, such as the importance and some unusual characteristics of slavery, do not fit easily into the most conventional God-bless-America comparative framework.

And for my purposes, in a short and highly thematic world history course, I want students to see that for the most part the United States can be grasped as an extension of Western civilization. This is not, I admit to them, an incontestable choice. American exceptionalism has some valid as well as exaggerated bases in fact, even if established on carefully comparative ground rather than — as is the wont of most Americanists themselves — merely asserted. Students should acknowledge some ingredients here, as in racial and frontier issues (including proclivity to violence and relatively weak government controls), or religious and family patterns that began to take shape as early as the seventeenth century. It might be desirable, where time permits, to develop a larger civilizational category that would embrace the United States, Canada, Australia, and New Zealand, admitting close connections to Western civilization but emphasizing distinguishing experiences not all of which, however, were those of the United States alone.

But I try to defend the extension of Western civilization hypothesis, arguing indeed that there are fewer problems integrating United States history into modern Western history than there are in treating Japan as part of a Chinese-inspired East Asian civilization, a comparative civilizations problem with which my course has grappled earlier. (Indeed, an essay assignment on precisely this topic has worked rather well.) Arguments about shared cultural origins — due reminders offered about non-Western groups in the developing North American population — here blend with the startling degree of chronological parallelism around such trends as the late eighteenth/nineteenth century demographic transition; the industrial revolution; new sexual behaviors and Victorianism; more democratic politics (though here with the vital caveat that the United States was unusual, and has seen unusual results, in establishing majority male universal suffrage prior to industrialization rather than afterwards, in contrast to most other Western countries).

The exact degree of United States participation in modern Western trends, and key qualifications such as the existence of slavery and its racial aftermath or the unusual persistence of religious belief in the nineteenth and twentieth centuries, must obviously be discussed and treated as interpretive problems rather than a set of tidy historical findings; but its analytical advantages, as well as the issues left dangling, can be indicated in a fairly brief discussion. The claim of shared Western-ness can be further discussed from the vantagepoint of more clearly different societies in the same period of time, including in many respects Latin America, from whose angle of vision the United States as a frontier outpost of the West would seem if anything more obvious than it does to most of us and our students.

With early United States history sketched comparatively, and its civilizational position — or lack of fully separate position — established, it is then possible to show United States participation in key world historical trends in the same three-century span. The simplest aspects involve showing United States inclusion in general Western evolution, through the industrial revolution, the growing fasci-nation with science, and participation in political upheaval. There are, however, crosscutting currents that among other things bring early United States history into different comparative contexts without vitiating (necessarily at least) the basic Western-ness argument.

The place of the North American colonies in Wallerstein's world economy is a case in point that allows contact with some familiar facts about colonial economic dependence. North America was in some sense a peripheral economy, though outside the South a less important and therefore less closely regulated one than Latin America at the same time. Relatively weak government and coercive labor systems established in the seventeenth and eighteenth centuries certainly follow from peripheral status as Wallerstein defines it, and this can in turn (where time permits) serve as framework for more extended comparison of slave systems both in this world economy and in relation to slavery in earlier societies. It is obviously true that to the extent the North American colonies were peripheral, they managed to pull out of this status, into industrialization, unusually rapidly. This may occasion a bit of student boosterism, but it can be explained, while the lingering effects of peripheralism, in the South-North relationship or in the ongoing United States indebtedness through 1914, should also be noted.

A second crosscutting trend context, again shared with Latin America and, later, with many twentieth-century societies, involves new nation status. While students will readily see that the United States avoided some new nations problems that beset Latin America slightly later, they can also see some classic new nations issues in, for example, the Civil War. Furthermore, some ongoing effects of new nations experience, suitably glossed with an exaggerated version of the Western ideology of liberal individualism, showed in the persistent weakness of the American state. Here is a striking United States departure from Western norms until at least the 1930s, and again an interesting similarity to Latin American patterns. I have found the theme increasingly useful as a followup to the civilizational comparison, not because it is more important than the world economy determination but because it is more complex. It jolts students more, and usefully. American government weakness, while not a total surprise given anti-statist ideology, deserves some careful statement as against dominant Western trends and despite the tendency of conventional United States history courses to treat the state as central actor from the revolution onward. Rates of crime and vigilantism, compared to Western trends, form one useful illustration. While American political characteristics did touch base with Western (particularly British) political ideology, they also deserve assessment in the light of new nations theory and the concurrent experience of new governments in Latin America.

It is important, obviously, not to chop up the United States patterns into too many discrete fragments. Indication of basic civilizational characteristics, however, can allow crosscutting participation in certain other world patterns where the United States position differed, at least initially, from that of the Western leaders. This in turn amplifies other comparative possibilities and simultaneously shows how world patterns really apply to our own society and not simply to more remote corners of the world where the absence of full historical free will is less surprising and (to most American students) less important, less jarring. The same process, of diverse comparison and insertion in larger world trends and relationships, helps students make United States historical data, new or previously acquired, coherent and assessable in world-historical terms. And, in broad outline at least, depending on student capacity and the level of detail which time permits, it can be sketched fairly economically, precisely because it calls on skills and concepts already utilized in other segments of the world course.

Elements of the same approach obviously can continue in the amplified treatment that becomes desirable from the 1870s onward. The comparative context must be retained. As the United States matured as an industrial society, and as Western Europe shed further vestiges of traditional structures that had never taken root in North America, from peasant agriculture to monarchical government, convergence in key features of the main segments of Western society became a leading theme. Some — though by no means all — of the qualifications necessary in the earlier period, in inserting the United States as part of a large Western civilization, now declined in salience. Indeed, from the 1920s onward the United States took a leadership role in defining many key features of the Western version of advanced industrial society, particularly in the realm of consumerism and popular culture. While political differences remained (indeed widened, in comparing the United States and Britain) during the twentieth century, the "new nation" limitations on American government waned somewhat and reduced the distinction in state functions.

Obviously, world economy analysis remains useful, as the United States moved more firmly into core status along with the rest of the West (and ultimately Japan).

The principle new theme to handle is of course the United States' ascension to superpower status. This evolution, familiar enough in many ways, can organize this

second of the chronological segments devoted to the United States-world interaction, centered of course on the twentieth century rather than the early-modern,
industrial decades. Quite apart from the narrative material to adduce — world war
roles, emergence from isolation, postwar diplomacy, the rise of multinational
corporations — the theme builds on the world economy approach, in linking the
more recent articulations of core status to the changing world power balance of
which the United States has been a major beneficiary. There is a link too, though
a more complex one, to the expanded Western civilization theme set earlier: to
what extent did the United States, in gaining new military and diplomatic power,
pick up distinctively Western interests and approaches? Tensions between United
States-Western affiliations and the actual geography of the United States usefully
inform a number of diplomatic trends in the twentieth century and shape some
questions about world politics (Pacific vs. Atlantic foci) in the near future.
Assessing the United States as a Western imperialist newcomer, though a distinctive
one because of twentieth-century world power realities and the revolutionary
heritage of the United States itself, is another useful application of earlier
comparative efforts to the new world power balance. American diplomatic mor-
alism, plus certain racist themes, obviously evoke Western impulses that were only
slightly more blatant a century ago.

At the same time, the United States' world power rise complicates earlier
comparisons in important respects. The United States has become, since 1945,
more militarized and diplomatically conservative just as much as the West has
become somewhat less so. Here, trends are at work which muddy the convergence
theme. And superpower status also invites a comparison with the Soviet Union in
attributes and goals beneath rhetoric; this comparison, like the new nations
analysis in the previous period, may highlight complexities in the United States-
as-Western model without necessarily overturning it.

The invitation, then, is to an adapted comparative approach that will build
upon the obvious shift in power position over the past century while utilizing the
comparative themes sketched a bit earlier in the world history course. This
approach allows some extensive narrative passages where time permits. It provides
students some opportunity to deal with major changes (including growing
attachment to more conservative international interests — from Yankee Doodle
to Great Satan in less than ten generations). It also establishes continuities with
earlier features of United States society, such as the close relationship to larger
Western patterns including now the movement toward a service economy and
new immigration streams. It yields, finally, a chance to discuss United States world
impact in something more than random fashion, by using themes from the world
economy, the new superpower concept and attendant comparison, and assessment
of relationships with earlier Western imperialist impulses seen not simply as
thrusts toward political or economic domination but also as assertions of cultural
hegemony.

Much is not covered in the scheme outlined here, given the emphasis on analytical frameworks rather than staples of the United States history game. There are surely many alternatives to the schema itself, in the whole or in part. Some instructors would doubtless find too much comparative complexity hard to handle for their student clientele and would prefer to limit the vantage points. What I do think can be widely urged, apart from some of the specifics already outlined, boils down to three main points. The first is that the United States should be discussed in the world history course for several good reasons. The second point is that this discussion can be manageable by using comparison, by dividing treatment into two basic chronological segments very simple to define in terms of world power roles, and by hooking into leading world history themes such as the unfolding of basic international economic relationships. The third point is that a variety of frameworks exist by which the inclusion of the United States can fit analytical goals and not involve an occasional, somewhat random narrative stroll through episodes. Frameworks exist, in other words, that can encompass discussion of United States history within other course goals. Furthermore, these frameworks can apply to the United States a rule that I believe must be fundamental in a world history course: societies worth discussing at all must not be simply popped in and out sporadically, but given enough character that major actions, such as diplomatic initiatives, can be interpreted in terms of causation and evaluated in terms of change and continuity in light of past trajectories. The frameworks applied to the United States may be evoked only briefly, for want of time, but a sketch at least is possible, so that students can begin to think of American history as part of a world pattern, in which some of the issues they discern in other societies can be carried over.

There is, then, a need to rethink the United States-world history relationship; the need can be manageably met, though various emphases are possible; and manageability can and should include coherence, not in terms of masses of detail but in terms of one or more analytical frameworks consistently applied.

Four final points must be made beyond these basic assertions. First, any new experiments with greater attention to the United States in world history should assume a certain amount of student obduracy. Beliefs about American separateness — a large if informal adherence to the exceptionalist school — die hard (and of course in some cases, carefully stated, they can be defended). It is easy to be disappointed about how much students can separate one framework of analysis from older habits that will crop up when a new topic or problem is addressed. Without pushing any particular conceptual agenda, it is worth noting that some points about reconceptualizing American history need to be hammered dramatically, if only to open a more questioning outlook.

Second, while good lectures and class discussions are possible around some of the points discussed above, it is obvious that some provocative reading matter that puts the United States into one or more comparative contexts would be a tremendous boon. World history books don't do this, because of their normally unanalytical approach and their particular uncertainty when it comes to United States history. Americanists tend to discourage the approach because of their normally blithe unawareness of comparative issues and possibilities (slavery and maybe why-no-socialism excepted). Some attention to relevant, and suitably brief, teaching materials would be timely, certainly feasible, and potentially a real advance in structuring history curricula.

Third, the task of relating United States and world history should be a two-way street. Without changing all their habits, Americanists should become more alert to the possibility of linking what they teach about to what students have learned or will learn in world history. This means some attention, from the more strictly United States perspective, to comparative issues and larger world trends; it means picking up systematically not only on changes in world power roles but also the impact of international influences on American life. Too much has been written of late about the problems of world history in diverting students from the values of their own society, without dealing with the total history package to which more students are exposed not only in college but in schools. While world historians can take up some responsibility for helping students to see how "our" history fits the world framework, the interchange must be mutual, as Americanists take fuller cognizance of what world history is about and how it bears on what they teach. The compartmentalization that students learn too well in history, which a world history course must attack to some degree, reflects lack of sequenced curricular relationships and, often, a real compartmentalization among historians. World historians must and can learn that their bailiwick is not "everything except the United States." American history teachers can correspondingly learn that one of their themes must be a positioning of United States development amid larger trends.

This leads to the final point, which can return us to the larger world history thrust. Until American history instructors convert to greater utilization of an international and comparative framework, world history teachers may justly fear that inclusion of United States topics will divert from their basic commitment to provide cultural breadth to a stubbornly parochial student body. Some students may indeed rivet on the United States entry into world affairs over the past century, as if this alone provided coherence in a global hodgepodge. This can be guarded against by restricting allocations of class time to reasonable proportions, and by the careful comparisons and application of larger themes already recommended. Focused discussion of the exceptional features of the United States position in the 1950s and 1960s, and the subsequent relative decline explained through a combination of American and world developments, can be a timely corrective. So can some exploration of views of the United States held by other societies, and how these link both to larger cultural diversities and to American behaviors.

Students need not emerge from a sensible presentation with a belief that the United States has become the pivot of world history, though it remains desirable if comparable attention to international influences and constraints, applied to coverage of the twentieth century in United States courses enhances this message. While risks exist of some lack of proportion, then they can be addressed. The current system, encouraging assumptions about United States-world connections to go almost entirely unexamined, is riskier still. Quite apart from its implications for properly balanced perspective on our own society, it misses opportunities for challenging analysis where students need it most, in seeing the relationships between "their" environment and the past and the wider world to which, happily, history teachers are increasingly trying to expose them.

Freedom in World History: Can Parachutists and Truffle Hunters Find Happiness Together?

Alan Wood

LET ME BEGIN BY giving an affirmative answer to the Question posed in the title of this essay — parachutists and truffle-hunters can find perfect happiness together, although at the moment they are not talking to each other, at least not in a language the other can understand. Parachutists, of course, are generalists, who take a broad view of matters, and truffle- hunters are specialists, who have an accurate understanding of very specific subjects. Their marriage, a once-blissful union which gave birth to many of the great teachers and scholars of the past, is now on the rocks. Ever since modern colleges and universities chopped up knowledge into bite size chunks known as departments, an academic aristocracy composed primarily of truffle-hunters has come to dominate higher education.

When H.G. Wells — an early parachutist — published his *Outline of History* in 1920, he complained that the study of history had become too partial and narrow, and that the volume of specialized research had become too much for one mind to absorb.

He could not have imagined then that the little mounds of monographs which dotted the academic landscape in his lifetime would grow by the end of the century to become vast and impassible mountain ranges, severing communication between disciplines of knowledge (and even between the sub-disciplines of history) and fostering the proliferation of mutually unintelligible dialects.

Faced with such daunting obstacles, the prospect of doing world history well, either in a classroom or between the covers of a book, would appear to be growing dimmer with each passing year. On the other hand, as our knowledge continues to fracture, the need for such a unifying device may be even greater. The fact that our microscopes can now peer at smaller and smaller objects on an elephant's hide does not mean we can forget about the whole elephant. One perspective is not better or worse than the other, simply different. In the same vein, if you want to find out how to get from Rockefeller Center to the New York Public Library, you look at a map of New York. If you want to find out how to get from Boston to

Bombay, however, you look at a map of the world. In the modern research university, unfortunately, there is no academic equivalent of a map of the world.

Let me try to put my own views on world history in the larger context of the profession as a whole. We live in a world dominated by science. The purpose of science is to investigate the behavior of objects in the natural world in order to predict and ultimately to control that behavior for the benefit of society. During and after the Enlightenment it was hoped that the "scientific method" might also be used to understand and improve the behavior of human beings. The social sciences were born. To be sure, Enlightenment thinkers got a little carried away when they anticipated that human nature could someday be perfected. But one does not have to believe in human perfectibility to hope that human suffering can be ameliorated through understanding more thoroughly the social and psychological forces which act upon us. To that noble purpose the social sciences committed energies.

There is one area that science does not treat, however, and that is meaning. If a scientist were to ask what the meaning of gravity is he would doubtless be retired early. Meaning is taken to be a matter best left to philosophers, whom nobody reads anyhow, at least in the United States (so said de Tocqueville, and little has changed since).

The academic study of history has understandably mirrored the assumptions of the larger society. In the United States, historical study came to be modeled on the nineteenth-century German institution of the graduate research seminar, which encouraged scholars to focus on a very small subject. The final product of the scholarly enterprise became the monograph, dealing with a single subject and limited in time and area. The bureaucratic imperatives of the modern academy have further narrowed that scope. All bureaucracies share certain characteristics. Among the least beneficial is a propensity to measure success in terms of quantity rather than quality, the former being more tangible and easily defensible if questioned, and more readily accepted as equitable and fair, than the latter, which is unquestionably messy and difficult to measure objectively. Since one can produce quantity more quickly by focusing on narrow subjects, the pressure to do so is irresistible. Those who are best at it rise to the top, from which lofty heights they survey the wreckage, pronounce it wonderful, and do everything in their power to ensure that the system which so wisely recognized their worth is supported to the end of time. The result is that the modern university stresses analysis at the expense of synthesis. The only time historians ever talk about synthesis is when they give the presidential address at the annual meeting of the AHA, after which the members of the audience, and the president, deploy back to their analytical foxholes. (I read through all the presidential addresses one summer. I highly recommend the experience, which I found to be inspiring.)

The intellectual energy of the university is produced by fission, not fusion, and the forces released by that energy are centrifugal, not centripetal. Robert Hutchins was not far off when he described the modern university as a collection of separate departments unified by a central heating system.

In any case, the ultimate object of a social science is to discover underlying patterns and laws of human behavior. Most of the views of world history which have appeared in the twentieth century have this same purpose: the organic metaphor of Spengler, the challenge/response paradigm of Toynbee, the Marxist view and its current permutation in the form of dependency theory, cultural diffusion, the various forms of modernization theory, applications of sociological or anthropological paradigms to the study of world history. I do not wish to deny the validity of any of these approaches. On the contrary, I have the highest regard for the insights which they have given us. Coleridge is supposed to have remarked once that men are usually right in what they affirm and wrong in what they deny, and in that spirit let me stress that my primary criticism of professional monographs is not that they are narrow — they have to be — but that there is no place for anything other than the monograph. To put it another way, historians are right in affirming the value of analysis, and wrong in denying the value of synthesis. My quarrel with specialists is not that they do not like generalists, but that they shoot them on sight.

Intellectual breakthroughs, after all, are the product of the synthesizing impulse. The analytical process is best suited for verifying or refuting insights originally arrived at through the free play of the imagination. Insofar as our institutions of higher learning discourage synthesis they threaten to dry up the springs of intellectual life in this country (or divert them into think tanks). The old cliché that the world is divided into problems and universities are divided into departments (with very little connection between the two) may have some truth to it after all.

My own particular approach does not pretend to have discovered a new pattern of human behavior, but is organized around a universal problem in the manner of a Greek play. The world history I have in mind is indebted to Greek tragedy, and to Thucydides. History is, among other things, a great drama, in which the human race is the protagonist who is endowed with prodigious gifts, who has free will, who encounters forces over which he has no control, as well as forces over which he does have control, who makes a serious error in judgment based upon a fundamental flaw in his own make-up, and who then suffers terribly — far more than he deserves — as a result. The suffering, as in *Oedipus Rex* (and *Oedipus at Colonus*), may be re-demptive, but that does not wash away the simple fact that the innocent are made to suffer along with the guilty. Thucydides carried out this basic plan, in which Athens — wonderful Athens, free and cosmopolitan, the fountain of democracy and philosophy — came to a grievous end because its citizens were corrupted by disease (over which they had no control) and power (over which they did have control) and brought about their own destruction as a result.

In Genesis, the temptation advanced by the reptile in the Garden of Eden was for Adam and Eve to become like God by eating of the fruit of the tree of knowledge of good and evil. As the inhabitants of paradise freely chose that fruit, so has the human race aspired to become like God through its mastery of the forces of nature, approaching ever closer to the divine prerogative to destroy all forms of life on earth, on the one hand, and to create life, on the other hand.

My focus is on freedom, tracing the development of the human race in all its cultural variety from very early times to the present, showing how free will and human genius have combined to increase man's control over the forces of nature but always with the tragic imperative at work. That control, from the domestication of fire on to the harnessing of nuclear energy, is available for good and for evil, for ameliorating suffering and for magnifying. The two go hand in glove.

Lord Acton, one of the most influential historians of the nineteenth century, was always on the point of beginning work on a universal history which he never quite got around to. Toward the end of his life his friends took to referring to the project as the greatest book never written. Instead, Acton acted as editor of the *Cambridge Modern History* — not too shabby an accomplishment, to be sure, but a work of specialists nonetheless. Had he written his own world history, I suspect he would have organized it around freedom, which he virtually identified with progress and human perfectibility. We ought to pick up where Acton left off (although not necessarily with his faith in the malleability of human nature — the intervening decades have, alas, rather tarnished those optimistic expectations).

My approach is to divide the activities of the human race into six categories: politics, economy, society, philosophy/religion, aesthetics (art, literature) and science/technology. In each of these areas, it seems to me, the notion of freedom can act as a kind of clothesline on which to hang the otherwise diverse expressions of human genius. The economic problem, for example, is how to gain greater control over the productive forces (and thereby expand the range of choice), and how to distribute their fruits equitably.

The political realm is more obviously one of increasing or decreasing freedoms. Incidentally it is here that many of my own colleagues in non-Western studies have often criticized my clothesline, saying that by focusing on freedom I am guilty of imposing my Western cultural assumptions on societies which do not have such values. I hope that the events in China in June, 1989, have put that argument to rest forever. One must make a clear distinction between the impulse to freedom, which I believe to be universal, and the existence or development of enabling institutions, which may vary a good deal from society to society and from time to time. That the Chinese have the desire, and not the enabling institutions, is now — courtesy of CNN — clear to all the world.

Freedom itself, of course, is not to be understood only in its negative forms as an absence of restraint, but also in its positive form as the opportunity to bring to fruition something which had previously existed in a potential state. In this sense, the outward expression of man's creative genius in art and literature, the deepened understanding of meaning which has developed as human religious and philosophical systems have grown, are all a part of this underlying system.

What I offer is an organizing principle for the study of world history which is based upon a fundamental pattern or law of behavior. This is clearly an understanding of history which departs from the professional assumption that history is a science, and only a science, focusing solely on the advancement of knowledge. Insofar as my view emphasizes meaning as well as knowledge, I suppose that what I offer is closer to art than science, but I stress again that my approach is not intended to be a substitute for the conventional way of organizing history but a complement.

The great French historian and sociologist of Chinese religion, Marcel Granet, who died shortly after the fall of France in 1940, is supposed to have declared to his class once (presumably *before* he died, though with some French intellectuals you can't be too sure): "I don't give a damn about China. What interests me is man." I suspect that if Granet were a recent PhD looking for a teaching job in the United States, with an attitude like that he would probably end up selling pencils on the street corner. If Granet meant what I think he meant, however, we could use a few more like him around now.

We know more about the world than we did, but we do not know the meaning of what we know, and it is that very meaning which is so urgently required. The problems brought about by rapid technological changes, by the struggles between religions and between a multitude of ideological surrogates for religion, by over-population, by environmental pollution, and by proliferating nuclear weapons, far transcend in their destructive potential those which confronted individual civilizations in the past. In the face of these circumstances, historians — who have a special responsibility for educating the public in their civic responsibilities — should address themselves, however peripherally, to these urgent questions, with a view to forging out of the diverse national traditions of the world a greater sense of common purpose. Only when the world realizes the degree to which each civilization manifests qualities and experiences common to all civilizations, only when it understands the ways in which the different forms of civilized experience give expression to a common impulse to order and meaning in life, will we be in a position to confront our problems with a reasonable prospect of success. The perspective gained from a study of world history is vital to this enterprise.

If such a pragmatic motive in the writing of history is criticized as imposing an unnatural burden of didactic morality on the interpretation of the facts, then I can only respond that facts, alas, do not always speak for themselves, and perhaps more interpretation would shorten the unnecessarily large gap between a public desperately in need of wisdom, and the historian in need of a public. In the words of Louis Gottschalk (in another presidential address), "let [the historian] also pray for the courage combined with the humility necessary to employ his historical training and insight as well as he can for the guidance of an unmoored society seeking firmer anchorage" (*American Historical Review*, 59 [January 1959], p. 286). We are all of us dependent, in one way or another, on the fortunes of the world around us. We must not allow that link, which binds the objects of our study to the need of the larger community for a clear statement of means and ends, to be permanently severed. Paul Gagnon's recently released report on high school textbooks in American history makes a strong plea for just this kind of approach to the teaching of history: "It takes a sense of the tragic and the comic to make a citizen of good judgment, as it does a bone-deep understanding of how hard it is to preserve civilization or to better human life, and of how it has nonetheless been done, more than once in the past. It takes a sense of paradox, not to be surprised when failure teaches us more than victory does, or when we slip from triumph to folly. And maybe most of all it takes a practiced eye for the beauty of work well done, in daily human acts of nurture" (*Democracy's Half-Told Story: What American History Textbooks Should Add* [Washington, D.C.: American Federation of Teachers, 1989], p. 157).

Here I seek only to remind the interested reader of the importance of a universal perspective in history, and to suggest that we should no more abandon the study of world history because of its inherent difficulties than we should cease trying to become better because we cannot become perfect. Recall for a moment Chesterton's marvelous remark (which should be carved in stone and hung around the necks of all academic perfectionists), that if something is worth doing, it is worth doing badly.

Most history departments in the major research universities in the United States devote very little if any attention to the subject of world history. Faculty members whose prospects for tenure and promotion are related to the number of publications they produce in their field of expertise are naturally reluctant to pursue a subject which might slow down the progress of their own careers. Added to this is their understandable hesitation to indulge in generalizations about areas of the world which lie outside the scope of their own academic preparation, and which would expose them to professional criticism by specialists in those areas. These obstacles cannot be dismissed lightly, nor do I know of any easy way by which they might be removed, and yet they do not diminish our responsibility to broaden and deepen the nature of the questions which we ask of the historical record. We now have within our grasp, because of the great contributions of the social sciences in the last two centuries in widening our knowledge of the past, the tools to undertake this great task; what we seem to lack is the vision and the will. We need, in short, more airborne truffle-hunters.

Chapter XI:

Social History

Social History and the Introductory European Course

Carolyn C. Lougee

THE COMMON INVOLVEMENT of college and secondary school teachers in introductory courses, exemplified by the Advanced Placement Program (AP), has become a source of strength in history curricula. AP courses in the schools offer students superior preparation for university-level learning and open to them higher levels of achievement in historical work.

Yet the success of such cooperative ventures depends upon effective communication between university and secondary school faculties: upon professors' familiarity with the capacities of students entering the university and upon secondary school teachers' familiarity with the research trends that continuously reshape college-level courses. What follows is an attempt to promote the latter, offered by a Europeanist who has taught the introductory survey for more than a decade at Stanford University and has recently been involved in test development for the Advanced Placement Program of The College Board and the Educational Testing Service. It reviews certain shifts in historical thinking that over the past two decades or so have changed the direction of historical research, reflects upon the reasons why these have not yet revolutionized the teaching of introductory European survey courses, and suggests some realistic aspirations for beginning to reshape those courses.

In the past twenty years, the ground has shifted massively under the European survey. As always, changing *interpretations* have revised our understanding of various portions of the past: for example, the recent ecumenical view of Luther as a Catholic saint in advance of his time, or the emphasis on the irrational in the so-called "Age of Reason." On a deeper level, however, certain inversions in historical philosophy have changed the very terms in which history itself and "historical thinking" are understood. The legacy of what are called the ' new social historians" in England and America and of the *Annales* school in France has turned upside down the conception of history that Tocqueville and Ranke honed and that for a century underlay the paradigm of European history on which European survey courses have been based.

Traditionally, the introductory European survey has been deeply rooted in a triangle of state, event, and analysis of causation. The traditional European survey has assumed with Sir John Robert Seeley that "history is past politics," with Thomas Hardy that "war makes rattling good history, but peace is poor reading," and with Thomas Carlyle that "the history of the world is but the biography of great men." Its framework has traced the succession of great public events (national elections, wars, civil strife, revolution), large-scale public transformations (the Renaissance, the Enlightenment, the Industrial Revolution); its actors have been the great figures in public politics, in public economic life, and in culture understood as the public world of art and ideas. Powerful social groups have been considered important; subordinate groups have been included only insofar as they interacted with elites.

Succinctly stated, the inversions of the past two decades have overturned the trio of state, event, and causation: elevating society over state, duration over event, and cohesion over causation. Looking first at state and society, the political and diplomatic history which has been the core of the traditional survey is in a sense an artifact of the nineteenth century, a time-specific feature of the nineteenth century, for this political history was defined and codified during the heyday of European nation-states and modern inter-state diplomatic systems. History as then defined fed upon the documents made available by the state and, more than this, served to legitimize the state by celebrating as historically significant the individuals and events within the public reality that the state itself recognized.

Since the Second World War, however, partly because of the experience of world war and partly because the flowering of social sciences greatly enhanced understanding of how human societies operate independent of state policy and in ways to which politics are irrelevant, European intellectuals (including historians) turned from a focus on state to a focus on society. Once subtracting the Leviathan from center stage of the past, these historians did not find a Hobbesean state of nature; they found, rather, community: a local or regional, private, spontaneous, self-regulating force that was even more important than the state in determining the direction of human affairs. And so turning from state to society, they came to focus on the common many rather than on the elite few, on the private reality rather than on the public, on the group rather than on the individual. As Lucien Febvre, founder of the Annales, said: history seeks "the collective historical person." "Jamais l'homme: les hommes [Never man, but men]." And we might update Febvre by saying "les hommes et les femmes [men and women]."

The second inversion raised the duration above the event. From the Annales in particular came the notion that change in human life across time takes place at different paces in different areas of life. In politics change can occur rapidly in an event; in economics change usually occurs at a moderate pace, often in generation-long trends; in mentality (the bases of thinking) change occurs much more slowly, "at a glacial pace," taking many generations or even many centuries for mental change to ripen. So the historian has to look at paces of change, at durations; above all, the historian has to avert his or her vision from the succession of events that traditionally had defined the framework of history just as he or she looks away from the state: the event, like the state, is simply not of capital importance. In the words of the late Fernand Braudel: "the event is explosive, it is something new. It blinds the eyes of contemporaries with clouds of smoke; but it does not endure, and its flame is hardly visible." "One is too accustomed in history to latch especially onto splendid, resounding, and ephemeral aspects of human activity, great events or great men … most facts labelled historical are to the true human history as waves that rise on the surface of the sea, colored for an instant by all fires of the light are to the deep and constant movement of the tides." The historian needs to plunge into the depths of the tides of human history, beneath the seductive but misleading event. [Braudel's seminal article on the durations of change, "History and the Social Sciences," has been reprinted in Peter Burke, ed., *Economy and Society in Early Modern Europe; Essays from Annales* (New York: Harper and Row, 1972), pp. 11-42.]

The third inversion might be called cohesion over causation. Whereas historical study had traditionally sought to identify chains of causation in human history (what were the causes of the First World War or of some other event of state), this new definition of history largely eschews the search for causation as inevitably oversimplifying the complex past. Conceiving human society as more analogous to a biological phenomenon than to a mechanical one, its goal is to find the *rapports*, the reciprocal relations within a society; not, for example, to ask why a particular population thought in a particular way, but rather to ask what social structure or economic organization coexisted with and thus corresponded to that way of thinking. Asking why a people think a certain way is an impossible task; but if one can identify the *Zusammenhang* [interconnection] of the various aspects of life, it is possible thereby to identify the character of a society.

Society, duration, and cohesion, then, are the assumptions that underlie the work that has excited historical circles during the past two decades and which has profoundly reshaped investigations into the European past. These are the assumptions underlying Fernand Braudel's *Mediterranean*, Le Roy Ladurie's *Montaillou*, Theodore Zeldin's *France*, Philippe Aries' *Centuries of Childhood* and *The Hour of Our Death*, and Natalie Zemon Davis' essays and *The Return of Martin Guerre*. These are the assumptions that underlie advocacy of social history and the importance attached to recovering the history of women and minorities. Social history, then, is more than a supplement to our knowledge of past politics, and the aspiration for "gender balancing" is not merely an artifact of present politics. Both are, rather, integral components in a novel vision of the way human societies work, an understanding that transcends and replaces state, event, and causation.

But if these inversions have reinvigorated historical research, they have also to some extent confounded and confused the introductory course. They have created a disjuncture between research directions, which have largely been running in these channels, and pedagogical practice, which has been slow to adopt social history, especially in the introductory course. In my experience, the abilities and familiarities of students to some extent militate against the reshaping of the introductory European course according to these inversions. By the time they reach college, students typically have firmly entrenched in their minds the notion that history is past politics; analysis of social development through time may strike them as interesting, but they do not think that it is history. (Here, by the way, is another inversion: the young more wedded to the traditional than their elders.)

Furthermore, abandoning the strict chronology provided by successive events often makes students uncomfortable. History by durations may seem "spongy," vague, and sprawling to their unpracticed eyes. For example, *Centuries of Childhood,* which ranges broadly in tracing mental change that occurred at a glacial pace, can bewilder students who cannot be sure from page to page precisely which century Aries is talking about. Whether because their previous training has been more narrow or because their cognitive abilities have not yet reached full development, beginning college students frequently have difficulty grasping *rapports* and multiple causations, which are far more complex than the succession of milestone events.

Finally, students are often put off by the numbers in quantitative approaches to analyzing entire societies. Students do not expect numbers in a history classroom and often are loathe to accept them. This reaction may be less pronounced at the secondary school level than in college, where greater self-selections have already taken place and the numerically inclined are less apt to take history courses at all than are those who prefer words to numbers. If so, secondary school history courses have a special role to play in accustoming students to social history.

Beyond the abilities and familiarities of students lies another kind of constraint on the adoption of this inversion of history, a very recent renewal of emphasis on the political that directly counters European historians' motivations for turning away from the state in the first place. In this country in recent months one certainly senses a renewing interest in the civic (interest in American patriotism) and also a renewing emphasis on history as civic education, as teaching with a civic purpose.

This same trend is discernible in Europe as well, at least in France. The Mitterand government has announced plans to return public school history to the traditional paradigm because the new history was not fulfilling its civic purpose. The new history was telling students much about food supplies and the experience of gender or ethnic groups but not much about what it means to be French. This governmental decision has challenged French intellectuals, who had turned to society and away from state precisely because two world wars on their own soil had led them to see the state as a divisive force that fragments humankind into artificial units of political loyalty. Their shift from state to society set out to use history less to consolidate nation-state identities than to unite peoples by emphasizing the universals of human experience (birth, love, subsistence, community culture) that men and women confront in all times and places.

In view of the changes in understanding wrought by social historians in the past twenty years and the persisting obstacles to teaching history in that way, what can or should up-to-date introductory European history courses consist of? This new history is much more comprehensive than the old; it has greatly expanded the past, but the school year has not expanded commensurately. So the teacher asks in bewilderment: "Who has time to include those new materials? I have too much else to cover." Or the teacher cries: "How can I include all that is now recognized as part of the European past and still have a manageable, coherent story?" The temptation to stick with the easily manageable will always be strong. Darwin's publisher, thinking his unprecedented ambitions had made his manuscript unwieldy, advised Darwin to confine the book to his pigeon data alone, since "everybody is interested in pigeons." As Darwin's example demonstrates, comprehensiveness makes for significance, the easily manageable is the easily dismissed.

The key to making a more comprehensive history manageable has to lie in judicious, even sometimes ruthless, selection. In order to construct a coherent story from the vastly expanded materials of European history, it will be necessary to lay aside much of the information that supplied the backbone of the old paradigm. [Two textbooks that endeavor to incorporate new understandings of social history are John P. McKay, et al., *A History of Western Society* (Boston, Houghton Mifflin) and Mortimer Chambers, et al., *The Western Experience* (New York, Knopf). Six models for introductory history courses appears in Kevin Reilly, ed., *Proceedings of the AHA Annapolis Conference* (Washington, 1984), which can be purchased for $6 from the AHA (400 A Street, S.E., Washington, D.C., 20003). Curriculum materials entitled *Restoring Women to History: Materials for Western Civilization*. prepared by Elizabeth Fox-Genevese and Susan Mosher Strard, can be purchased for $16 from the Organization of American Historians (112 N. Bryan Street, Bloomington, IN 47401)].

The analysis of society cannot simply be grafted onto the story of past politics; it cannot be inserted in the empty spaces in political history surveys, even if such empty spaces could be found. In order to do justice to the new historical totality, one will have to apply a revised conception, revised principles of selection. And though the new social historians have not offered a fully-articulated pedagogical blueprint, they have suggested three principles of selection: society, duration, and cohesion.

In principle at least, and practice has often borne this out, once past the initial blocks in the students' understanding, the more comprehensive history of the social historians has an appeal that is stronger and more universal than the appeal of the traditional paradigm, for it relates to every person's experience as the old did not. Few of our students will ever wield political power, formulate or articulate state policy, or create great ideas. But everyone is born, everyone thus becomes part of a community, everyone lives in a household or institution, marries or remains single, has children or not, migrates or stays put, and eventually dies; that is, everyone participates in and makes the patterns of private experience that the new history looks to. So the new history at one and the same time makes historical actors of us all and allows us to extend our personal acquaintances beyond the pitifully narrow chronological range of our own lives. Surely, few would be able to resist the appeal of a brand of history that does that.

Teaching Social History: An Update

Peter N. Stearns

DURING THE PAST DECADE a number of history educators have discussed the reasons for including social history approaches and findings in mainstream history teaching, and also the various mechanisms by which this can be done. The subject was compelling because of social history's surge on the discipline's research agenda. Currently more than one third of all research historians in the United States add the "social" label, and there is little question that the bulk of the most innovative and widely-noted research in the past twenty years has fallen in this category. (Think back, for example, to how little was known or taught about slavery in U.S. history surveys just a generation ago.) The subject was also compelling because social history added both a list of new topics to the understanding of the past — from demographic behavior to basic leisure forms — and a sense of excitement that more conventional staples were often missing. Finally, it was compelling because it posed some obvious challenges: 1) Social history topics did not fit neatly into the established agenda—how, for example, can one combine an analysis of the rise of soccer with a narrative of late-nineteenth-century British politics? 2) Many social historians borrowed methods and concepts, ranging from quantification through sociology to — most recently — anthropology, that were different from standard descriptive political or intellectual history. 3) And finally, social historians, quite apart from their topic choice, had a style and focus that were distinctive: they examined trends and processes as their empirical core, rather than events and individual personalities.

In sum, teaching social history meant a good bit of new learning. It meant deciding what familiar topics to curtail in favor of wider coverage, and figuring out how to juxtapose event-based chronology, such as the series of wars, reigns, or presidencies that form the backbone of traditional textbook history, with shifts in processes, such as the advent of a new birth or death rate pattern, where hundreds of thousands of separate events — decisions about children, sex, and health — accumulated over a decade or more into a new demographic framework. Clearly, teaching social history in the classroom was not easy.

Yet there were also some obvious reasons to make the attempt. The field was vibrant. It produced undeniable new knowledge which could add to students' factual fund and also stimulate historically-informed thinking about a host of topics significant in their own lives and society, such as the nature of adolescence and its emergence as a discrete life-phase in the nineteenth century. Social history provided potential links with other social sciences, though the interdisciplinary promise was sometimes more rhetorical than real. In dealing with topics such as the family, social history might incorporate components of a larger social studies curriculum with students benefiting from improved integration. Finally, social history topics might bring a wider range of students into the field of history than the staple diet of politics and high culture by themselves achieved. Serious study into the history of key groups such as women, workers, and Afro-Americans spurred the new research and also could engage various sectors of the student population. New topics, such as leisure or family, might similarly draw some students into a serious discussion of the problems of change and continuity because of their immediacy in contemporary life. For a host of reasons, then, the urge to deal seriously with social history as a teaching area has remained strong despite undeniable practical and conceptual problems.

As a result, social history has been frequently defined and justified, and its major subfields outlined as subjects for classroom use. College Board recommendations have urged serious attention to the field as prerequisite for successful college work. The National Council for the Social Studies has issued a number of valuable how-to pamphlets, as have numerous other organizations. (Matthew Downey, *Teaching American History: New Directions*. Washington, 1982; College Entrance Examination Board, *Academic Preparation in Social Studies*. New York, 1986; Linda W. Rosenzweig, ed., "Teaching About Social History." *Social Education* 48 [1982]; James B. Gardner and Rollie Adams, eds., *Ordinary People and Everyday Life*. Nashville, 1983.) After a slight lag when focus riveted on research strategies, social historians themselves began producing textbooks and supplementary materials, particularly, but not exclusively, at the college level. (As examples, see Gary B. Nash, Julie R. Jeffrey et al., *The American People: Creating a Nation and a Society*. New York, 1986; Constance Bouchard and Peter N. Stearns, *Life and Society in the West*. 2 vols. San Diego, 1987; and at the high school level, Linda W. Rosenzweig and Peter N. Stearns, *Themes in Modern Social History*. Pittsburgh, 1985.) Workshops, along with revisions in college curricula, helped spread the word to many innovative teachers both old and young. Any discussion of social history in teaching by now proceeds along a well-trodden path.

Indeed, given the coverage, why return to the subject of social history teaching? There are three reasons. First, suggestions for altering some time-tested teaching strategies take time to sink in, perhaps particularly in a discipline that many practitioners fancy precisely because it seems familiar — the intellectual equivalent of well-scuffed slippers. Second, a recent surge of counter-attacks continues to require comment. Third, and most important, significant bases for synthesis, developed in social history as a research field, offer new promise for historical teaching in settings that require some means of linking the novelty of social history to the staples of political and intellectual coverage.

A social history update, skimming over the now-familiar groundwork, is timely in several senses. It allows response to some recent distractions and distortions in a number of educational policy statements, and it uses this criticism to improve the articulation of social history's teaching purpose. It permits a clear acknowledgment of important maturation in thinking about the field and its relationship with other history teaching goals. An evaluation of social history teaching today cannot and need not be confined to the valid but often slightly abstract sketches offered a decade ago; gratifyingly, there is progress to report.

Reconsidering the Standard Menu

An update report must begin, however, on a more prosaic note: a comment on the lags and disjunctures in introducing social history to the teaching repertoire. Development has been real, but uneven, and some initial efforts at simplification proved misleading.

There is no question that the teaching of social history has advanced far more rapidly in college curricula than in secondary schools. While this disparity was initially unsurprising, given social history's research-driven impulse, it has become counter-productive. Among other things, we are failing to introduce students to history's real range when their attitudes toward the discipline are being formed. A host of imaginative high school teachers have, to be sure, pressed forward into at least some aspects of social history, not only in survey courses, but in social studies offerings where the interdisciplinary potential can be tapped. Some social history staples have even entered more widely; units on slavery and immigrants have important social history content. But for all the achievements, the hesitations are even more striking. Teachers of high-prestige offerings, including Advanced Placement United States history (despite serious College Board encouragement to the contrary) and, even more frequently, Western civilization courses often perversely insist on strictly political and high-culture definitions. They add college-level, but highly dated, readings to testify to their advanced level rather than catch up with the field. Consequently, survey textbooks and their publishers remain timid.

Furthermore, in courses and texts alike, some initially understandable transitions have not been adequately rethought, despite their limitations. Some school curricula, responding to well-intentioned guidelines, define their social history curriculum in terms of almost every conceivable American ethnic group to demonstrate that all the ingredients of the melting pot have a significant past. The proposition is correct but at the teaching level unwieldy, producing unnecessary, and highly vulnerable, incoherence. Larger themes, such as particularly significant or exemplary groupings, or integrative categories such as a comparison of the histories of "new" and "old" immigrants and their receptions, can and must be found.

Another approach, still more frustrating, is the addition of an occasional social history snippet to an otherwise conventional survey. In texts the snippet approach shows an occasional "this is how they lived" insert, or tacked-on segments on such subjects as women in colonial society. In actual courses, the same filler approach shows the odd day devoted to a social history topic, with no coherence or system applied. Students, of course, readily perceive the change in tone, often correctly assuming social history is intended as light relief and that they will not be tested. Here too, the experience of teaching social history suggests some corrective guidelines: deal with social history topics with a seriousness equal to other coverage; return to topics in each key time period so that the family, for example, can be seen in terms of changes and continuities over time, rather than as an institution evoked haphazardly; provide some opportunity to discuss the relationship between social history topics and other developments; show how family change results from new political or economic forms or affects these forms in turn.

Social history teaching at other educational levels has moved forward more rapidly. As a means of introducing young students to the past, social history topics have long been a primary school staple, and one recent report urges an enhancement at the concentration at this level (Bradley Commission on History in Schools. *Building a History Curriculum*. Westlake, OH, 1988). Social history courses, and subfield topical courses on family, work, women, and a host of other subjects, dot college curricula, usually paralleling more conventional national history or period offerings, but in some cases increasingly upstaging them. Even here, however, curriculum problems have by no means entirely been resolved. Much of the task of pulling the past together is left to students themselves as social historians merrily spin off one topical course after another, not even stopping to talk about what ties their field together in terms of central causal forces or periodization, and conventional courses, including many surveys, introduce serious social history analysis warily if at all. The past, at the college level, is much richer than it once was, and the return of students to history courses in new numbers in recent years reflects the excitement. But opportunities to discuss coherence or interrelationships are, too often, few and far between.

In fact, at both high school and college levels, two satisfactory, well-tested, integrative approaches are now possible, and simply require wider awareness and utilization. In a high school or collegiate freshman survey course, or in a larger college-level history curriculum, social history topics and analytical styles (with their focus on trends and processes) can be carefully and systematically alternated with narrative coverage, providing opportunities to discuss interrelationships and interpretive problems in each major period. Or the processes approach can be applied to political and intellectual history as well as the social residue, so that students are introduced to major changes in governments' forms and functions just as they are to new patterns of work, major shifts in demographic balance, or changing beliefs about children. Periodization, in this second and more ambitious rendering, involves discussion of what kinds of change take a leading role — allowing the possibility that at some points the state holds center stage but at others, less overtly political beliefs and behaviors are more significant. (Realistic teaching strategy options are explored in Bernard R. Gifford, ed., *History in the Schools: What Shall We Teach?* New York, 1988.)

A social history teaching update can, in sum, note the obvious: there has been more routine-mindedness in the teaching of history, and more token or incoherent experiments in embracing bits of social history, than seems either necessary or justifiable. It can also note serious teaching strides and some frameworks, available in the better college-level texts and in courses at several levels, that provide a systematic presentation of major sociohistorical patterns and illustrate their connection to the more standard historical fare. It remains necessary to exhort, lest the teaching of history lag needlessly behind available historical knowledge and insight, but it is also possible to cite significant improvements in experience and pedagogical conceptualization. Models exist to guide more and more teaching programs past the toe-wetting stage. (See Downey, *Teaching American History*; Rosenzweig, ed., "Teaching About Social History; " Peter N. Stearns, "Social History and the American History Course: Whats, Whys and Hows," in Gifford, ed., *History in the Schools*.)

Counter-Countering

But is the need to rethink still valid? Have we perhaps gone too far? The second facet of the social history teaching update must recognize a recent mood of counter-attack, as teachers held back by a sense of routine are joined by powerful voices urging that conventionality is precisely what we need and should return to. Critics such as Gertrude Himmelfarb argue that social history distracts students from the lessons of rational policy actors, whose example can teach the validity of reasoned political action. A host of pundits urge that history education should consist of a series of factual staples, mainly Western and derived from politics and high culture alone, otherwise, the educational process has failed. Reports point out contemporary students' abysmal ignorance of political institutions and the salient features of the constitution, geography, and other time-tested subjects. (Though, interestingly, they fail to venture any historical comparisons, such as the familiar examples of World War II inductees who were not exactly paragons of political knowledge themselves, even though uncorrupted by social history.) The implication is that social history is one of a series of faddish innovations that have fatally distracted students from the past's right stuff. Reaganite federal agencies, spearheaded by the National Endowment for the Humanities, have taken up the charge, withdrawing earlier support from social history educational projects in favor of an emphasis on great texts and other monuments of our uniquely privileged past (Gertrude Himmelfarb, *The New History and the Old*, Cambridge, MA, 1987; Allan Bloom, *The Closing of the American Mind*. New York, 1986.)

Amid this barrage, and having admitted that social history gained less than consistent ground as a teaching subject even before the assault, can there be any response?

The answer is a ringing, though carefully phrased, affirmative. The attack on social history has three prongs and, though they are linked in the minds of some critics, they must be disassociated. The first is purely political. Conservatives do not like social history's emphasis on the common man or on any derogation from a consensus political past. They must have a right to their views, but dissent is easy even by political moderates. Social historians have argued for rationality, though on the part of ordinary people, for example in protest action or family decisions, and not just in the behavior of a chosen elite. History education should be designed primarily to teach students a certain analytical and factual perspective, not a single set of values including some convenient political myths. Social history contributes to this analytical process, while embracing no single political perspective of its own. Reaganites may wish students to ponder Plato and believe our institutions are jointly sanctified by the ancient Greeks and by God, and they may manipulate educational money to this end, but they can be contested.

The second prong to the critical attack involves an assumption that new historical knowledge cannot be combined with necessary elements of more conventional fare and so history education must be defined in terms of the latter alone. Again, it seems to me easy to disagree. History is not simply the study of new topics like crime patterns and sexuality, but it is not simply a list of presidential administrations either. To fix the historical canon in a single list of facts is to deny the contribution of history to the store of knowledge about how humans and human societies function — thereby ultimately limiting and sterilizing the discipline's teaching appeal. The list of necessary facts from the past has changed, and should continue to change, and while the result may indeed downgrade some of the less significant conventional staples, it does not therefore lead to educational deterioration.

Himmelfarb's criticism, among other things, singled out a statement of mine urging that students must know the history of menarche along with that of monarchy. Obviously I was trying to be amusing in linking the two terms, but I would still defend the fundamental thought. A historical understanding of basic demographic shifts is arguably as important as grasping changes in monarchical styles — not more, but as, important. The past has more varied corners, and hence more varied uses, than some recent critics even remotely glimpse.

This leaves the final prong, which social historians must indeed attend to and not simply refute: students do not know enough about history of any sort, old or new. It is unquestionably dismaying to find a substantial ignorance of geographical and historical basics in entering college students (or even worse, in departing students) otherwise bright. History teachers, social or otherwise, have an obligation to try to repair the worst omissions, and this without any doubt means devoting serious attention to some items besides the staples of a social history diet. But an extension of this undeniable problem into a statement that social history should be dismissed as an unwarranted distraction is incorrect.

Student ignorance is not, empirically, the result of large doses of social history teaching in the schools, since, in the main, these doses have yet to be administered. A fairly conventional regimen of largely political history continues to prevail, and if it is not doing the job, then other remedies must be sought. Attention to some serious social history in school curricula will distract students from some details of conventional coverage; there is no denying that some choices must be made. But it need not, and should not, detract from adequate coverage of essential features of political history. To the extent social history can liven a history classroom and improve analytical skills, it might even facilitate coverage of the basics. But the main point is that with social history the basics have changed, not completely, but in part, and require a different definition of what students should know and different criteria for lamentations about ignorance.

There is a problem here, in other words, consisting of inadequate student knowledge of conventional essentials but also newer historical essentials. The problem must be addressed by better and more rigorous teaching at many levels. It should not, however, excuse teachers from attending to social history curriculum components. It should not obfuscate the extent to which educational conservatives are attempting to maintain or reconvert history teaching not to an exploration of the past, but to politically-useful mythmaking; an agenda that should be modified by teaching a good historically-critical sense — that social history can help provide.

The New Coherences

This brings us to the third, and most positive, element of the update on social history teaching. Educators, including social historians, who have worried about including social history components in teaching at various levels have long and correctly cited two related issues: the centrifugal tendencies of social history itself, as it splinters into hosts of difficult-to-relate subtopics, and the barriers to contacts with most conventional history raised by the proliferation of new topics and enhanced, for a time, by social historians who proudly proclaimed their independence from political subject matter. While issues of synthesis and integration have by no means been entirely resolved, approaches are under elaboration that move forward in exciting ways.

One advance consists quite simply of asking historians, in presenting any large view of the past, to define what "big changes" were occurring in any major time period. This approach was first put forward by Charles Tilly, who defined the big changes in modern Western history in a particular way, but it can be appropriated by others whose range of definitions might differ. (For a convenient introduction to the Tilly approach and other integrating essays, see Olivier Zunz, ed., *Reliving the Past: The Worlds of Social History*. Chapel Hill, NC, 1985.) The point is not to claim a single interpretive formula — which pre-social history never provided either — but a basis for a coherent line of argument that pulls together older history coverage, in its essentials, and newer social history topics alike.

Take, for example, the emergence of a new, propertyless proletariat in Western Europe in the sixteenth and seventeenth centuries. This emergence obviously altered social structure and redefined issues of social mobility. It helps explain new patterns of crime and political response, including the rise of the prison. It called, in other words, for new state functions. It contributed to new attitudes about poverty and to major cultural eruptions such as witchcraft persecutions. It obviously affected the nature of economic activity and work, and even began to play a role in redefining family life. Here is, furthermore, a phenomenon that would undergo important elaboration over time, allowing a periodization into the later twentieth century that does not lose sight of a central basic phenomenon; and it would extend geographically, affecting United States history, for example, increasingly from the late eighteenth century onward with some effects similar to those that had already emerged in Western Europe (Pieter Spierenburg, *The Spectacle of Suffering. Executions and the Evolution of Repression; From a Preindustrial Metropolis to the European Experience.* Cambridge, 1984; Pieter Spierenburg, "From Amsterdam to Auburn: An Explanation for the Rise of the Prison in Seventeenth-Century Holland and Nineteenth-Century America." *Journal of Social History* 20 [1987]: 439-62; John R. Gillis, *For Better or Worse: British Marriages, 1600 to the Present.* New York, 1985). Proletarianization does not unlock every modern historical door, but it links a number of apparently disparate developments and cuts across sociohistorical and conventional historical domains. It contributes to greater manageability in a sociohistorically-sensitive curriculum.

In addition to the big changes approach, of which the rise of a proletariat is only one example, two new interest areas have been developing, in teaching and research alike, that have similar integrating qualities. They are indeed compatible with a "big changes" line of inquiry, but merit separate consideration.

The first involves the growing interest in the history of mentalities, defined in terms of intensely-held beliefs and attitudes (as opposed to casual or fickle opinions) on the part of large groups of people. (For basic approaches to mentalities, James A. Henretta, "Social History as Lived and Written." *American Historical Review* 84 [1979]: 1239-1322; Richard Brown and Sanford Lyman, eds., *Structure, Consciousness and History.* Cambridge, 1978; Patrick Hutton, "The History of Mentalities: The New Map of Cultural History." *History and Theory* 20, no. 3 [1981]: 237-59.) Mentalities history meets key sociohistorical tests: it applies to ordinary people, though also to the elite; it accommodates new topics (such as the study of emotional change); it deals with values about many facets of social life — family, self, sexuality, leisure — and not simply about the state or Newtonian laws. But mentalities history is not simply another in a long list of topical innovations. It pulls together disparate strands. It forces the historian to deal with relationships between ideas about family and, say, ideas about physical nature — to look for basic elements. And it forces the historian also to deal with large swathes of conventional history. When popular beliefs change, as was the case in Western society in the late seventeenth and early eighteenth centuries, what relationship does this change have to formal intellectual activity covered by such terms as Scientific Revolution and Enlightenment? (The answer, not surprisingly, turns out to be reciprocal: new beliefs helped spur formal intellectual change at the creative summit, but were further affected by new elite ideas.) Mentalities history, in other words, pulls serious intellectual history into a new and more meaningful context, while doing careful justice to its essentials. Finally, despite the undeniable bias toward cultural causation, mentalities history must also consider political and economic changes as sources of new popular beliefs. Growing commercialism and the expansion of state functions turn out to feed early modern mentalities transformations, along with new science. (Keith Thomas, *Religion and the Decline of Magic*. New York, 1986; Peter Burke, *Popular Culture in Early Modern Europe*. Brookfield, VT, 1988.)

Finally, along with mentalities history has come a new concern for a "state and society" approach. (For discussion of the state-society approach, Theda Skocpol, ed., *Vision and Method in Historical Sociology*. Cambridge, 1984; Gareth Stedman Jones, *Language of Class Studies in English Working-Class History*. Cambridge, 1984; Charles S. Maier, ed., *Changing Boundaries of the Political: Essays on the Evolving Balance Between the State and Society, Public and Private in Europe*. Cambridge, 1987.) This involves utilization of the new findings and approaches of social history while resolutely putting the state back into the overall equation. As with mentalities, the result can pull in a host of sociohistorical facets. Families mirror power relationships, and childhood socialization must be particularly considered. Leisure activities relate importantly to political expressions or serve as their surrogates. Mentalities obviously have a strong political component, since people have political attitudes along with other fundamental beliefs: crime, social structure, work relationships — the list is long. But the state is an important actor as well, which necessitates serious examination of changes in state form, constituencies, functions, and key policies. The result of a state and society approach is not simply conventional political history. Certain kinds of detail (e.g., about cabinet machinations) become less important. Attention to government function, and to the real impact of the state in addition to the professed intent of its policy, looms larger, as does the relationship of large groups to political power and political expectations. But political coverage is a central piece in the puzzle.

The big changes approach, mentalities history, and state-and-society coverage are by no means entirely worked out, nor do they dictate a single set of judgments about how particular societies change. In this sense, teachers must still be prepared to carve something of their own synthesis, aided by selection of appropriate scholarship, old and new. But the bases for valid synthesis have been laid in recent work. It is no longer either necessary or valid to dismiss social history's teaching role with knowing asides about lack of integration or a hopeless distance from the other aspects of the past that must be taught. Important progress in synthesis translates directly to the classroom and makes insisting on routine coverage less excusable than ever before. The Holy Grail of a total history, in which every piece of the past's puzzle is neatly interlocked, escapes us still and always will. History instruction, like history scholarship, must remain a creative endeavor, calling for and teaching the art of interpreting an often-elusive reality. The signposts are nevertheless in place for a further redirection of history teaching that can combine new and old ways of finding challenge and coherence in the past.

Gender, Reproduction, and European History

Bonnie G. Smith

A DECADE AGO Carolyn Lougee of Stanford University presented an elegant new syllabus for a Western civilization course. It integrated women into reading, lecture, and discussion material in striking new ways. From then on, Stanford's Western civilization program incorporated Lougee's directions, especially a three-fold set of themes. Western civilization courses, Lougee proposed in the AHA-published version of the syllabus, should present "as accurately as possible the 'condition' of European women." In addition the courses needed to highlight "contributions made by women individually and as a gender group to the develop-ment of European civilization." Finally, the introductory survey would "resurrect" and "heed" women's voices as found in their autobiographies, fictional writing, letters, and elsewhere.

Lougee's proposals were inspiring, especially to those with the energy to search out material for presenting those voices. It took time for teachers to find women contributors to Western civilization and to learn enough about those contributions to make changes in curricular materials. As for determining the "experience" of women, that was and remains a tall order, for women's experience ran the gamut. From women influential in courts or queens responsible for reproducing dynasties to market women, members of disorderly crowds, women marrying and maintaining agricultural life — the abundant experience of all of these has filled up entirely discrete courses on European women, to say nothing of providing sound enrichment to the subject matter of Western civilization surveys. The only excuse for not integrating has been time — the material is so vast that one can no longer keep up.

A decade has passed, and in those few years yet another revolution has occurred in thinking about women and the Western civilization course. This revolution developed in part from the sheer mass of information and the premonition that despite the abundance there was still more to be discovered about women. The anticipation of more to come, more crucial books and articles still to read, ever more material to integrate into courses already teeming with kings, wars, great philoso-phers, and literary men, awakened an urgent need to figure out what the "knowledge explosion," when it came to women, meant for history. Was history a democratic

phenomenon in which everyone should have a "voice"? Was women's "experience" a discrete narrative line tacked on in special sections on women and the
family as part of "covering" their world in a representative way? When faced with
substituting women's voices and narratives for wars and kings, how did one justify
such a decision? Indeed, many commentators began to think that research on
women had gone far enough; some even claimed that it was time to stop. The mass
of material threatened to overwhelm the teacher, the student, and indeed Western
civilization itself.

In the midst of this anxiety new interpretative paths opened, offering ways to
control the growing tension between traditional syllabi and the material about
women. The most influential idea — not unconnected to what had gone before —
announced that the ways of marking out the masculine and the feminine constituted the fundamental work of society, economics, and politics. Rather than
maintaining the singular importance of such a thing as "women's voice," the
interpretation that society rested on an ongoing process of "gendering" suggested
that history was distorted if it did not take account of so basic a process. Creating
definitions of masculine and feminine amounted to marking out "difference."
Political, economic, and cultural power was founded on such definitions, such
markings, and on revising or maintaining the ensuing systems of gender difference.
This insight gave new urgency to understanding what women's history was about,
for it meant that traditional history based only on knowing which king followed
which had something missing. Exclusive attention to the chronology of politics
often masked precisely those social issues involved in the creation and organization
of political power. By contrast, the integration of gender with traditional historical
subject matter helped one understand more of the content of politics.

A second insight is now emerging to accompany and inform this first one. From
lesson one, some Western civilization surveys are beginning to see replenishment
of the human population as a fundamental historical category. Just as the production of goods for human sustenance occurs in a matrix of social and political
arrangements, so too reproduction constitutes a major endeavor from which
political, social, and cultural power evolve. In addition to the topic of hunting and
gathering, the matter of how the reproduction of the species operated is becoming
indispensable to understand social, political, and cultural history. Formerly it was
convenient to think of reproduction as "natural" and thus happening beyond the
realms of power and social arrangements; such a supposition, therefore, placed it
outside historical narrative and analysis. Yet reproductive experience, changes in
population, and demographic behavior in general have a history and have influenced history. So basic a category has yielded power and produced politics.

During the last three decades, for instance, history realized that the family was
not "natural" but rather historical. Old and young, men and women had different
kinds of power, different duties, and so on. Familial rules at any particular time
involved assigning tasks so that productive work would sustain the family unit,

while reproductive rules (e.g., age at marriage, courtship, or breast-feeding patterns) worked to arrange just the right number of children to permit familial and community survival. The development of women's history has forced us to consider how the organization of reproduction may work differentially in the lives of men and women both in so small a unit as the family and in so large a one as the state. In this endeavor we encourage our students to connect the history of reproduction with insights about gender. By making these connections they can discuss how the differentials in reproductive arrangements yield differentials in power, whether that of the father, of the tribal chief, or of a national leader.

Specific areas where material about gender and reproductive organization can fit into the survey course are abundant, so I mention a few by way of suggestion. Conclusions about even these few are still in the formative stage, however, and teachers and advanced students can share in pursuing them further. Over the past decade, for instance, historians have come to consider the condition and experience of women in the ancient world. They note that the transition from the so-called dark age in Greece to that period when classical institutions arose involved a transition from a perilous population situation after wars and an accompanying agricultural decline. Textbook writers, newly aware of looking for women's experience, have also begun to note that women were disadvantaged when it came to participating in that new construct of the "polis" and specifically in what is called "Athenian democracy." Indications of women's condition are usually presented following descriptions of how Athenian democracy operated and after assessments of that democracy's conceptual importance to the development of future political systems. Democracy was not yet complete, new accounts proceed, because for the moment it excluded slaves and women. In this way Western civilization serves as a Whiggish celebration of an expanding democracy, made complete when slavery ultimately disappeared and women could vote.

Understanding the concept of gender and its constitutive social import allows us to rewrite such a scenario. The exclusion of women from the polis was not incidental to democracy; rather it was intrinsic to democracy. The idea of including women and slaves, or of "liberating" them, was outside the Athenian conceptional framework. Rather, a fundamental social and political process was at work in defining rights and access to politics in terms of male and female. Serving as warrior, as free landholder, as citizen, as theatre-goer, and as lover were the attributes of masculinity. In that particular society "adding" women or "liberating" them would have destroyed the social and political edifice because gender definitions would have collapsed. Moreover, the sexual segregation involved in the gendering of classical Greek society helped restore population and political order. Political regulations marked off spaces for masculine and feminine functioning and defined reproductive duties so that population growth would reoccur tranquilly.

The period of the French and Industrial Revolutions provides another specific instance during which demographic change and the reorganization of reproductive habits seem crucial to understanding the cataclysms of those years. In the eighteenth century population surged as never before; people wandered the countryside homeless and begging in ever greater numbers. In the midst of this disorganization a concern for population restraint appeared not just among political economists like Malthus. Segments of the European population began reorganizing the reproductive system and reducing fertility still more. Should we not ask our students (and ourselves) whether these conditions affected the shape of the Age of Revolution? One friend, hearing this suggestion, emphatically maintained that despite all the new information about women during the French and Industrial Revolutions, those events were about less faddish, more transcendent matters like liberty, class, and so on. Yet one can hardly ignore that the revolutionary epoch redefined masculinity and femininity and that new conditions of population and the replenishment of the species existed. Thus the conscientious teacher will make some attempt to see the relationship between the political and productive revolutions on the one hand and the demographic and gender revolutions on the other. Only such considerations allow us to make sense of French revolutionary legislation proscribing women from attending political clubs, from meeting to talk politics, from gathering in groups of more than three. Only such considerations help us make sense of the regulation of women and reproduction in the provisions of the Civil Code. Husbands were made all powerful economically while married women had no right to property; they had to follow their husbands wherever they might move and legally had to reside with them. Instead of seeing these provisions as mere expressions of transcendent ideals, as whimsical acts, or predictable expressions of Napoleonic misogyny, we need to consider revolutionary legislation as part of an effort to regulate population and to redefine the terrain of men and women. What, as all of us know, was the result of the legislation of equal inheritance except the early onset of the birth control revolution in France? A modern political ethos arose through the impulse to regulate and reshape society along these lines.

Another modern historic situation — that of imperialism — adds to our sense of how the relationship between masculine and feminine constructs is crucial to historical understanding and pertinent to the Western civilization survey. We are now able to teach our students how such a phenomenon as imperialism intersected with ideas of masculinity and femininity. Europeans by the late nineteenth century had created an identity that depended on controlling other races. But gender also structured the idea of what "European" meant. White men forged identities as colonial soldiers and administrators, hunters, and journalists or scholars expert in the ways of native peoples. In a complementary way, politicians maintained the imperialist domination, and thus the survival of entire nations like Britain depended on the efforts of wives and mothers. To preserve the nation, they had to create an imperial race by nourishing, clothing, and otherwise tending their families more vigorously and more successfully than they had in the past. This was no task incidental to imperialist nations, for those very nations as then organized would collapse without the gendered roles of masculine and feminine carrying out the imperial mission. Finally, imperialism reached its crescendo precisely when one of the most central developments in Western history was taking place: the precipitous decline in the birthrate by approximately fifty percent and the concomitant creation of a dramatic new approach among couples to reproduction. Politicians in France questioned the potency of French men; other European leaders felt that women in general had rejected their maternal identity for the sake of being "new women." Without doubt the ethos of imperial society and the history of its politics were intertwined with gendered and reproductive concerns.

Analyzing the rise of Adolf Hitler and Nazism for Western civilization classes calls for an understanding of gender, race, and ethnicity as pivotal to politics. Even the most conservative historians will note that Nazis and fascists displayed misogynist tendencies. Such misogyny, however, was hardly incidental to Nazism but rather permitted the deployment of the rest of its program. The Nazi ideologue's power rested on his distinction from the women around him, on redefining himself as warrior and male after the shattering experience of World War I. Hitler's first year in power saw major legislation working toward reestablishing gender clarity and the power of masculinity. That legislation mandated the removal of women from civil service and university jobs (male professors in particular responded with gusto) and provided subsidies for women who would stop working to have families. Not just legislation but the demeanor and speeches pointed to the ways in which Nazism built on the power derived from rebuilding the difference between men and women.

Nazism also depended on anti-Semitism in word and deed to heighten its power and to provide a motor force for its policy. Throughout history misogyny and anti-Semitism have been conjoined. The Western civilization student will see Chaucer, for instance, putting the vicious anti-Semitism of his society in the prim mouth of the distasteful prioress. For the modern period we see nineteenth- and twentieth-century Jewish men often described in feminine terms and thus defined as threatening to masculine definition. The Jew had the metaphorical power to destroy gender definition and thus society. By the twentieth century anti-Semitism increased in potency as the gender order and the reproductive order (given the birth control revolution and the blows at traditional definitions from the experience of war, feminism, and economic catastrophe) weakened. Genocide was so primal a matter because it worked to reorder all that. It signalled renewed control over the entire reproductive order as whole groups could be racially defined and then encouraged to reproduce, or, alternatively, be destroyed. Nazism, and ultimately the Final Solution, were about determining how biology would work. Aryans would be encouraged to reproduce; Slavs, Jews, Gypsies, and other peoples marked out by those with political power, would be destroyed as racial groups. Below the ethical outrage at the Final Solution, the naked display of the most fundamental but unnamed power over the forces of being terrified the world, and still does.

The suggestions above should indicate that an air of intellectual adventure still presides over women's history. Even as teachers continue the important task of finding women's voices and describing their experiences, even as we try to make the Western civilization course more democratic in terms of gender, race, and ethnicity, new interpretative frames have freshened our approach to integrating the ongoing results of scholarship on women. This new material and these new frames have transformed the way we look at everything from the conduct of government and political power to the conduct of the household. Intellectual life as displayed in, say, literary works or scientific institutions can benefit from considering their connections with gender definitions or their involvement in theorizing about structures for replenishing human society. Politics, low and high culture, the world of work, the social order — none of these exists outside the always fundamental definition of what is male and what is female, or beyond the concern for how human society will shape and control its own regeneration. Integrating such vital categories into our understanding of civilization's history is the measure of our educational mission and the challenge for this generation of teachers.

Teachers wishing to start thinking about these issues may consult the following recent works. On the issue of how to frame historical questions concerning women and men see Joan Scott, "Gender: A Useful Category of Historical Analysis," *American Historical Review* (1986); Judith Bennett, "Patriarchy," *Gender and History* (1989). Texts, anthologies, and collections of primary material now exist in abundance, for instance: Susan Groag Bell, *Women from the Greeks to the French Revolution* (1980); Eleanor S. Riemer and John Fout, *European Women: A Documentary History 1780-1945*; Erna Olafson Hellerstein et al., eds., *Victorian Women: A Documentary Account of Women's Lives in Nineteenth Century England, France and the United States*; Susan Groag Bell and Karen Offen, eds., *Women, the Family, and Freedom: the Debate in Documents*, 2 vols. (1983); Marilyn Boxer and Jean H. Quataert, eds., *Connecting Spheres: Women in the Western World, 1500 to the Present* (1987); Renate Bridenthal and Claudia Koonz, eds., *Becoming Visible: Women in European History*, 2nd ed. (1987); Bonnie Anderson and Judith Zinsser, *A History of Their Own*, 2 vols. (1989); Bonnie G. Smith, *Changing Lives: Women in European History Since 1700* (1989).

Chapter XII:

History of Science

History of Science in the European History Survey Course

Bruce Eastwood

TO INTRODUCE THE HISTORY OF SCIENCE, a useful gambit is a quick review of definitions. The *Oxford English Dictionary* notes that in the Middle Ages the word *science* (*scientia*) was commonly equivalent to the word *art* (*ars*), whereas there is an implied and real contrast in the modern academic phrasing: arts and sciences. While the ancients and medievals would subscribe to the *OED*'s general definition, "a particular branch of knowledge or study; a recognized department of learning," the most frequent modern usage of *science* is "restricted to branches of study that relate to the phenomena of the material universe and their laws, sometimes with implied exclusion of pure mathematics." The ordinary modern usage conveniently allows us to begin the historical study of science without a lot of agonizing over the principles behind our definitions and interpretations.

Historians of science usually look for explanations or orderly descriptions of past appearances of what we would call science today. However, as soon as they look beyond the recent past or outside long-established scientific disciplines, science historians will tend to bend or even disregard the modern assumptions about the nature of scientific knowledge as well as its location.

Astrology, for example, was both distinguished from and intimately tied to astronomy until about 1650. Only then did astrology come to appear opposed to astronomy as a branch of knowledge. Similarly, within theological studies about angels, grace, and the Eucharist one can find very intelligent discussions of physical motion, quantification of heat, and basic characteristics of physical matter during the Middle Ages. The history of science, seen over the long haul, becomes as much a history of what preceded science as we now categorize it as a history of what we now call science. More precisely, the history of science has become the study of earlier investigations of natural phenomena as characterized by those investigators rather than as labeled by modern science. For the more adventurous student, the history of science becomes also a history of the frameworks and purposes of past questions about the world of natural phenomena as understood then.

While the history of technology sometimes catches the attention of students more quickly than science, technology in Western culture is much more difficult to characterize as distinctively Western. The history of technology in China, for example, appears at least as advanced and rationalized as that in Europe prior to the scientific revolution of early modern times. Consequently, my attention here will be limited to the history of science alone — a history which is intrinsically and characteristically Western.

The place of the history of science in European history survey courses will be determined by the kind of history being taught. I believe the most fruitful approach at the beginning level will be one presenting science as investigations, or questions, about nature that bear witness to a set of social constraints or cultural commitments. Thus we may gain insight into the almost heroic self-confidence of mid-nineteenth-century physiology by observing the support given to those like Emile Dubois-Reymond, who believed that all animal processes would ultimately be explained by electromechanical forces. Certainly the invocation of standards of "scientific objectivity" or simply the reference today to idealized science as a model has persuasive power; witness the common notion that "true" science is a valid basis for resolving political disputes about such matters as environmental pollution. How long has this been so? What are its implications? What are the roots of our apparent faith in science?

Insofar as science holds a central place in our culture, we omit one of the essential driving forces and normative constraints in Western culture if we treat science as extraneous and having no history. Indeed, from a modern point of view there is a strong defense for the thesis that the history of science in its broadest sense is part of the core of the history of Western culture. One of the most striking characteristics of Western culture for well over a century has been its view that scientists are the "wise men" of our civilization, able to explain the fundamental causes and forces in nature as well as to solve all manner of economic, social, and political problems with applications of scientific knowledge.

Among the topics from the history of science that can be made part of a Western civilization survey the following would be likely to arouse interest:

1.   Ancient Greek concepts of ideal reality (Parmenides on absolute Being, Platonic Ideas, Euclidean geometry);

2.   Greek reasonings from experience (Hippocratic study of diseases, historical patterns in Thucydides, Aristotelian classification of animals);

3.   Hellenistic astronomy from Apollonius to Ptolemy: science for the specialist;

4.   Stoic and Epicurean views of nature: new philosophies in the Hellenistic empires;

5.   Digests of knowledge and the decline of science in late Antiquity;

6.   The condemnation of 1277 at Paris: theological impetus to science in the Middle Ages;

7.   Artists as scientists in the Renaissance;

8.   The trial of Galileo: Copernicanism, atomism, and the authority of the Church;
9.   The science of Galileo: cosmology and terrestrial mechanics;
10.   The "mechanical philosophy" of the seventeenth century (esp. Descartes, Hobbes, Newton);
11.   Newtonian physics and its meanings for eighteenth-century culture;
12.   The economies of nature and of human society in the late eighteenth and nineteenth centuries;
13.   Debate on the age of the earth: from religion to science;
14.   Darwin on species: What are they? Where do they come from? Where are they going?
15.   Scientific analysis of the material world: chemistry from Lavoisier, Dalton, and Wöhler to the industrial world of 1900;
16.   Atoms of life: cell theory, Pasteur, and nineteenth-century scientific medicine;
17.   Forces of nature: energetics and thermodynamics of the nineteenth century;
18.   The paradoxical world of the quantum;
19.   The non-Euclidean world of relativity;
20.   Molecular biology: birth of a new science from physics and biology.

It may be said that these topics fit well into the general developments in the history of ideas in the higher culture. The first five, for example, follow a traditional pattern in the history of art and drama in classical antiquity, and these in turn have usually been said to mirror to some degree the religion and politics of the successive centuries from the sixth B.C. to the fourth A.D. Topics 7-11 deal with the transformations that made possible modern Western science. Topics 12-16 reveal the progressive rationalizing and even "scientizing" of major aspects of the everyday world we inhabit. This is a central thrust in the history of modern thought. Topics 18-20 introduce ideas that have transformed science again, producing "post-classical" science. We can look at a couple of topics long enough to observe ties to the general culture and themes for emphasis in teaching.

Item 6 in the list is the only medieval theme, largely because medieval cultural and intellectual history in general receive a limited place in the European survey course. Item 6 offers an excellent opportunity to broaden students' understanding of scholasticism as well as to see the utility of investigating religious subjects in search of information and attitudes on ostensibly (to moderns) nonreligious matters.

It was not simply the translations of scientific works from the Arabic in the twelfth century nor even the translations of Aristotle and commentaries on his works, more specifically, which occasioned the concern of ecclesiastical leaders regarding rationalistic doctrines about the material world. The condemnations of

1277 are a part of the intellectual history of the universities, specifically the University of Paris, and the internal conflicts regarding the proper subjects of study. A general background can be found in the essay of William A. Wallace, "The Philosophical Setting of Medieval Science," in D.C. Lindberg (ed.), *Science in the Middle Ages* (Berkeley, CA, 1978, 91-119). Edward Grant's essay, "Science and Theology in the Middle Ages," in D.C. Lindberg and R.L. Numbers (eds.), *Gods and Nature: Historical Essays* ... (Berkeley, CA, 1986, 49-75), focuses on the science vs. theology issue, while his earlier article, "The Condemnation of 1277, God's Absolute Power, and Physical Thought in the Late Middle Ages," *Viator: Medieval and Renaissance Studies* 10 (1979, 211-44) (also published as ch. 13 in E. Grant, *Studies in Medieval Science and Natural Philosophy*, [London, 1981]) focuses directly on the scientific questions. The 219 propositions condemned by the bishop of Paris in 1277 are translated in Ralph Lerner and Muhsin Mahdi (eds.), *Medieval Political Philosophy* (New York, 1963, 337-54); a selection from these, especially relevant to science, appears in E. Grant (ed.), *Source Book in Medieval Science* (Cambridge, MA, 1974, 45-50).

Topic 12 shows the transformation of economics from human systems of power and wealth to more general biosystems of rationalized mutual interdependence. In short, humanity becomes no more than a part of nature, and nature becomes for some an object of sympathetic concern, not simply manipulable property. Yet the old attitude of domination remains. Clarence Glacken, *Traces on the Rodian Shore* (Berkeley, CA, 1967, 501-654), covers the eighteenth-century emergence of a new natural history from natural theology and the concerns for an environment fit for various inhabitants. The story told by Glacken concludes with Malthusian population doctrines and the idea of limits on environmental support systems. Keith Thomas, *Man and the Natural World: a History of the Modern Sensibility* (New York, 1983, esp. 143-91), describes the affective, emotional side of this new awareness of nature as human habitat. The human material economic environment as analyzed by Adam Smith is nicely comprehended in excerpts presented by Peter Gay (ed.), *The Enlightenment: a Comprehensive Anthology* (New York, 1973, 576-616). The story of ecology in the later eighteenth century, both Arcadian and rationalistic, and the conflict of these two outlooks through Darwin's contributions is attractively told in Donald Worster's *Nature's Economy: a History of Ecological Ideas* (New York, 1985, pts. 1, 3).

For the two topics just discussed, as well as the others in the list, the connections with the European history survey must come from within the individual topics. There is no simple formula for integrating all or even most themes on the history of science into the course. At a general level — and this can be pushed too far — the institutional framework provides connections that help: university, governmental agency, industrial employer, private or public patronage, etc.

Furthermore, cultural correlations, while showing no causal connection, are useful teaching devices, and these may appear in motivation, content, or purpose of scientific work. Such correlations are better left as tentative bases for further inquiry than as evident facts. Examples are: the parallels with political uncertainty in the discussions about the uncertainty principle in quantum mechanics, the presentation of idealized forms in Platonic physics and Greek sculpture of the fifth century B.C., the rather ideological trumpeting about the virtues of the method of experimental science in many seventeenth-century responses to radical religious and philosophical skepticism.

Science has a social history and a cultural history, but the discipline of history of science at present seems to offer the most uniform support for students looking for expositions of the development of scientific ideas. Like the history of a political theory, the history of a scientific theory is of marginal significance in the absence of connections with its contemporary history, but the teacher (or student) must sometimes bend the available expositions of an idea or theory to realize its potential for historical significance. The student in a European survey course will be doing well to gain the basic idea of a scientific theory or achievement and a reasonable notion of the relevance of this to the rest of history. Equally important is the recognition, through the introduction of science history at many points in the course, that science has as long and as meaningful a part in the Western tradition as, for example, religion or art.

An introductory bibliography for teachers will necessarily omit some desiderata. The basic bibliography for both teaching and research is the annual *Critical Bibliography* published as the final number each year in *Isis*, the official periodical of the History of Science Society. This has been put into more convenient reference form in the *Isis Cumulative Bibliography 1913-65* (London: Mansell, 1971-82); volumes on 1966-75 also published by Mansell (1980, 1985). Information on persons in the history of science appears in the sixteen-volume *Dictionary of Scientific Biography*, ed. by C.C. Gillespie et al. (New York: Scribner's, 1970-80). "The Scientific Revolution" (July 1986) is the first of a series of teaching guides for selected topics, to be published initially in the *History of Science Society Newsletter* and then as separate pamphlets.

Articles of general interest to European history teachers appear from time to time in the periodical *History of Science*, which takes a special interest in the intellectual and social context of science and in reviews of scholarship on a topic. A recent example is D.R. Oldroyd's "How Did Darwin Arrive at His Theory? The Secondary Literature to 1982," in vol. 22 (1984, 325-74).

A useful outline of thirty lecture topics, with readings, from the sixteenth century to the beginning of the twentieth, can be found in S. Shapin's "A Course in the Social History of Science," *Social Studies of Science*, 10 (1980, 231-58).

Unlike the Western civilization course, the history of science survey has not been inundated by a variety of often successful textbooks. Quite the contrary, there seems no general recognition of the success of even one such textbook. For want of a replacement, Stephen F. Mason's *A History of the Sciences* (New York: Macmillan,

1962) is still used by some, though it is almost thirty years old. For the period up to ca. 1600 Richard Olson's *Science Deified and Science Defied* (Berkeley: U. Calif. Press, 1983) is useful for teachers but is not confidently recommended for students. John Marks, *Science and the Making of the Modern World* (Portsmouth, N.H.: Heinemann, 1983), covers the period from ca. 1600 to the present in thirty-seven short chapters; only the final chapters of this book make good use of research published since the 1960s. L.P. Williams and H.J. Steffens, *The History of Science in Western Civilization*, 3 vols. (Washington, D.C.: University Press of America, 1979), provides historical introductions to a well chosen set of readings from the sources of scientific thought. A volume still useful, originally published in 1971, is Joseph Ben-David's *The Scientist's Role in Society* (Chicago: U. Chicago Press, 1984). Dependable surveys of important eras and themes in the history of science are available. Among these are the following:

Geoffrey E.R. Lloyd. *Early Greek Science: Thales to Aristotle*. New York: Norton, 1974;

Geoffrey E.R. Lloyd. *Greek Science After Aristotle*. New York: Norton, 1973;

Marie Boas. *The Scientific Renaissance 1450-1630*. New York: Harper & Row, 1962;

A. Rupert Hall. *From Galileo to Newton*. Mineola (N.Y.): Dover, 1982;

Garland Allen. *Life Science in the Twentieth Century*. New York: Cambridge Univ. Press, 1978;

C. Chant and J. Fauvel (eds.). *Darwin to Einstein: Historical Studies in Science and Belief*. Chicago: Longman, 1981;

N.G. Coley and V.M. Hall (eds.). *Darwin to Einstein: Primary Sources in Science and Belief*. Chicago: Longman, 1981;

D.C. Lindberg and R.L. Numbers (eds.). *God and Nature: Historical Essays on the Encounter between Christianity and Science*. Berkeley: U. Calif. Press, 1986.

The History of Science and the Survey Course in American History

John W. Servos

AN ENTERPRISING PUBLISHER recently issued several volumes containing course syllabi used by prominent American historians in universities across the United States. They make interesting and, on the whole, encouraging reading. The political, economic, and social history of the United States is treated with great skill.

Consequently, a serious student could not take any of the survey courses described in these volumes without learning a great deal about the origins of the various wars and reform movements that have punctuated American history, about race relations and foreign relations, about the rise of big business and the history of the labor movement. The assorted "isms" of intellectual history, although rarely spotlighted, usually occupy a few sessions: Puritanism, transcendentalism, pragmatism, socialism, and liberalism among others.

But one dish is notably absent from this banquet: the history of science. To judge by these survey courses in United States history, it would seem that science was and is a very minor part of American culture, occupying a position somewhat inferior to that of history itself.

Our students of course must know otherwise. Science buildings dominate academic campuses; science is touted and condemned on the nightly news; foreigners fear, admire, and emulate American scientific and technological achievements; the newsstands hawk scores of more or less reputable science magazines; advertisers use science to flog their products; and politicians and industrialists debate science policy. Even those unconscious of the past find in the present overwhelming evidence testifying to the importance of science to our economy, politics, and culture. Alert students will naturally wonder about when, how, and why science came to occupy this position; our history courses give them few clues.

The disparity between the role of science in our lives and its role in our history courses demands some explanation. It would be easy to say that general historians lack the technical sophistication to understand the history of science or that historians of science lack the literary skill to attract readers from the humanities.

Yet neither of these arguments carries much force. Few historians have managed to evade all contact with science during their educations, and many have strong scientific credentials.

More important, much history of science is written for the non-scientist. There is nothing forbiddingly technical in Charles E. Rosenberg's sparkling essays on the interplay of science and American values in the nineteenth century or in Daniel J. Kevles's magnificent book on the development of the discipline of physics in America.

Just as in any special branch of history, the history of science offers a spectrum of approaches and styles. General historians may find little use for a close analysis of Thomas Hunt Morgan's fruit fly experiments or Robert A. Millikan's cosmic ray research, but they will benefit from studies that set the lives and works of such scientists within the broader context of American society, institutions, and culture. Most historians of science are today far closer to general historians in their values and interests than they are to scientists; it makes little sense to array historians of science opposite humanists along C.P. Snow's two-culture divide.

If mutual antipathies between science and the humanities do not explain general historians' peculiar neglect of the history of science, what does? Here, as historians are wont to do, it is useful to look to the past. A generation or two ago, when the history of science was just beginning to coalesce as an academic discipline, scientists and non-scientists alike held firmly to a few simple generalizations about the nature of science and its role in history. Science was seen as a logic machine that worked according to its own laws. It was objective and impersonal; it stood above and beyond the realm of human action.

Indeed, science was believed to be progressive in ways that other human enterprises were not because it transcended the foibles and stupidities of individual actors. It needed only freedom and money to prosper, and of these freedom was most important. Religious dogma and totalitarian ideology were its enemies. Science was the powerful engine of progress; it pulled in its train technology, medicine, and the other arts that shared science's progressive character. Francis Bacon's aphorism was little doubted: "Human knowledge and human power meet in one, for where the cause is not known the effect cannot be produced."

Leaving aside the interesting question of why near unanimity existed on these issues, it is worth noting that these beliefs made pedagogy simple. By invoking a few simple bromides, general historians could relieve themselves of their duty to integrate science into the story of civilization. Those teaching United States history could explain America's rise to scientific leadership in the twentieth century by referring to the money and freedom the United States afforded its scientists. The integration of science into American culture could be described as a kind of warfare in which science won inevitable victories over theology and ignorance. The lengthening of life spans could be described as a logical consequence of the development of scientific medicine; the quickening pace of technological change could be explained as a natural consequence of the infusion of science into industry. Science, according to this view, transformed America during the late nineteenth and twentieth centuries, but the nature of science and the way in which it accomplished these results seemed so mechanical and so obvious as to be historically uninteresting. Historians ignored the history of science a generation ago because so much of it seemed so dull. In truth, it was dull.

During the past thirty years, however, all of the simple and seemingly self-evident verities cited above have been called in question by historians and philosophers of science and by historians of technology and medicine. Science no longer appears as impersonal and objective as it once seemed. If scientists achieve progress, Thomas Kuhn tells us, it is not because they obey special and inflexible rules but rather because they work within social structures that are unusually efficient in defining and solving problems. Others, more extreme, assert that scientific progress is illusory and that science is simply a tool used by interest groups to maintain and extend their political and social power.

Just as the progressive nature of scientific knowledge has been challenged, so too have old assumptions about the relations between science and technology, medicine, and religious belief. Today, few specialists in the history of technology would accord science a central role in the development of technology prior to about 1870 or argue for a simple uni-directional model of the relationship between science and technological change in the decades since. Scientific knowledge is one among many resources that inventors or engineers may draw upon, but the precise contribution that science makes to technology varies from case to case. Engineers often work outside the realm within which scientific theory has useful guidance to offer. Where once simple answers sufficed, historians of technology now struggle to find ways to express the complexity of the issue with which they deal.

Much the same could be said of recent scholarship on the relations between science and medicine. Where there was once consensus there is controversy. How and why medical doctors began to identify their profession with the basic sciences is now hotly debated; some deny that scientific medicine had a major impact on mortality rates, some even question whether the basic sciences have made significant contributions to therapeutics.

As for the warfare between science and religion, those patient enough to search will find many shades of opinion in the secondary literature. By and large historians of science seem far more interested in understanding the role of religious values in nurturing the scientific enterprise than in developing or supporting the old warfare thesis. Careful studies of the relations between science and religious belief, pioneered by Robert K. Merton, have shown that scientists, as often as not, have shared the values and religious assumptions of their times and that science and religion have often reinforced one another and drawn strength from common sources.

What was once a picture so simple as to be dull has very rapidly become so complex as to be bewildering. Faced with so much uncertainty about such basic issues, it is understandable why historians teaching survey courses might wish to skirt the history of science. The risks of crossing such terrain are great, and there are always fields in political or social history which, complex as they may be, are more safely and easily traversed by both teacher and student.

A little reflection, however, is sufficient to show how wrong this response is. We do not typically organize our courses around the material that is easiest for ourselves and our students; nor do we typically eschew that which cannot be expressed by a few simple maxims. The controversy, the counter-intuitive findings, and the uncertainties of the history of science should be seen as opportunities and not headaches by those teaching survey courses. Unsettling as it may be — or better, because it is unsettling — students deserve to be acquainted with some of the questions defined and explored by historians of science, technology, and medicine from recent years. At the very least, they should be led to examine those old verities which, despite recent scholarship, are still uncritically accepted by most young men and women entering college: that science is an impersonal and objective force that is independent of the politics, values, and beliefs of its practitioners and patrons; that basic science undergirds technology and always has; that scientific medicine had an integral role in the demographic revolution of the past two centuries; and that science and religion have historically been implacable adversaries. Liberally educated men and women should not only know that science has an important place in our society, but that we are only beginning to understand why that is so and how it came to be.

▼

There are as many ways to integrate these issues into survey courses in United States history as there are teachers of such courses. Nevertheless, it seems safe to say that most teachers of United States history already deal with such topics as industrialization, the secularization of thought and society, and the growth of the professions. It takes little effort to imagine how one might move from these topics to a consideration of the issues outlined above. It is, for instance, quite natural to discuss technological change in connection with the growth of industry.

On the other hand, challenge students to name a science-based invention developed prior to 1870. Unless one adopts an exceedingly loose definition of science, the list will be very short. A question like this breeds discussion of the separability of knowing and doing. It suggests that links between the enterprises of science and technology are historically contingent. And it prepares students to ask how and why the relations between science and technology changed during the past century or so — queries that are best treated by following the development of a specific industry or technology. It is equally natural to weave a discussion of the relationship between science and religious belief into a treatment of the secularization of American culture or a discussion of the role of science in medicine into a treatment of the professions.

However one chooses to integrate the history of science into the history of the American people, there are certain books and articles that should make the task easier for both instructors and students. On the history of science as a field of scholarship, readers will do well to read Thomas S. Kuhn's lucid essays, "The History of Science" and "The Relations between History and the History of Science," in *The Essential Tension: Selected Studies in Scientific Tradition and Change* (Chicago: University of Chicago Press, 1977). Kuhn's well known *The Structure of Scientific Revolutions*, 2nd ed. (Chicago: University of Chicago Press, 1970) was enormously influential in shaking traditional beliefs about science. Barry Barnes develops a more radical view of the nature of scientific knowledge in *Scientific Knowledge and Sociological Theory* (London: Routledge & Kegan Paul, 1974).

The best introduction to the history of science in America is Daniel J. Kevles's *The Physicists: The History of a Scientific Community in Modern America* (New York: Knopf, 1978). Constructed around the question of how an avowedly elitist enterprise grew and prospered in a democratic culture, Kevles's work is unsurpassed for its breadth and literary style. For the period prior to the Civil War, readers should begin with John C. Greene's *American Science in the Age of Jefferson* (Ames: Iowa State University Press, 1984).

Among recent biographies, two are especially notable for the skill with which scientific lives are used to illuminate larger issues in the development of science in America: Robert H. Kargon, *The Rise of Robert Millikan: Portrait of a Life in American Science* (Ithaca: Cornell University Press, 1982) and Garland Allen, *Thomas Hunt Morgan: The Man and His Science* (Princeton: Princeton University Press, 1978).

The development of the electrical industry affords perhaps the best case through which to study historical relations between science and technology, both because of the rich secondary literature and because of the importance of electric power in American economic development. Several recent books are of special value here: George Wise, *Willis R. Whitney, General Electric, and the Origins of Industrial Research* (New York: Columbia University Press, 1985); Leonard Reich, *The Making of American Industrial Research: Science and Business at GE and Bell, 1876-1926* (Cambridge: Cambridge University Press, 1985); and Thomas Hughes, *Networks of Power: Electrification in Western Society* (Baltimore: Johns Hopkins University Press, 1983). David F. Noble's *America By Design: Science, Technology, and the Rise of Corporate Capitalism* (New York: Knopf, 1977), although marred by errors of fact and exaggerations in interpretation, raises exciting and challenging questions about both the relations between science and technology and the influence of corporations upon the development of American science.

E. Richard Brown, *Rockefeller Medicine Men: Medicine and Capitalism in America* (Berkeley: University of California Press, 1979) shares many of the virtues and flaws of Noble's book. His Marxist analysis, however, will provoke readers to reexamine their assumptions about the foundations of scientific medicine. Competing interpretations are available in John Ettling's *The Germ of Laziness: Rockefeller Philanthropy and Public Health in the New South* (Cambridge: Harvard University Press, 1981) and Paul Starr's *The Social Transformation of American Medicine: The Rise of a Sovereign Profession and the Making of a Vast Industry* (New York: Basic Books, 1982). Thomas McKeown's *The Role of Medicine: Dream, Mirage, or Nemesis?* (Princeton: Princeton University Press, 1979) assesses the role of therapeutics in the modern decline of mortality rates. Although based upon analysis of the English experience, McKeown's argument should also find application in the discussion of American demographic patterns. On the relation between basic science and therapeutics, see Gerald L. Geison's provocative essay "Divided We Stand: Physiologists and Clinicians in the American Context," in *The Therapeutic Revolution: Essays in the Social History of American Medicine* (Philadelphia: University of Pennsylvania Press, 1979).

Questions about the relations between science and religious belief in America arise in the study of Puritan New England and reappear in various forms up to the present. Among the better recent works on this subject are: Theodore Dwight Bozeman, *Protestants in an Age of Science: The Baconian Ideal and Antebellum American Religious Thought* (Chapel Hill: University of North Carolina Press, 1977); Charles E. Rosenberg, *No Other Gods: On Science and American Social Thought* (Baltimore: Johns Hopkins University Press, 1976); James R. Moore, *The Post-Darwinian Controversies: A Study of the Protestant Struggle to Come to Terms with Darwin in Great Britain and America, 1870-1900* (Cambridge: Cambridge University Press, 1979); and David C. Lindberg and Ronald L. Numbers, eds., *God and Nature: Historical Essays on the Encounter between Christianity and Science* (Berkeley: University of California Press, 1986). As the title suggests, Robert K. Merton's classic *Science and Society in Seventeenth-Century England* (1938; reprint ed., New York: Harper and Row, 1970) is about England, but his thesis — that proponents of experimental science and Puritanism held common values — is well worth study in relation to the scientific and religious traditions of America.

Readers seeking more information about the issues discussed in this article or for a fuller bibliography should consult Sally Gregory Kohlstedt and Margaret W. Rossiter, eds., *Historical Writing on American Science, Osiris* 2nd ser. 1 (1985); especially valuable are the essays on science and medicine by John Harley Warner, on science and religion by Ronald L. Numbers, and on science and technology by George Wise.

Chapter XIII:

Local History

Finding the Layers in Your Town

Mary Joan Cook

HAVE YOU EVER WONDERED how your hometown got its name, or the elementary school you attended or the street on which you lived? A few years ago I decided to use that kind of wondering as the motivation for my student's freshman reseach paper.

James Michener's *The Source*, the fascinating story of an archaelogical dig through a fifteen-layer fictional site at Makor, in the Holy Land, suggested my "find the layers of your town" assignment. At each layer of the dig an object was discovered, and around this object Michener created a story related to and incorporating the historical and scriptural persons and events of that layer's period. Michener's fecund imagination gave life to the bare archaeological remains. The excavated objects took on a new significance when their "story" was told.

In my first assignment for this research/term paper, I talk about Michener's book and its layers. I explain that the layers of a town's history are actually evident, that if one reads the signs carefully, the past is present. One need not dig physically to find a town's history. Most of its "layers" are, in fact, visible today. They surround us even as we walk or drive down its streets or lanes; we need only to learn to look. The alert observer can detect evidence which suggests the town's political, economic, religious, social, and educational history and its founders, developers, educators, political leaders, and industrialists.

I ask the students to look around their own town at the names of streets, buildings and parks, at monuments and plaques, at houses of worship, to visit old cemeteries and to jot down any observations they make or any questions they may have. Since almost all of our students either commute or return home regularly on weekends, this assignment can easily be carried out. Students from neighboring states also participate, but since this research project does demand some on-site time it would exclude students who could neither fit this in nor substitute another appropriate site for their research. In my own experience, no student has been unable to carry out the assignment.

One major premise of this "layers" study is that the signs of the past are readily visible. Throughout, the students are reminded that the layers they are looking for are not hidden away inside buildings. A few illustrative slides of significant local street names, monuments, cemetery headstones, and old buildings in Hartford are shown in class to help the students see the kinds of evidence they will be seeking. I might use, for instance, two Indian street names (Wawarme and Sequassen), several Dutch street names (one commemorates Adrian Block, the seventeenth-century Dutch navigator whose ship traveled up the Connecticut River), a statue of Thomas Hooker, the city's founder, a bronze plaque (mounted on a large boulder) which summarizes the three-centuried history of Hartford's original high school, the Wadsworth Atheneum, the 1847 plaque on a major department store, and a statue of the nineteenth-century industrialist, Samuel Colt, in the park named for him.

As I show the objects pictured, I explain that they and many others like them preserve Hartford's story, taking us from the river and Indian layer up through the centuries to the skyscrapers and bridges of our own day.

In introducing the project, I also often use a film called *The Long Tidal River*, narrated by Katherine Hepburn and produced by her brother-in-law Ellsworth Grant; in it one sees the central role played by the Connecticut River over the centuries. It is a good introduction to the significance of the terrain as a piece of evidence to be noted in studying a town's history. For comparable films and videos focusing on other parts of the country, the two-volume *Education Film/Video Locator* (3rd ed., 1986) is a helpful tool.

Having shown the students how slides graphically present historic monuments and other evidence of the town's story, I strongly recommend that they use slides in their final oral presentation. Although the use of slides is not required, some kind of illustrative material is. Most of the students in fact take slides which they use for their final presentation and then keep for themselves. Those who do not incorporate slides use overhead transparencies (which can easily be produced at our media center), maps, drawings, and/or displayed photographs.

A class session is devoted to sharing orally the students' notes on the "look around your town" assignment. Typically, in this sharing, someone will mention observing that several cemetary headstones bear the same names as certain streets or that the local Congregational church has a sign which dates the church back to the seventeenth century or that a lake in the area has an Indian name. (I remember one student who, at this point, wondered why there was a "College Street" in Old Saybrook and who later discovered that Yale University itself was originally located in that spot.) As one listens to these observations, the speaker's voice rings with a tone that says, "I want to find out more about this."

In their next assignment, the students are asked to interview someone in the town who has lived there many years or who has studied its history. I usually suggest the town historian, a librarian, an elderly resident (perhaps a relative or friend of the family); lately I have added that one might visit a local nursing home and ask a member of the staff to recommend a knowledgeable person. At least one interviewee must be cited in the final research paper.

My reasons for requiring such a citation are varied. To begin with, most students do not spontaneously turn to interviewing as a means of research; they rely, rather, on written materials. Assigning the interview leads them to this means and introduces them to its effectiveness as a source. Moreover, the interview for this "layers of your town" project focuses on the knowledge of the elderly and on their lived experience. One goal of the assignment is to encourage interaction between the student and the interviewee and thereby to encourage the student's appreciation of the elderly person's knowledge gained through lived experience. Thirdly, by listening, the researcher is able to share the perspective of how one can personally remember the town as it was, who can bridge the past and the present, for whom riding the trolley down Main Street to the end of the line was a Sunday adventure.

High points of the interview are shared orally with the class. Almost always, the student conveys the results of this interview with a great deal of enthusiasm and appreciation of the experience. The interviewee has obviously enjoyed reminiscing about the town with an interested listener. I can remember one student describing a drive through the town of Enfield. In the car with him was an elderly informant who excitedly poured forth into a tape recorder the story of building after building. And another student comes to mind who heard from two women in their nineties the story of working as teenagers in the town magnate's textile factory. Just a few simple questions, such as "What was Main Street like when you were young?" evoke a heartwarming response and one which will add valuable details to the young researcher's essay.

The students, equipped now with their own lived experience in the town, their recent observations, and the information gained from interviewing, turn next to books, journals, newspapers, and other written sources, seeking documentation and verification for their interviewee's comments and answers to their own questions concerning street names or old buildings or the dates for the coming of various ethnic or religious groups. Now they must find out if what they guessed or heard is true, whether it is legend and hearsay or recorded fact. What do historians write about the famed "Charter Oak"? And is the capitol actually built on the original site of Trinity College? Is the street name "Navillus" truly a disguised tribute to the Sullivan immigrant? The students enter readily into this phase of research. If they expect their readers to accept their assertions about the town's past and about the significance of the signs which they have observed, they must find and cite authoritative sources in addition to their interviewee's recollections.

They are advised to take notes carefully and from a variety of sources. In addition to their using the local and college libraries, I suggest they try the state and local historical societies, the town hall, the Chamber of Commerce, and the State Library in Hartford. Each of these sources has proved helpful to students. Old maps of the early settlers' land allotments, property deeds, newspaper articles written for the bicentennial celebrations, up-to-date brochures on the town's development, all serve to document the student's research.

Recently, one student, curious about the number of French street names in her neighborhood, ferreted out the answers she needed from land records, old newspapers, and parish church bulletins. When she drives by Caya, Burgoyne, and Levesque streets now, she knows well the intriguing story of the young Canadian developer who named them.

About midway in the semester, several class hours are devoted to three-minute talks by the students. Students each choose an interesting facet of their study; this may be a notable person in the town's history, a house, a local legend, a historic event, or a particular institution; the possibilities are varied. It is important that the student narrow the subject of this talk lest it become identical with the scope of the entire paper. By this time, the speakers are apt to be so enthusiastic and so knowledgeable that I use a handbell to signal that their time is up.

At the conclusion of these talks, all students are asked to write for about thirty minutes from their notes on what they have heard. These essays, written in class, may focus on any aspects of the talks. The principle of organization is up to the student. I do, however, suggest considering points of comparison and/or contrast in the material heard. All must also strive for an engaging opening and satisfying closing. As a set of in-class essays, these, which I do grade, are apt to be very successful.

When the research on the town's history is complete, the students must decide on their focus for the final paper. Most are eager to discuss their choice of a focus with me, and we do this either formally in a scheduled conference or informally before or after class. At this point in the process, I also ask them to develop a thesis statement and topic outline. To help them, I present, on an overhead transparency, an effective outline and thesis statement of a former student. Students submit their outline to me about four weeks before the research paper is due. I return the outline with comments, suggestions, and/or corrections. They develop their final paper from this outline. I do not ask to see their preliminary drafts, although this step could easily be added to the process.

The selection of a focus or theme encourages originality in the organization of the paper and is one of the ways in which the student impresses on it her/his own perspective. Usually during the research, the student becomes especially interested in a particular facet of the story. It might be a family's contribution over the centuries; one student, for instance, traced her family from the founding of the little Connecticut town to her own residence there now. One chose to focus on contemporary evidence of the Shaker community's history in Enfield; another on the tradition of their town's independence. Still another did a sensitive study of the Little River that ran through Hartford and emptied into the more majestic Connecticut River. Using the rhetorical figure of personification, she pictured the "giving river," changing over the centuries until it was literally buried under a new highway.

Another important original aspect of the paper lies in the students' explicit linking of today's evidence of the town's history with their own research. The students are frequently reminded that in their essay they must refer to the *still-visible* evidence of the people, events, topographical features, buildings, and institutions that formed the town they know today. The student writing on Hartford, for instance, would point to the still evident remains of the Little River, to the statuary on Burr Mall depicting a pioneering family and labelled "The Safe Arrival," to the plaque on Center Church commemorating its first pastor and date of establishment, to the streets named Potter, Asylum, Pratt, Wyllys, and Morgan, to the Amos Bull House, and to Mark Twain's mansion in Nook Farm. Explicitly referring the reader to observable signs of the town's story, of its chronological layers, is essential for the successful completion of this research paper.

Near the end of the semester, students each use their own set of fifteen to twenty slides or other types of illustrative material and share their research with the class. The illustrations picture the terrain, the historic buildings, public monuments, street signs, cemetery headstones, ruins, and other evidence of the town's layered history. The time allotted to each presentation varies with the size of the class. Typically, four, fifty-minute class periods are devoted to these presentations. The class size ranges from fifteen to the low twenties and the time of each presentation from nine to twelve minutes. Several slide-projector carousels are provided, and students can follow one another smoothly.

The presentations are always enthusiastic as the students point out with considerable confidence and authority the historic aspects of their town. The use of slides or other illustrative material lessens the student speaker's self-consciousness and heightens the attentiveness of the listeners. The latter, having researched their own towns, appreciate the work that has gone into their classmate's presentation and they form a supportive, interested audience.

In giving the presentation, too, originality surfaces. In my experience, the most creative was an amateur videotape in which the student, costumed elaborately as Wethersfield's traditional symbol, the red onion, was pictured parading through the town's center, pausing here and there to comment on selected historic sites.

During the presentations themselves, I am basically a listener. Occasionally I make a general recommendation to a speaker or help a student who is having difficulty with the slide projector. In addition, of course, I take notes and evaluate each student's work. At the end of the course, I meet individually with each student for a fifteen-minute conference whereupon I review with them my judgment of both the research paper and the oral presentation.

This "find the layers of your town" topic has without doubt worked far better than any other topic in my twenty-plus years of teaching the research paper. It has proved to be one that interests the students, lends itself to research, is not too esoteric, and demands originality. I have tried it with at least one-hundred students, both traditional age and older. The older students, men and women, many of whom are just beginning or returning to college, carry out this assignment as a part of Communication 104, a course intended to help them make the transition back to school. The assignment enables them to combine research with their own experience as mature adults, as well as residents of the town. And in the excitement of learning and communicating the answers to their questions about their town's history, they overcome some of their fears about writing and speaking in an academic setting.

The traditional-aged freshmen in my classes (all young women) find that their research interests the whole family; often this includes grandparents, whose knowledge on this topic is a joyfully recovered resource. The topic, and the research involved, may even provide a wholesome link between home and college life. In addition, the in-class sharing on their hometown, its special places and meaning, introduces these young people to one another at a level which is not readily reached in a formal academic setting.

In closing, it is important to mention one or more outcomes of this "finding the layers of your town" assignment; that is, the application of historical imagination. Our imagination, by which we can picture that which is not present to us, frees us from the restrictions of the here and now and allows us to transcend our immediate environment. Imagination enlarges our world. It enables us to picture other times, other places, other people. It helps us to extend ourselves, to understand what we have not personally experienced, to bond with those from different times and places. It is imagination which can help us envision a past we have not experienced. With it we are able to place ourselves in another time and identify more easily with those who have preceded us.

The students who have been researching the layers of their towns can, with imagination and newly acquired knowledge, frequently picture the town as it was in its different historical periods. They "see" the Town Green in the eighteenth century, the mainstreet, or the country roads. They can picture the coming of the railroad, the Civil War regiment commemorated in the monument on the green as it departed for camp, and the Saturday night dances in the little wooden hall, still standing on Pearl Street. They hear the bustling factory summoning its workers with a shrill whistle.

The student of Hartford's story may stand on the bank of the Connecticut River at the site of the seventeenth-century Dutch fort and can imagine off to the west, clearly visible from this vantage point, the great oak, and beyond that the beginnings of the English settlement.

Such imaginings brings the past to life and a new understanding of the present. It enlarges one's perspective as the surface view is deepened with a knowledge of the layers which have formed the town and an appreciation of its centuried human story.

This appreciative awareness of the past, which adds a new dimension to the students' surroundings, is a major goal of the "find the layers of your town" assignment, an awareness which I hope will enrich their daily lives and the lives of those with whom they share their research.

Communities of Collaboration: Sources and Resources for Teaching Local History

Terrie L. Epstein

ON A SATURDAY EACH SPRING during the Organization of American Historians' annual meeting, a series of sessions focuses specifically on issues involving the teaching and learning of history. At the 1989 St. Louis meeting, one of the sessions centered on the teaching of local history at the precollegiate level. The session's three panelists presented information on projects that were far reaching in format and content. A common denominator, however, factored into all three projects: each had originated through the collaborative efforts of educators in schools, universities, and historical societies.

The first panelist, Mary Seematter, described her work at the Missouri Historical Society on the American History School Project. With the aid of a grant from the National Endowment for the Humanities, she and others have developed teaching materials on the history of St. Louis. The project aims to present the city's past through the use of concrete and comprehensible primary sources and to relate the history of St. Louis to national events and experiences.

To date the staff has published two units and will complete another eight in the next two or three years. The complete set will span selected topics on St. Louis' history from the eighteenth through the twentieth centuries. Each unit includes a narrative which relates local events to national themes, a set of one- or two-day lesson plans centering on students' interpretations of one or more primary sources, and a set of visuals, reproduced as slides and paper prints. The images include photographs of people, paintings, buildings, maps, and artifacts. A written explanation accompanies each one.

Missouri Historical Society staff members and secondary school history teachers from the St. Louis area worked together in creating the completed units. They began by exchanging ideas on potential materials and activities. Staff members then selected primary documents and images from the Society's collections and wrote the narrative, lesson plans, and explanatory texts accompanying the images. The secondary school teachers tested these materials in their classrooms and made suggestions for revisions. These revisions are reflected in the materials' final form.

Examples of individual lesson plans illustrate the project's goals of teaching students to interpret primary sources and to relate those interpretations to significant historical themes. One plan, for example, centers on the interpretation of an early twentieth-century state senate report on the working conditions of women. The document vividly portrays the experiences and expectations of working women, as well as businessmen's and reformers' attitudes towards women and work. In addition, a teacher can relate the information students acquire in examining the document to broad questions about reform in the progressive era, women and the struggle for suffrage and equal rights, and labor and its battles over wages and working conditions.

Other lesson plans illustrate how primary sources relating to local matters can complement and complicate traditional textbook accounts. One plan on antebellum St. Louis includes a long excerpt from a narrative of a St. Louis slave. Students are encouraged to compare and contrast William Well Brown's urban slavery experiences with the more commonly depicted textbook image of slaves on southern plantations. Brown's narrative also can serve as a springboard for discussion of national political events, such as the Missouri Compromise and the Dred Scott Case.

Overall, staff members at the Missouri Historical Society, in consultation with classroom teachers, have created the kinds of high quality resources teachers alone rarely have time to produce. Moreover, teachers who make the effort to integrate into their courses the materials from the Missouri Historical Society's American History School Project most likely will find it is well worth their time.

The second panelist, Marla Marantz, described how she enables her secondary school students from Joplin, Missouri, to relate the history of their local communities to the broad themes of America's past. She does this by encouraging them to complete research projects on local topics and to compete in National History Day competitions. National History Day is an annual contest in which over 200,000 middle school and secondary school students participate. Like science fair exhibits, students' history projects are judged at regional, state, and national competitions. Projects can take the form of research papers, performances, museum-type displays, or media presentations. Marla Marantz's involvement with the program is intense and long standing; over the past six years, more than 100 of her students have won over sixty-five district, state, and national awards.

Because they work on topics relating to local communities, Ms. Marantz's students spend considerable time doing research at local and state libraries and historical societies. And because this is the first in-depth research project most students have pursued, they at times rely quite heavily on the assistance of library and historical society staff members. Ms. Marantz noted that the time these professionals spend supervising secondary school students has paid off in the past. Seven of her students' displays are exhibited permanently at local and state museums and historical societies, while three other displays have become part of traveling exhibits.

Ms. Marantz then showed slides of some of her students' award-winning displays. One young man, in an effort to find out why a creek near his home had been designated by the Environmental Protection Agency as the worst polluted area in the country, interviewed residents of surrounding communities and miners who had worked in area mines. He then researched the region's economic development, the state's laws and regulations on pollution control, and the technological changes affecting the mining industry. His research resulted in his winning first place in the district and state competitions; he finished fourth at the national level.

Another student documented the life of a Joplin, Missouri, industrialist. To detail his financial, civic, political, and personal activities, the student interviewed the industrialist's descendants and examined documents at local and state archives, museums, and government offices. Her final display, entitled "Thomas Connor: Frontier Capitalist," illustrated how one man's involvement in local affairs both influenced and was influenced by national events. The young woman's project won first place at the district, state, and national levels.

For classroom teachers like Marla Marantz and other professionals who take the time to train secondary school students in the rigors of historical research, the rewards can be significant at more than one level. Not only do students learn valuable research skills, they also come to recognize the relationships between the history of their local communities and larger contexts.

The third panelist, T. Harri Baker, a historian at the University of Arkansas, explained the production and dissemination of *The Arkansas News*. Proudly making its claim as the state's third largest circulated newspaper (55,000 copies printed per issue), *The Arkansas News* is coedited by Mr. Baker and Judy Dalton, a staff member at the Old State House Museum, Little Rock. Resembling a nineteenth-century newspaper in format and print, *The Arkansas News* is distributed biannually to public and private elementary schools, museums, and other public agencies. Each issue is filled with stories, editorials, advertisements, crossword puzzles, and other items of interest pertaining to a particular period or topic of the state's history.

The paper began in 1984 with the aid of a grant from the Arkansas Endowment for the Humanities. The contents of the first and subsequent issues are planned jointly by the paper's editors, university historians, and area teachers. The copy for each issue is then researched and written by historians and museum staffers. Each issue also contains a crossword puzzle, composed by an associate justice of the Arkansas Supreme Court.

The spring 1989 issue is representative of the paper's content and format. Focusing on developments in transportation, articles range in topic and time from the first poorly traveled and unpaved territorial trails to the use of state and federal funds for highway construction and improvement. Photographs and graphics of all kinds accompany the text. There are, for example, reproductions of stagecoach and steamboat advertisements from the 1850s and 1860s and automobile advertisements from the 1920s and 1930s.

The paper also includes three state maps. The first details early nineteenth-century trails and river transportation routes, the second illustrates late nineteenth-century railroad lines, and the third demarcates the state's present-day highways. It is clear from these maps that the physical location of the state's major transportation routes have changed little over time, yet the change in modes of transport have made long and arduous travel a thing of the past.

In addition to the paper, the editors publish an attending Teachers' Guide. Along with a solution to the crossword puzzle, the guide includes bibliographical material on events or persons mentioned, suggestions for field trips to state museums, and a chronology of state and national events relevant to the topics covered in the paper. Attractive in its design and comprehensive in its content, *The Arkansas News* is the type of tool teachers can take into their classrooms for years to come.

The perspectives on teaching local history presented by the three panelists reflect national and state efforts to improve history instruction in the schools. Reports written by the Bradley Commission for History in the Schools and the National Commission for Social Studies in the Schools, as well as the History-Social Science Framework adopted by the California State Board of Education, recommend that school districts include as part of a middle school or high school curriculum a course in local or state history. Copies of or information on the above-mentioned reports — each of which emanated from Commissions or Advisory Boards comprised of classroom teachers, historians, and educators — can be obtained from the following addresses: Bradley Commission on History in Schools, 24898 Fawn Drive, North Olmsted, OH 44070; National Commission on Social Studies in the Schools, 11 Dupont Circle, Suite LL4, Washington, DC 20036; and History-Social Science Framework for California Public Schools, Bureau of Publications Sales, California State Department of Education, P.O. Box 271, Sacramento, CA 95802-0271. The reports suggest that the inclusion of such courses not only enables students to understand the evolution of their local communities but may encourage them to participate in community affairs.

There are other opportunities characteristic of and perhaps unique to the study of local history. Like those who have worked with the Missouri Historical Society's American History School Project or *The Arkansas News*, teachers can design or create classroom materials from accessible primary sources. In planning field trips or independent student projects, teachers can take advantage of their proximity to historical museums, homes, or other sites relevant to the topics being taught. For guidelines and activities for teaching local history, see Fay Metcalf and Matthew Downey, *Using Local History in the Classroom* (Nashville, TN: American Association for State and Local History, 1982). The aims of these efforts are to enable students to create connections between past and present, cause and consequence, local and national event or experience. These continuing collaborations among classroom teachers, historians, and educators serve to further such aims.

Chapter XIV:

Teaching Teachers: Cooperation

Meetings and Minds: The La Salle College AP History Conference

George B. Stow

ONE OF THE INCIDENTAL BENEFITS of serving as a reader of Advanced Placement history essays concerns the sharing of experiences and perspectives in teaching courses in history. It was in the course of an informal colloquium during the 1981 reading that one reader, an AP European history teacher at the high school level, outlined the benefits he had derived from meetings with instructors in history at a local university in his area. As the newly elected chairman of La Salle College's Department of History, I became interested in presenting a similar program for AP teachers in the Philadelphia area for two reasons: 1) discussions of this kind would be mutually beneficial; AP instructors would, it was hoped, benefit from exposure to current teaching practices at the post-secondary level, and 2) La Salle's history faculty would gain valuable insight into the instructional techniques employed on the secondary level, and thus into the level of preparedness of entering freshmen as well. And, more pragmatically, La Salle's history program would achieve some degree of exposure and recognition among area secondary schools.

With all of this in mind I sought assistance in organizing an AP history conference from Professor John S. Grady, director of La Salle's honors program. While reviewing student records, Professor Grady discovered some interesting data regarding those entering students who had completed the AP history courses while in high school (each entering class consists of approximately 750 students; total day-school enrollments at La Salle number around 3,300 students). For example, of the approximately 100 students in this category, the majority scored a "3" or better on the examination, and were awarded credit for United States or European history when they matriculated at La Salle. It was also found that not only had most of these students distinguished themselves academically at La Salle, but also, of the thirty-seven undergraduate Fulbright Fellowship winners at La Salle during the past ten years, thirty had entered with AP history credit.

Quite apart from these considerations were the questions: From which schools should we invite teachers of AP history? Should the invitations go only to those schools that have traditionally served as "feeder schools" for La Salle? Or should the program include representatives from schools — especially private schools — not accustomed to sending students to La Salle? Beyond all of this, how should we determine which schools in the latter category offer AP history? And for all schools, how should we identify individual teachers of AP history?

As an initial step toward resolution of these problems, I requested from the Educational Testing Service (ETS) a listing of all schools in the geographical area from which most of our students come: Pennsylvania, New Jersey, Delaware, and Maryland. I also asked for the names of individual AP teachers in each of the institutions listed. From the list sent by ETS of approximately fifty schools, Professor Grady and I began to narrow our focus according to specific criteria. First, there was the consideration of manageable proportions. An ideal size for the sort of panel program we had envisioned would be around twenty-five participants. Buttressing this figure were budgetary considerations. Although at no time did the administration of La Salle impose strict fiscal guidelines, Professor Grady and I decided that an outside figure of $500 should be our limit. As it turned out, this figure was projected as an estimated cost by La Salle's Director of Food Services; the final bill amounted to $499.25. A second concern was that, at least for the initial program, we ought to involve those schools and teachers that had, over the years, developed especially close ties with La Salle. Thus, a survey of all students with AP credit currently enrolled at La Salle revealed that ten institutions were represented among the student body, having from two to thirteen representative students each. Yet another factor in our deliberations was that of time and distance. Not only might it prove unfeasible for a teacher from, say, the Pittsburgh area to travel 300 miles to La Salle for an afternoon and evening program, but also it might prove economically impractical for us to invite him. As a final matter, Professor Grady and I did think it worthwhile to extend invitations to schools within a fifty-mile radius that had not traditionally delivered strong students to the college.

At this stage we decided to solicit prima facie indications of interest in the program. To this end, I telephoned selected teachers from a variety of schools, both those with long-standing affiliations with La Salle and those with no previous connections. Without exception, those in the former category responded enthusiastically to the idea; those in the latter category showed little or no interest (one teacher from an affluent, suburban preparatory school even snapped, "I've been teaching AP history for thirteen years, and I don't have to come to La Salle to learn how to do it!"). Finally, invitations were sent six weeks before the program's date to thirty schools. We hoped for acceptances from twenty-five; twenty-two eventually attended the conference.

The format of the program was designed to emphasize collegiality between history instructors on the secondary and postsecondary levels. Therefore, the program was structured around two principal events: an afternoon panel discussion, "The Teaching of History: Yesterday and Today"; and an evening presentation —

following a reception and dinner — by Dr. Lawrence Beaber, consultant for the Advanced Placement European History program at ETS.

The afternoon session featured two presentations, each focusing on two subjects: recent historiography in United States and European history; and problems and perspectives in the classroom. Professor Joseph P. O'Grady made the presentation in United States history. After reviewing trends and developments in historical literature, he shared his perceptions concerning the teaching of United States history on the college level, giving special attention to what he described as "fads" in history and their impact on the historical profession. Professor John P. Rossi then delivered some remarks on approaches to European history, including a comparison of the old war-horse course of history departments — Western civilization — with the more modern course in "global" history. A spirited discussion followed, in which invited teachers and other members of La Salle's history department participated.

The evening session began with brief remarks by La Salle's president, provost, and dean of arts and sciences, followed by a presentation by Dr. Beaber entitled "Recent Developments in Advanced Placement History." With accompanying handouts Dr. Beaber outlined the process by which AP examinations, especially essays, are graded. Additional comments concerned changes in the examination formats in 1981 and 1982. The principal concern during the following question-and-answer sessions was about the testing and grading procedures employed by ETS.

Reaction to the program was overwhelmingly positive. La Salle's history faculty were impressed with how well-educated and informed the secondary school teachers were, and found that they had a great deal more in common with them than they had originally thought. Moreover, they were pleased with the teachers' enthusiasm about the future of history as a subject in the secondary schools, and the impact that "gifted and talented" legislation is having on fostering AP history programs.

La Salle's administrators were similarly impressed, especially with the potential of the program for other disciplines. As the provost remarked:

> Concerning a repeat of that program next year, at this time I would suggest that we place that issue on an agenda for our review in the spring semester — perhaps during the annual departmental review. I have in mind the appropriateness of our seeing whether we can interest other humanities departments in sponsoring such a program; that direction would indicate some need to cycle such programs.

The AP history teachers were equally enthusiastic; many sent unsolicited responses to the program. They had learned a great deal from the afternoon programs on historiography and they had developed contacts with the college faculty that they might use when they were planning their courses for 1982-83 or for advice on organizing specific aspects of their courses. One teacher wrote that he found the program "informative, stimulating, and encouraging." He added that "it is nice to know that the work of high school instructors can be beneficial and is worth the extra effort." Another teacher wrote that he had "benefited immensely from the presentations and interactions, as well as from the opportunity to discuss cogent issues with colleagues." Yet another thought that "too often the role of a teacher is overlooked. It is gratifying to know that you in the history department at La Salle are recognizing the teachers' contributions to the program." Perhaps the best summary of the results of the program was offered by Sister Dorothy Connor, S.S.J., who related that she "found it a rare treat to listen to and participate in the question-and-answer session with Professors O'Grady and Rossi. In an age that so glorifies science, math, and technology on one hand and wonders about the utility of history on the other, I was and still am extremely delighted that you and your colleagues saw fit to honor this happy history teacher."

There was finally a response from Dr. Beaber himself, who believed that the La Salle program might serve as a model format for other areas of the country:

I believe the format developed by La Salle could be easily and relatively inexpensively replicated at other colleges where AP history candidates enrollment is increasing and where the history departments have an interest in developing better relations with outstanding AP history teachers, and not incidentally, in attracting more of these fine-calibre history students to their institutions. Although the huge national public and private universities might not be interested in this model, I would suspect that the history departments at smaller institutions where they are just beginning to get sizeable numbers of AP history students matriculating would be very interested. I would like to see ETS Program Direction and College Board central and regional Program Service Offices suggest the "La Salle Model" to institutions as a way for fostering better secondary school-university history teacher contacts, and as a means of attracting more AP history candidates."

A short while after the program's conclusion, members of the history department conducted an open and freewheeling postmortem of its positive and negative points, along with suggestions for any future programs. Some thought the program needed no improvement. Others, however, believed that the afternoon panel presentations by Professors O'Grady and Rossi were too one-sided, and that they could have been designed to offer more practical information for our colleagues on the secondary level. Thus, two attractive ideas were suggested: the next program should focus on matters of bibliography, calling attention to the latest monographs and articles in European and United States history; future sessions should also emphasize new offerings in audiovisual aids (including university lending libraries and possibilities for securing relevant television documentaries.)

There is a postscript. Professor Grady submitted a proposal outlining La Salle's AP history program for inclusion as a panel session at the Middle States Association of Colleges and Schools annual meeting in Philadelphia in fall 1982. Entitled "AP — A Shared Perspective," the proposal was accepted, and included as panelists Dr. Beaber, Sr. Dorothy Conner, Professor Grady, and me. Each participant summarized his or her perceptions of the program at La Salle; this was followed by a lively question-and-answer session with the overflow audience. As a measure of the interest in the topic, the room originally designated by the Middle States program committee quickly proved too small, and the panelists were forced to interrupt the proceedings until a larger, more suitable room could be located. Among the audience were many high-ranking teachers and administrators from East Coast schools and colleges, including the Commissioner for Higher Education for Pennsylvania, Dr. James P. Gallagher.

The Summer Institute for Teachers of Talented High School Students at Carleton College

Clifford E. Clark and Diethelm Prowe

EXCELLENCE IN EDUCATION has once again become a major national issue. Advanced Placement teachers in high schools have never lacked commitment to either excellence or the right of talented students to receive the kind of education appropriate to their level of motivation and intelligence. But what has often been missing is the support for such teachers beyond the classroom. Even when parents and school administrators have expressed their approval, the hard-pressed teacher of Advanced Placement or accelerated courses has received only meager help from colleagues in colleges and universities.

High school teachers attempting to introduce their students to college-level materials have been isolated because typical secondary school texts are often inappropriate or out of date. They also have not had an opportunity to communicate and share their needs and experiences with college faculty. College teachers, for their part, have known little or nothing about the previous educational experiences of their best students who have taken Advanced Placement or accelerated courses. And this lack of knowledge has compounded the problem of placing these incoming high school students in courses at an appropriate level of sophistication and difficulty.

Four years ago some faculty and administrators at Carleton College set out to do something about this situation. We decided to create week-long workshops to be conducted during the third week of June, when high school faculty could escape the pressure of their demanding teaching schedules and, working closely with college teachers in small seminars, explore recent developments in their own disciplines. The object was to foster an environment in which ideas could be shared and course materials revised and brought up to date.

Although a historian was the prime mover in establishing the first contacts with high schools in Minnesota and in setting up the first workshops, these were never restricted to history alone. By the summer of 1983, the Carleton Institute for Teachers of Talented Students offered seminars in no fewer than seventeen disciplines, ranging from art history to problem solving and from computer science to humanities. From the beginning, however, the program has included courses in both United States and European history, each taught by one United States and one European historian from our department, and in one case from a neighboring institution. In all, some 600 high school teachers have attended at least one of the workshops over the last four years. The Carleton Summer School Office makes the first contacts with high school teachers in late February or early March, when it sends out brochures containing brief descriptions of all the workshops and application forms to department chairs of high schools in the Upper Midwest and selectively beyond; the cost is approximately fifty cents per announcement. Advertisements are simultaneously placed in newsletters of the appropriate professional and teacher associations. More specific information, about readings and assignments, is sent to applicants by the individual instructors as the applications come in. All assigned books or other materials are conveniently available by mail through the Carleton Bookstore. After that point, and until graduate credit is awarded formally through the Registrar's Office, the individual disciplines and workshops function independently.

The challenge we have faced in the two annual history seminars was to engage teachers in at least some of the most significant new areas, approaches, and debates in the discipline, and to explore together how these ideas might be integrated into the typical year-long accelerated high school course. From the beginning, we did not try to tell the high school teachers how to teach these materials. Nor did we advise them on the technical aspects of how to set up an AP course. Rather, our goal was to provide the kind of academic environment in which high school teachers could debate some of the most important and exciting ideas in the discipline with an eye to using them in their own courses.

The particular topics covered have varied somewhat from year to year. The European history workshop has emphasized the modern and contemporary period. We have striven for balance among new areas, new approaches, and recent developments in traditional topics, which have remained of central interest both to historians and students. The most obvious were the chronological and gender extensions: Europe since 1945, which until recently was generally omitted in European/world history courses and is still only barely present in the AP European history examination, and women's history for which classroom materials have been developed only recently. Most popular and probably of greatest practical value for teachers and students have been the units on recent interpretations of the great European social revolutions, the French and Russian Revolutions, and the phenomena of Nazism, fascism, and totalitarianism in our century.

Lest the workshop become all too utilitarian, we set aside time to delve into nontraditional AP materials such as the history of technology, the political economy of economic development and decline, and governability and interest groups in the corporatist state. As foci for the discussions, strong thesis books were assigned, among them Pierre Ayçoberry, *The Nazi Question;* Theda Skocpol, *States and Social Revolutions;* Renate Bridenthal and Claudia Koonz, *Becoming Visible;* E. O. Hellerstein, L. P. Hume, and K. M. Offen (eds.), *Victorian Women;* Daniel Headrick, *The Tools of Empire;* Mancur Olsen, *The Rise and Decline of Nations.*

In the United States history workshop, we have followed a similar pattern, focusing on recent interpretations in the fields of the new social history, intellectual history, the history of women and the family, slavery and minority studies, American studies, the Cold War, and Vietnam. Particularly popular have been the units on the American Revolution, women's studies, and Vietnam. Like the European class, the United States historians also spent some time on nontraditional AP materials. A particular concern was how to use novels, short stories, paintings, music, films, and architecture in the survey course. The seminar began with a discussion of textbook strengths and limitations, prompted by the reading of Frances Fitzgerald's *America Revisited.* Other readings were then used to suggest the spectrum of possible approaches to the study of political and social history, including Robert Gross, *The Minutemen and Their World;* Allen Weinstein and Frank O. Gatell, *American Negro Slavery;* William Chambers and Walter D. Burnham, *The American Party Systems;* and Gerda Lerner, *The Majority Finds Its Past.*

The practical format of both workshops has been adapted as far as possible to the circumstances and needs of the high school teachers. The letters from the instructors, detailing seminar objectives, assignments, and approximate daily schedules, were sent out about two or three months before the sessions. Included in these letters were the titles of the four to five major books that would serve as starting points for the discussions each day. During the workshop week, the seminars met every morning from 8:30 to noon, with a common coffee break for all institute participants from 10:00 to 10:30. Afternoon sessions varied in length and format, but usually ran from 1:30 to 4:30, with some time set aside for individual consultations and coffee or library breaks. In the later afternoons and evenings, participants were free to read assignments or begin work on their course outlines and lesson plans.

In the daily routine, the college instructor normally took the lead at the start of the class and introduced the context for the book under discussion. The group then proceeded to explore the broader implications of the particular interpretation and to investigate sources for further study. During that discussion and in the early afternoon, the teachers commented further on ways in which these perspectives might be integrated into an accelerated high school course. Later in the afternoon, time was set aside to share practical experiences with different approaches, materials, and methods in AP or other advanced courses. Here participants have appreciated extensive suggestions by the college instructors for further reading and for books that might be used effectively in the high school classroom. Beyond that, however, the high school teachers played the leading role in this part of the workshop by sharing their experiences with certain topics and materials, and by asking each other about different options of course organization, emphases, teaching aids, and reading materials in open discussion.

The written assignments have been similarly tailored to the needs of the participants. Generally, teachers were asked to write course plans or prepare particular units that would integrate some of the new perspectives discussed in the workshop. In practice, the end products have ranged from completely new syllabi to revised units on particular topics. In European history, for example, one participant did a sophisticated revision and expansion of his unit on Nazism and the Holocaust, which was of particular interest to the students in his suburban school. Another designed a topical unit on autocracy vs. totalitarianism, which allowed her to try a wholly different thematic approach. The new course plan ranged from a completely new syllabus of a new AP teacher to a revision of a fine traditional course emphasizing the classics to include the materials that would enable his students to take the AP examination and gain Advanced Placement credit in college. Most plans in one way or another incorporated new approaches and fresh readings, especially in relatively new areas such as women's history and changed fields such as history and technology. All syllabi included major revisions and expansions of the reading lists.

In United States history the pattern has been similar. Individual participants wrote syllabi for entirely new courses or created new units for established courses. One teacher developed a set of primary sources on the Pullman Strike, including extensive statistical information. Two teachers from suburban schools worked up annotated reading lists for new units on the Cold War and Vietnam. Yet another, seeking to focus on concerns that were central to her own students' experiences, designed a new unit on youth in the 1920s. And a teacher from a parochial school created a 'diplomat game' that allowed his students to role play and understand the dynamics of diplomatic history.

Economically, the workshops have not been overwhelmingly profitable for the college. Our goal from the beginning was, at best, to break even financially. This goal has been reached consistently. At a cost, in 1983, of $180 tuition and $95 room and board for those who chose to stay on campus — as did most participants — the program has been self-sustaining, and the college has not sought outside funding. A number of the teachers have been sponsored by their school districts, usually in connection with planning new Advanced Placement courses. Faculty salaries have been modest, but we have felt richly rewarded by the experience. The history workshops, which have each drawn between eight and fifteen participants a year, have attracted some of the most interesting and lively minds among history teachers from all over the country. They have been ready to debate, challenge, and rethink historical materials from the moment they arrived on campus until the moment they left. They have been highly stimulating to teach. We have gone back to our college classrooms in the fall, and especially to our freshman classes, with enthusiasm and a fresh outlook.

To judge from the formal (and anonymous) evaluations by the secondary school teachers at the end of the Institute, the workshops were as successful as we had hoped in at least several related ways: they offered fresh perspectives on old and new topics in history, expanded old reading lists and, above all, refreshed the minds of all the participants. Several of the evaluations commented specifically on this last point. The experience has similarly allowed those of us in our department who have taught workshops — two of the five Europeanists and one of our two Americanists have been involved until now — to share with our colleagues the insights we have gained into the Advanced Placement program and the high school teaching of gifted students generally.

Thus, both the high school faculty and the college instructors have benefited from the workshop experience. The intense week of work has demonstrated that teachers from both levels can work cooperatively together, helping bridge the gap that too often exists between high schools and colleges. Perhaps more importantly, both high school and college faculty have come to believe that this type of program can encourage the kind of quality education for the most talented students that in recent years has all too often been neglected in this country's public schools.

Teaching Teachers:
A Reflection on the Use of
Sources in a Seminar Setting

Augustus Burns

IN 1983, MY COLLEAGUE Kermit Hall at the University of Florida created the History Teaching Alliance. That organization has since become a national enterprise supported by the American Historical Association, the Organization of American Historians, and the National Council for the Social Studies. It has developed and encouraged summer seminars and colloquia for secondary school teachers in a wide variety of programs nationwide, seeking to invigorate and enrich the teaching of secondary school history courses. In addition, the Alliance effort has built a partnership between academic historians and their secondary school colleagues that will extend beyond occasional summer programs.

In the beginning of the Alliance collaboratives, the substantive focus in these programs was constitutional and legal history, a subject chosen because of the then impending Bicentennial of the Constitution. Professor Hall, who directed a pilot seminar in the summer of 1983, in Gainesville, Florida asked that I assist him in that effort, and in 1984 I became director of the Alachua County Collaborative.

As I began my duties, I had only an intuitive notion of how to proceed, supplemented by my own distant experience as a public school social studies instructor. I knew that teachers would benefit from a seminar setting, but that our emphasis should not replicate a graduate seminar. We should not stress bibliography and interpretation to the exclusion of factual and thematic substance, because our participants would be people who were not conversant with constitutional and legal history. We needed, instead, the structure of a good seminar, with wide participation in informed discussion — the type of effort I associate with an advanced undergraduate course. Such an approach, I concluded, would give our participants the substantive enrichment they need to improve their knowledge of the subject at hand. We also intended to provide participants with a variety of source materials and written works. We wanted teachers to have an opportunity to hone their analytical and interpretive skills and, especially, to examine works of history in an inquiry-based format. Finally, we wanted to bring them into contact with legal professionals, people who work daily with modern variations of the fundamental questions that have helped shape this republic and its legal and constitutional history.

The University of Florida has offered this program for five years and I have directed four summer seminars. We began our sixth year in July 1989. We are the oldest continuing collaborative in the nation, of those begun under HTA auspices. Our program, in addition, is one that has continued to offer constitutional and legal subjects in its summer institute.

Over these five years, our focus has enlarged, and the program has invited the participation of teachers from adjoining school districts. Approximately seventy-five teachers from four school systems have now participated in our program.

Certain premises informed our effort from its inception. First, we decided to spend out time exclusively focused on substantive concerns, omitting pedagogical matters altogether. We wanted academic rigor to be the hallmark of these seminars. Second, we have sought to establish a climate of cooperative inquiry, stressing the shared professional concerns of participants and faculty. We have discouraged any hint of academic intimidation, such as one might find in an occasional first-year graduate seminar or even in a random law school course. Finally, one of objectives of the program has been its eventual absorption into the University of Florida's Department of History, as part of a renewed university effort to invigorate the subject of history in the state's secondary schools.

We planned from the beginning to use a variety of materials in our study of the Constitution itself: selections from the *Federalist Papers*, the Articles of Confederation, and the Massachusetts Constitution of 1780; and court cases, in such subsequent topics as the origins of judicial review or the power of the president. For some of these subjects, we would rely on John Patrick's and Richard Remy's superb *Lessons on the Constitution*, one of the study manuals produced by Project '87, developed under NEH grant support as a joint project of the AHA and the American Political Science Association.

From our first summer program, the participants responded enthusiastically to our effort. They found the subject of constitutional history both invigorating and challenging. We knew they did, because they told us so. Their evaluations uniformly confirmed their sense of accomplishment in our enterprise.

After our first summer seminar some participants gave us informal opinions that suggested deficiencies in our curriculum. They made clear that the seminars could be improved in part by rethinking the appropriateness of some of our course materials.

In planning our program we had assumed that all our social studies teachers had, minimally, a few history courses in their academic backgrounds. We further assumed that at least some of them had been undergraduate history majors. But the teachers pointed out that many of them, in fulfilling state requirements for social studies certification, had taken few history courses. In some instances, teachers had

gained certification with no history work at all. (Changes in certification requirements in Florida in recent years make such a meager subject background impossible
for new teachers.) As a consequence, several of our participants lacked the
historical background necessary to provide an informed analysis of some of the
materials our course utilized. In short, the complaint was not that the seminar was
too sophisticated, or too demanding. It was, instead, a discontent over meager
academic preparation on the part of the participants. The teachers suggested,
therefore, that they be provided not only with course materials similar to those
assigned in the previous collaborative, but with additional or supplementary
materials to be read prior to the summer meetings. (All our materials are mailed to
participants approximately one month before our session begins.)

These concerns produced several modifications in our seminar. We surveyed the
academic background of our participants by having them describe to us their
undergraduate history course work (and graduate coursework as well). We did not
use this information to screen applicants, however, because our approach to
participant selection throughout has been inclusive: to make our program available
to all interested teachers in the school systems we serve. Indeed, we hope that the
teachers who have weaker subject backgrounds will participate; we would be likely
to select participants *because* they lacked previous history study.

We have used the information gleaned from personal discussion to adjust our course
materials and to provide additional reading for participants who might lack an
understanding of, for example, the origins of American constitutionalism. We might
now make available Bernard Bailyn's chapters in *The Great Republic*, on reserve at the
University of Florida's library, or Gordon Wood's chapters in the same volume. We
might include the early chapters in Herman Belz's revision of the Kelly and Harbison
constitutional history textbook, or a chapter from Esmond Wright's *Fabric of Freedom*
(revised edition) explaining British politics in the age of the American Revolution. In
every instance, the purpose is identical: to assist seminar participants in their effort to
become more skilled analysts of a wide variety of constitutional source materials by first
acquiring a basic familiarity with the history of the period. One simply cannot assume
that such an historical awareness already exists.

Perhaps no illustration better demonstrates this problem than the attempt to
introduce the concept of judicial review. Our initial plan was to study this idea in
the context of American constitutionalism in the same manner that first year law
students take up the subject: we would begin with *Marbury v. Madison*, then assign
an edited version of John Marshall's opinion, give the participants a twenty-minute
lesson on how to brief a case, and, on the following day, use participant briefs to
initiate a discussion of Marshall's immortal ruling. Such a process should insure
clear understanding of the constituent elements of judicial review as Marshall
developed them.

How could this plan fail? Is it not time tested? We discovered, of course, that it
could fail very easily, especially if our participants had never read the case before

or, in fact, had never read any court case prior to our seminar meeting. Nor could they read a truncated version of Marshall's opinion and deduce a definition of judicial review. In short, for many of them, this exposure to *Marbury* was their first exposure to judicial opinion of any kind. Our participants were as vexed by *Marbury* as first-year law students often are. And their confusion could not be clarified through a Socratic exchange — try though we did.

Our problem was compounded because our participants had no clear notion of the meaning of the term judicial review in any historical context. Moreover, they had a confused idea of the procedures whereby cases come to federal courts, and they were especially perplexed when asked to explain how cases ever got to the Supreme Court.

In the face of this confusion, we retreated and reevaluated. We determined first that an understanding of the *Marbury* case is essential to the concept of judicial review. On that rock we stood with every constitutional law textbook author who has ever taken up a pen. But we also concluded that in subsequent seminars we would present *Marbury* with materials that prepared our students for the case. We would still do a brief, identify the legal issues, and try to reproduce Marshall's line of legal reasoning — but only after a more purposeful introduction to the subject of judicial review. Such a practice would, we hoped, give our teachers the introduction they required to this important subject, and would enable them to read the case with greater understanding.

Propitiously, the American Historical Association had initiated a series in 1984, edited by Professor Herman Belz, entitled *Bicentennial Essays on the Constitution*. The first volume appeared in early 1985, authored by — who else? — Kermit Hall, entitled *The Supreme Court and Judicial Review in American History*. In this essay, Hall traces the historical evolution of the idea of judicial review, from early colonial and British musing on the subject, through the American Revolution and the Constitutional Convention. The pamphlet continues, of course, into a discussion of the evolution of the idea into modern-day judicial decision-making.

In his narrative, he provides his readers with a lucid explication of judicial review as it was understood in the late eighteenth century. He then proceeds to a two-page discussion of *Marbury*, which sets the case in its proper context and emphasizes its primary theoretical importance. Hall's discussion in no way replicates the case itself — that is not Hall's intention — or substitutes for a careful reading of Marshall's opinion. But Hall does accomplish a critical task. He prepares the untutored to grapple with one of the primary texts of American constitutional history — the great case itself. Having read and discussed Hall's essay, students find *Marbury* manageable, and instructors find the case discussion much more illuminating and rewarding. Such investigation, when combined with carefully crafted discussion, enabled our seminar participants to understand judicial review in a way they had not grasped it previously. They became sufficiently conversant with the principles of Marshall's argument to enable them to present the case to their own students, with clarity and even drama. I had occasion, on two subsequent classroom visits, to observe secondary colleagues conducting classes on the establishment of judicial review, and can attest that the teachers who conducted the classes knew whereof they spoke. They both acknowledged to me that prior to our examination of judicial review in our seminar, they had glossed it over in their units on the Constitution.

By relating this experience, I am trying to suggest that in some contexts, and especially when teaching subjects with which teachers and students are unfamiliar or unknowledgeable, primary materials are better taught when they are joined by distilled scholarship. In this instance, neither source can replace the other, nor can the primary document stand alone.

One additional historical source deserves some mention when discussing ways to teach constitutional concepts to secondary teachers. We confront them with living historical sources: a judge, a state attorney, or a public defender. In our program we arrange each summer for two such guests to visit our proceedings. In the course of our deliberations over these five years we have utilized two federal judges, one district judge, and one member of the Eleventh Circuit Court of Appeals; two state's attorneys; a state circuit judge; two public defenders; and one former judge now in private civil practice.

Prior to each visit, we discuss with the guest speaker, usually in telephone conversation, the focus of study in our seminar. We send our guests an instructional outline and study materials, and we suggest a specific topic for discussion. We seek to offer our participants a focused presentation which will bear directly on our substantive concerns. The guest presentations, in other words, are intended to supplement our study, not to divert from it.

It has not been necessary for our guest teachers to prepare extended remarks. They can discuss such topics as contemporary judicial review, or the court system of Florida, by explaining their professional duties and concerns. On two occasions, our guests have sent reading materials ahead of their visit, at the offer of the instructors, to be distributed to the participants. In the course of a morning's work, these "living sources" have challenged our students and enriched our seminar. Judge Gerald Tjoflat of the U.S. Eleventh Circuit Court of Appeals, for example, explained how, in September 1971, as a federal circuit judge, he had written the order that dismantled the dual school system in Jacksonville, Florida (Duval County). He then traced the history of the federal court litigation that had led to his order, and outlined a theory of modern judicial review that went back to the pathbreaking Supreme Court decision of *Palko v. Connecticut*, 1937 and *U.S. v. Carolene Products*, 1938. In his discussion, Judge Tjoflat confirmed the development of what Kermit Hall has called the "judicial monopoly theory" of federal jurisprudence.

Judge Tjoflat's presentation profoundly impressed our participants, in part because he is a dynamic personality. But equally importantly, the teachers were prepared by their own seminar work to understand his remarks in their proper constitutional context. They were intrigued as well because the judge was discussing constitutional law, judicial review, and the public schools — a nexus that teachers could readily grasp. Every participant commented subsequently that Judge Tjoflat's appearance at our seminar was the supreme intellectual experience of the summer.

I do not challenge this view. Indeed, other speakers have been equally effective. I would simply observe that the examination of these "living sources" is little different from the use of any other historical source. The participant must be prepared to interpret. History is, after all, an interpretive art, and skillful interpretation is a learned enterprise. Historical sources, examined by the unlearned or the unskilled, yield very limited insight; sources explored in historical context can provide an experience that excites the intellect and advances historical understanding. Such activity may even make one a better teacher.

Notes on Contributors

Mildred Alpern is an AP European history teacher at Spring Valley (NY) Senior High School. She is a former member of the AHA Teaching Division, a former coeditor of the "Teaching History Today" and "Teaching Innovations" columns in *Perspectives*, and a former Chair of the Development Committee of AP European History.

John C. Bartul teaches AP European history at Jericho (NY) Junior-Senior High School.

Robert F. Berkhofer, Jr. is Professor of History at the University of California, Santa Cruz.

Robert Blackey is Professor and Chair of the Department of History at California State University, San Bernardino. Currently, he is Vice President of the AHA, in charge of the Teaching Division, and coeditor of the "Teaching Innovations" column in *Perspectives*. He is a former Chief Reader of AP European History and a former Chair of that program's Development Committee.

Augustus Burns is Associate Professor of history at the University of Florida. He has directed the University of Florida/National Endowment for the Humanities constitutional seminars for secondary teachers.

Clifford E. Clark is Professor of History and M.A. and A.D. Hulings Professor of American Studies at Carleton College.

Mary Joan Cook teaches American studies, writing, and oral communication at Saint Joseph College.

James E. Copple teaches AP U.S. history and is an Assistant Principal at Garden City (KS) High School.

Roderic H. Davison is Professor Emeritus of History at George Washington University.

Bruce Eastwood is Professor of History at the University of Kentucky-Lexington. He is a former member of the Committee on Education of the History of Science Society.

Terrie L. Epstein is Assistant Professor of Education at Boston College. Currently, she is Chair of the Organization of American Historians' Committee on Teaching.

Lanny Fields is Associate Professor of History and Acting Associate Dean of the School of Social and Behavioral Sciences at California State University, San Bernardino.

John A. Garraty is Professor Emeritus of History at Columbia University. He is a former Vice President of the AHA, in charge of the Teaching Division.

Phyllis A. Hall is Professor of History at the University of Richmond.

Charles F. Howlett taught AP U.S. history at Amityville (NY) Memorial High School when he wrote this article. Currently he is an school administrator in West Islip, NY.

Russell Hvolbek was recently a Visiting Professor of History at the University of California, San Diego.

R.E. Johnson is Associate Professor of History the University of Toronto, Erindale College.

Ray W. Karras teaches AP U.S. history at Lexington (MA) High School. He is a former member of the Development Committee of AP U.S. History.

Eve Kornfeld is Associate Professor of History at San Diego State University.

James Lance was completing his dissertation, in African history, at Stanford University when he co-wrote this article.

James A. Litle is an instructor in history and social sciences at the North Carolina School of Science and Mathematics.

Carolyn C. Lougee is Professor of History at Stanford University. She is a former member of the Development Committee of AP European History and a former member of the AHA Teaching Division.

William H. McNeill is a Professor Emeritus of History at the University of Chicago and a former President of the AHA. He served on the Curriculum Task Force of the National Commission on Social Studies in the Schools.

Donald Mattheisen is Professor of History at the University of Lowell.

Patricia Matuszewski teaches AP U.S. history at Franklin (Somerset, NJ) High School.

Donald G. Morrison teaches AP European history at New Rochelle (NY) High School.

Gary B. Nash is Professor of History at the University of California, Los Angeles and Associate Director of the National Center for History in the Schools (UCLA). He is a former chair of the AHA's Nominating Committee.

Ruth F. Necheles-Jansyn is Professor of History at Long Island University.

Diethelm Prowe is Professor of History at Carleton College.

Vera Blinn Reber is Professor of History at Shippensburg University.

Richard Roberts is Associate Professor of History at Stanford University.

Lisa Rosner is Assistant Professor of History at Stockton State College.

Ann McCormick Scott teaches AP U.S. history and has chaired the Department of History at The Madeira School, Greenway, Virginia.

John Anthony Scott has taught history at the Ethical Culture Schools in New York and at Rutgers University School of Law. He is co-chair of the Committee on History in the Classroom.

John W. Servos is Associate Professor of History at Amherst College. He is a former member of the Committee on Education of the History of Science Society.

Bonnie G. Smith is Professor of History at Rutgers University and chair of the Development Committee of AP European History.

Peter N. Stearns is Heinz Professor and Head of the Department of History at Carnegie Mellon University. He is editor of the *Journal of Social History*. He is a former chair of the Development Committee of AP European History as well as a former member of the History Achievement Committee of ETS.

John E. Stovel teaches AP European history at Mt. Greylock (Williamstown, MA) Regional High School. He is a former member of the Development Committee of AP European History.

George B. Stow is Professor of History at La Salle University.

Gerald L. Wilson teaches U.S. history and is Senior Associate Dean of Trinity College, Duke University.

Virginia S. Wilson teaches history and is Head of the Department of Humanities at North Carolina School of Social Science and Mathematics.

Shirley Wilton is Professor of History at Ocean County College.

Alan Wood is Assistant Professor of History at the University of Washington

Teaching Articles from Perspectives, 1982-93

THE FOLLOWING is a list of the "Teaching History Today," "Advanced Placement Teaching," and "Teaching Innovations" columns since September 1982, including several that are tentatively scheduled to appear in 1992-93.

1982-1983

September: Steven A, Riess, "Sport History in the Classroom."
Kelley, Hamm, "The First Years."
Calvin Harris and Larry Wilson, "Reflections on Teaching AP American History."

October: Mary L. Lifka, "History as a Genre."
Luther Spoehr, "AP American History: Expanding a Traditional Approach."
Alice Duffy Grant, "AP Course Criteria and Development."

November: Robert Blackey, "How Advanced Placement History Essay Questions Are Prepared—and How Yours Can Be Too."

December: Brian C. Mitchell, "Teaching Local History: Lowell and the Adult Evening Experience."
Peter N. Stearns, "Back Toward School: Links in the Stages of History Teaching."
John Howe, "'New Social History': The Introductory Course in U.S. History."

January: E. Bradford Burns, "Teaching History: A Changing Clientele and an Affirmation of Goals."
Allan M. Winkler, "Grading the AP American History Exam."
Kathleen Weiler, "At the Reading: The European History Examination."

February: Kim Phillips, "Some Thoughts on American History Textbooks."

March: Richard Place and Christopher Johnson, "Teaching History to Social Work Students."

April: Francis Jennings, "The Newberry Library Center for the History of the American Indian: Its Impact on School and Community Constituencies."
Mildred Alpern, "Considerations in Planning and Revising an Advanced Placement or Survey Course."

May/June: Michael D'Innocenzo, Martin Melkonian, and Sandra Mullin, "Special Studies in History: War and Peace in a Nuclear Age."
Stephen F. Klein, "The Genesis of the Shorter Document-Based Essay Questions in the Advanced Placement American History Examination."

1983-1984

September: Christine Naitove and Barbara Bartle, "A European History Course that Stresses Writing and Reasoning Skills."
Mary Lifka, "Old Chestnuts and New Acorns: Trends in AP European and American History."

October: Terry A. Cooney, "Drawing History: Working with Student Attitudes from the First Day."
John W. Crum, "AP and College Teachers: Cooperation and the Growth of Acorns."

November:	David L. Porter, "Debating the Great Historical Issues."
	Charles F. Howlett, "Two Minds, One Thought: The Creation of a Students' History Journal."
December:	John J. Appel, "Postcards: More Than Just 'Wish You Were Here.'"
March:	Virginia S. Wilson, James A. Litle, and Gerald L. Wilson, "Blending the Two Cultures: The Role of History and the Social Sciences in the Education of Future Scientific/ Technological Leaders."
April:	Patricia Matuszewski, "Is There Life After AP?"
May/June:	Fraser Harbutt, "A Course on the History of U.S.-Soviet Relations."

1984-1985

September:	Anthony O. Edmunds, "Is the Grading of AP Exams Fair to all Concerned?"
October:	Neal McGoldrick, "History in the Classroom: Drama and Film in Juxtaposition." Repeat of article by F. Harbutt, May/June 1984.
November:	John A. Garraty, "Teaching and Textbooks."
December:	Muriel Nazzari, "Introducing a Gender Perspective to the Teaching of American History."
January:	No column.
February:	Paul S. Holbo, "American History and the History Major."
March:	Clifford E. Clark and Diethelm Prowe, "The Summer Institute for Teachers of Talented High School Students at Carleton College."
April:	Frederick E. Hoxie, "The Indian Versus the Textbooks: Is There Any Way Out?"
May/June:	Virginia S. Wilson, James A. Litle, Gerald L. Wilson, and Robert N. Sawyer,"Anytime, Anyplace: The By-Mail AP American History Course."

1985-1986

September:	David F. Krein, "Teaching History to the Unprepared College Student."
October:	No column.
November:	Barbara Oberg, "Editing and the Teaching of History: Notes from the Gallatin Project."
December:	Mildred Alpern, "AP European History for Able Sophomores."
January:	Donald Johnson, "Integrating Asia into the World History Curriculum."
February:	Michael S. Henry, "The Intellectual Origins of the Document-Based Question."
March:	Richard L. Schoenwald, "History is About Art, Too."
April:	James E. Copple, "AP History in the Small and Rural School."
May/June:	Robert Blackey, "Writing in the Major: A Novel Approach that Works."

1986-1987

September:	Carolyn C. Lougee, "Social History and the Introductory European Course."
October:	Victoria Chandler, "What We Can Learn from 'Chuck Oozo.'"
November:	No column
December:	Mario D. Fenyo, "Columbus and All That: 'Discovery' and 'Expansion' in American Textbooks."
January:	John W. Servos, "The History of Science and the Survey Course in American History."
February:	James Axtell, "Forked Tongues: Moral Judgments in Indian History."
March:	Bruce Eastwood, "History of Science in the European History Survey Course."
April:	Harold D. Woodman, "Do Facts Speak for Themselves? Writing the Historical Essay."
May/June:	"Reuniting the Historical Profession: The National Commission on the Social Studies."

1987-1988

September: James D. Heffernan, Jr., "Traditional or Inquiry: Why Not Use Both?"

October: Donald G. Morrison, "Students as Historians: A Convention."

November: Jonathan J. Liebowitz, "Reflections on Teaching Engineers."

December: Shirley Wilton, "Art as Social History in the Western Civilization Survey."

January: Glen Jeansonne, "Teaching a Course in Writing Biography."

February: Robert F. Berkhofer, Jr., "Demystifying Historical Authority: Critical Textual Analysis in the Classroom."

March: Ron Briley, "What Are the Responsibilities of the Colleges and Universities to the Schools: The Professionalization of the Classroom History Teacher."

April: Gerda Lerner, "Priorities and Challenges in Women's History Research."

May/June: David R. Beisel, "Teaching Psychohistory."

1988-1989

September: No column.

October: Eric Rothschild, "Simulation: Stimulation for Scholarship."

November: No column.

December: Phyllis A. Hall, "Using Your Research in the Survey Course."

January: Ruth F. Necheles-Jansyn, "Building Critical Thinking Skills in an Introductory World Civilizations Course."

February: R.E. Johnson, "History by Numbers."

March: Joshua A. Newberg, "Sins of Omission."

April: Peter N. Stearns, "Teaching the United States in World History."

May/June: Charles Hart, "Teaching the Enlightenment with a Student Solon."

1989-1990

September: No column

October: Peter N. Stearns, "Teaching Social History."

November: John Bartul, "Teaching the Value of Inquiry through the Essay Question."

December: Donald Matthiesen, "Finding the Right Film for the History Classroom."

January: Phyllis A. Hall, "Teaching Analytical Thinking through the 'AHA Forum' and '*The Return of Martin Guerre*'"

February: Virginia S. Wilson, James A. Litle and Gerald R. Wilson, "No Solo Venture: Essay Writing in History."

March: Jack E. Stovel, "HELP—New Tricks for Old Dogs."
Augustus Burns, "Teaching Teachers: A Reflection on the Use of Sources in a Seminar Setting."

April: Nancy Nicholas Barker, "Teaching the French Revolution."
Vera Blinn Reber, "Teaching Undergraduates to Think Like Historians."

May/June: Paul Hanson, "Teaching the French Revolution in the Core Curriculum."

1990-1991

September: Eve Kornfeld, "Representations of History."

October: Lisa Rosner, "Teaching Quantitative History with a Database."

November: Roderic Davidson, "Teaching History with Song and Doggerel."

December: Mary Jane Cook, "Finding the Layers in Your Town."

January: Alan Wood, "Freedom in World History: Can Parachutists and Truffle Hunters Find Happiness Together?"

February: Jonathan Zophy, "Student-Centered Learning."

March: James Lance and Richard Roberts, "'The World Outside the West' Course Sequence at Stanford University."
Lanny Fields, "Some Thoughts about the Course, 'The World Outside the West.'"
William H. McNeill, "Teaching World History."

April: Terri L. Epstein, "Communities of Collaboration: Sources and Resources for Teaching Local history."
Peter N. Stearns, "The Challenge of 'Historical Literacy.'"

May/June: John Anthony Scott, "There Is Another Way: United States History Texts and the Search for Alternatives."
Gary B. Nash, "Response to John Anthony Scott's 'There Is Another Way.'"

1991-1992

September: Bonnie G. Smith, "Gender, Reproduction, and European History."

October: Peter B. Levy, "Teaching the History of the Modern Civil Rights Movement."

November: Carl Degler and Robert Kunath, "Is Research the Whole Enchilada?"

December: John F. McClymer and Paul R. Ziegler, "Lost at Sea: A Proposal for Countering Information Overload in Introductory Courses."

January: Ann K. Warren, "Biography and Autobiography in the Teaching of History and Social Studies."

February: Donald L. Wasson, "Mr. Chips Goes to Jail: Teaching History in a Correctional Environment."

March: Patricia J.F. Rosof, "*Mentalité* in the Advanced Placement Curriculum."
Samuel S. Wineburg, "Probing the Depths of Students' Historical Knowledge."

April: Linda Kelly Alkana, "Teaching Critical Thinking with Historical Methodology."
Patrick Manning, "Methodology and World History in a Ph.D. Program."

May/June: Sara Joan Miles, "At the Sound of the Beep: Teaching Through Electronic Mail."

1992-1993 (tentative)

September: Richard White, "'*Far West*. See also *frontier*': The 'New Western History,' Textbooks, and the U.S. History Survey Course."

October: James J. Lorence and James G. Grinsel, "Amen: The Role of Religion in History Teaching."

November: Marvin Lunenfeld, "'The Play's the Thing': Students Write Historical Fiction."

December: Joel Beinin, "Remapping the West: Teaching the Middle East in World/Western Civilization Courses."

January: Ellis L. "Skip" Knox, "The Electronic Renaissance: A Course in the Ether."